THE UNITED NATIONS AND U.S. FOREIGN POLICY

*A study from the United Nations Project
Center for International Studies
Massachusetts Institute of Technology*

The UNITED NATIONS and U.S. FOREIGN POLICY

A New Look at the National Interest

by

LINCOLN P. BLOOMFIELD

 Little, Brown and Company
Boston · Toronto

BY THE SAME AUTHOR:

Evolution or Revolution? The U.N. and the Problem of Peaceful Territorial Change (1957)

The editors of *Foreign Affairs* kindly granted permission to adapt for use in this book portions of the author's article entitled "The U.N. and National Security," which appeared in the July, 1958, issue.

*Published simultaneously in Canada
by Little, Brown & Company (Canada) Limited*

PRINTED IN THE UNITED STATES OF AMERICA

Preface

THE POSTWAR YEARS effectively dissipated many of the extravagant and utopian ideas which the American people and some of their leaders earlier entertained about the United Nations. But the process of disillusionment, as so often happens, left a void. So long as the earlier notions were not replaced with more serviceable attitudes, the American view of the United Nations in the succeeding years has tended to become increasingly mechanical. We have gone through the motions of pledging support, making speeches, and voting on resolutions. At crucial moments—Korea, Suez, the Congo—the United Nations suddenly seemed to dominate American policy making. The remainder of the time it existed in a backwater of policy. But in neither case did American performance reflect an entirely rational view of the place of international political organization in world affairs. The reason for this, I believe, is that we have not as a matter of national concern comprehensively reappraised the United States national interest in the United Nations, nor have we figured the real cost of sustaining that interest. In a period when the Soviet Union has begun to grasp eagerly at the opportunities offered by the United Nations' world-wide forum, the United States has devoted little or no official attention to reviewing systematically the connections that exist—or should exist—between the United Nations and other, better understood sources of national strategy.

The relative isolation of the U.N. sector of American foreign policy is, however, intelligible only as part of a far greater problem. I refer to the difficulty the United States has in identifying its general political goals and objectives, and acting upon them. The relationship between the two problems was brought home to me strikingly from a position of modest official responsibility for policy planning in regard to American U.N. participation during eleven years of postwar service in the State Department. It became increasingly clear that until the United States acquired a better over-all strategic doctrine in the political realm, until its broad and sometimes vague goals were made more explicit and backed by a more purposeful program of action, this country could not have the assurance that it was employing such instruments of diplomatic and political action as the United Nations with maximum effectiveness to achieve desirable ends. In the absence of a more meaningful over-all program of national strategy, the United Nations—both as a symbol and as a place of business—has appeared to many Americans a baffling mixture of ward politics and high morality—stepchild of foreign policy one day and prodigal son the next.

The conviction grew upon me that there was only one logical way in which to examine afresh the strategic uses of the United Nations for American policy over the next decade. That was to spell out systematically the foreign policy objectives of the United States, across the board, and to relate them to the capabilities and limitations of the United Nations as best those could be estimated from the available evidence.

The Center for International Studies at the Massachusetts Institute of Technology offered an opportunity for just such an assessment at a crucial juncture in the history of the United Nations. It had just been sorely tested by the Suez and Hungarian crises of 1956. And within the U.S. national security community the ordeal of planning and policy making in the late fall of that year revealed once again the lack of adequate bridges between multilateral diplomacy and the other vital elements of strategic planning and action.

The Center's United Nations project made it possible to commission a number of inquiries in this general field of study. As director of the project, I sought to answer the question: What is the American national interest with respect to the United Nations as we go into the 1960's? This book thus concentrates on the larger political aspects of U.N. policy rather than on its technical or administrative aspects. Its focus is on strategic issues of policy rather than on the tactics of face-to-face, day-to-day diplomacy. (The organization of American participation is discussed in the Appendix.) Its underlying thesis is that a better understanding of the general strategic connection between U.S. policy imperatives and U.N. potentialities—and limitations—is the indispensable basis for reconsidering what relevant uses this important world instrumentality may have for American and free world interests in the period ahead.

MY GRATITUDE must be first of all to the Center, and above all to its inspiring Director, Max F. Millikan, for affording me the opportunity to apply scholarship to experience in a uniquely satisfying environment. Max Millikan, Norman J. Padelford, and Walt W. Rostow offered invaluable substantive advice and encouragement in the present enterprise, while Donald L. M. Blackmer and Arthur L. Singer, Jr. smoothed the administrative ways throughout. Elizabeth Park Hoban and Joan Narcus shared patiently and loyally the burden of seeing both the author and his work through the always painful stages of production.

I join a goodly company in reserving a very special acknowledgment for the Center's Editor-in-Chief, Richard W. Hatch. His talents can, I believe, be fully appreciated only by those who have enjoyed his friendly editorial whiplash and seen him evoke form and clarity out of the most disorderly raw materials. My own debt to him is literally unpayable.

L.P.B.

Cambridge, Massachusetts
September, 1960

For: **PAMELA**
LINCOLN, JR.
DIANA

who will inherit
the world we make.

Table of Contents

ix

III *The United Nations and the Cold War*

IV *Toward a More Stable World*

Part **I**   **THE UNITED NATIONS
AND THE NATIONAL INTEREST**

CHAPTER ONE

The Place of the United Nations in National Strategy

INTRODUCTION

For fifteen years the United States has been a member of the United Nations. During that time the leaders of both political parties in this country have proclaimed American fidelity to the Purposes and Principles of the U.N. Charter. The Congress of the United States has consistently appropriated funds for U.S. participation, averaging about one-third of the organization's total budget. It has affirmed through other legislation the nation's basic decision to play a leading role in the organization. Public opinion, however fickle through alternating national crises of panic and overconfidence over a fifteen-year period, registers general approbation of the United Nations and faith in its prospects. Citizens' organizations through the country publicize the United Nations and its family of specialized agencies on a scale unparalleled elsewhere in the world. There can be no question that in terms of words, hopes, and promises, the United States, certainly of all the great powers, has been the prime supporter of the United Nations from the beginning to the present.

But the actions of the United States over the whole period of

3

the existence of the United Nations tell a somewhat different story. The United States has exerted itself strenuously to develop outside the structure of the United Nations diplomatic and military machinery responsive to the need for defense of the non-Communist world against the new imperialisms of Soviet Russia and Communist China. Major attention was transferred outside the United Nations before it was two years old, with the formulation of the Greek-Turkish Aid Program, followed quickly by the Marshall Plan, N.A.T.O., and a host of bilateral or regionally based policies. In terms of the pressing short-run problems the nation suddenly confronted, the United Nations as an agency of action seemed not to be proving valuable or even relevant except in a minor and sporadic way.

The U.S. government never made a conscious decision to abandon the U.N. effort. It was proving of utility in certain limited areas, even in aspects of the cold war. More important, it stood for the more distant future on behalf of which the short-run strategies were presumably directed. But the degree of American attention to the United Nations as a significant agency of national strategy sharply declined, and the decision was made, never explicitly but with ample clarity, that the United Nations was "on ice" indefinitely until the entire world situation changed. The United States remained officially and publicly attached to the United Nations as a symbol of a better world. To the extent that it could handle lesser matters it would be encouraged, as a practical matter, to do so. But the main thrust of American diplomacy moved in other directions. It focussed instead on bilateral and regional arrangements geared to the possibility of overt Soviet Russian and Communist Chinese military aggression or subversion. Korea and Suez were major exceptions to this studied inattention, but they were deviations from what had become a normal pattern. On almost any scale—financial, military, economic, or diplomatic—the proportion of official American attention and effort focussed on the United Nations, by contrast with the total effort of American diplomacy, has been minor.

Americans have sensed—rightly, in the author's opinion— that an important coincidence of interests exists between the

United States and the United Nations. They are aware that the Charter in effect spells out American aspirations about relationships among nations. The American people have sometimes understood better than their own government that the prospects of the Western world and of mankind itself are tied in vital ways to the prospects for world organization. Their feeling has suffered in the light of events, although it has persisted. Without a better defined set of national aspirations, it still lacks the strength and quality of a wholly rational conviction. But the greatest obstacle to understanding has been self-inflicted. For the American government, through two major administrations, has publicly described its attachment for the United Nations in a tone which has not made it easy for the American people to gauge with any accuracy the true nature of the relationship.

A sharp division between ideal and reality, between official platitude and official policy, has thus characterized the American relationship to the United Nations. This in turn reflects a well-recognized paradox in the historic American style—a style which favors the pragmatic and the seemingly expedient, which rejects planning from abstract or theoretical premises, but which is invariably accompanied by top-level assertions about the moral nature of international politics and the American vision of a more perfect world. It is with respect to the United Nations that this duality has reached its most extraordinary level; that the most abstract sentiment and lofty goals have been given voice and the profoundest human aspiration evoked; and that as a consequence the contrast between hopes and results has been the most acute.

The downgrading of the United Nations has of course been a world-wide phenomenon. But the most dedicated—and least sophisticated—proponents of world organization and order have been found principally among Americans, and their own government has often been the target for their frustration. The commonest criticism of American policy has been that it "bypassed" the United Nations. Sometimes this accusation has been justified. But at other times it has been doctrinaire and unhelpful, urging multilateral action for the sake of internationalism, so it seemed, even when the requirements of American security dictated the opposite course.

The American record regarding the United Nations has not been blameless or consistent or at all times enlightened. But in the light of events following the 1945 peace it has had almost a quality of inevitability. The fact that, while in office, both major parties subscribed to the same general strategic pattern strongly suggests that American policy in and out of the United Nations tended to follow its most natural and logical course during the postwar years.

Indeed, many can be found to argue that the United States has done all it could—or should—to act in accordance with the U.N. Charter, to support the organization financially and morally, and to depend significantly on its acts and decisions. If we were faced with nothing more than a continuation ad infinitum of the postwar pattern, there would be strong arguments for continuing as before in the United Nations, correcting unprofitable tactics where they exist but continuing to starve it, as it were, in the process of allocating major diplomatic, economic, and military resources.

The situation is not, however, standing still. Shifts have already taken place in the equations of world power and in the atmospherics of the international climate. It is precisely because things have not stood still that there is an urgent need for reappraisals of strategies and policies which have served us reasonably well under different circumstances. The postwar years have already given way to a different era. Not only are external power relationships altering; significant changes are visible in both Soviet and Western societies. Outer space and other technological developments in what has been called the "Age of Acceleration" are outmoding recently perfected military weapons systems. Whether we wish it or not, we are facing certain strategic choices of policy goals and actions which are crucial in a sense that never fully applied before. The shape that has been assumed by the East-West conflict and the nationalist movement in Asia, Africa, the Middle East, and Latin America demands new decisions, new directions of policy, and new styles of thinking and planning from the richest and still most powerful nation in the world.

It is in such a context—one of revolutionary change and increasing political complexity—that we must now formulate national plans. A traditionally ambiguous posture toward the United Nations offers no assurance that in the quest of national objectives the most effective use will be made of the world's only presently available global diplomatic institution. At a time when each sector of national policy that has a bearing on the shape of the future must be scrutinized, and, where necessary, reordered, the sector of American diplomacy and action involving the United Nations calls for re-examination no less than any other—and perhaps more.

THE OBSTACLES TO PLANNING

The difficulties in reformulating national strategy with respect to the United Nations are striking.

One major difficulty arises from the image held by some Americans of the United Nations as an interesting and hopeful experiment that exists apart from the mainstream of strategy and diplomacy. This image is an unhelpful one, for it leads to two common errors. One is the neglect of useful possibilities for action; the other is the occasional departure in its name from the strategic moorings which otherwise anchor leadership to reality.

Perhaps the most important single thing about the United Nations is the picture of it that responsible statesmen carry in their minds. There were two critical junctures in recent history—Korea and Suez—at which the United Nations suddenly and for a brief time acquired an overwhelming importance in the consciousness of the highest levels. Even while believing that the basic policies followed in both instances were the correct ones, one can ponder the fact that two American Presidents at times in these two crises acted as though the United Nations were somehow a substitute for responsible national decision making and for the American diplomacy and power without which the United Nations is an

empty abstraction. Leadership and public alike were not prepared with a sound concept of the relationship, and much of
the subsequent criticism of U.S. and U.N. actions was
grounded in that failure.

Another major difficulty in focussing on the United Nations
as a central instrument of U.S. policy arises not so much from
conflicting ideas and ideals in the minds of men as from trends
in the changing international scene, faithfully reflected and
sometimes magnified within the United Nations. I refer above
all to changes in the nature of Soviet-Western relations and
to the rapid upsurge of the underdeveloped and dependent
countries. These two factors have combined to raise important
questions about the value of the United Nations for Western
coalition diplomacy, and about the future position of the West
in an organization increasingly composed of non-Western nations. In the early days of the cold war, it was not uncommon
for the vote in the U.N. General Assembly to be 55 to 5 on a
whole range of issues. The lines were sharply drawn; the balance of power was so rigid and bipolar in structure that little
flexibility for maneuver was left within the United Nations
(or, for that matter, outside). In such a setting, the presence of
Soviets and Americans under one roof posed a novel problem
for Western diplomacy. At a time when we were struggling
to organize a world-wide defensive coalition against the Communist threat, we had to meet and negotiate with our allies
in the presence of the enemy. Each issue and each vote thus
came to represent a separate test of free world unity, and often
it was more important in this sense than because of the actual
question involved. As time went on, the unity of the non-
Communist states was put under increasing strain by the
growing split between the poles of what might be called North
and South, primarily on issues arising in the colonial field. But
the over-all alliance held together, albeit with difficulty.

In 1952 the tone and mode of Soviet diplomacy, both in
and out of the United Nations, began to alter. The political
effect of this was acute, coming at a time when the bipolar political world was itself beginning to splinter. With
the development of something like a military standoff between

the United States and the Soviet Union, forces within the two coalitions began to assert their freedom of maneuver and to move toward positions relatively independent of the two leader states. Britain, France, India, Yugoslavia, Poland, Egypt, Japan, China, and Germany suddenly began to emerge as actual or potential foci of new independent action and even leadership. "Automatic majorities" and "automatic leadership" in the United Nations, if they had ever really existed, became things of the past. The world was changing, and the United Nations was changing with it.

With the growing strength of the uncommitted countries, the success of the West in gathering support through the United Nations has become increasingly dependent on the stands which Western nations take on issues of primary importance to the peoples of those areas. These have not been such issues as capitalism vs. communism or German unification or liberation of the Eastern European satellites, but colonialism, "self-determination," economic development, and racial discrimination. Out of the present membership, approximately half the members for one reason or another see these as the crucial issues and put the United States to the test in regard to them with increasing frequency. The issue often is purely symbolic; it may reflect an accumulated heritage of resentment or be designed to play off the East against the West. But in the United Nations these issues take concrete shape in resolutions and action programs in which Soviet and American performance is constantly made the measure for a host of other attitudes.

The way in which we have restructured the United Nations itself has added to the American dilemma. The United States urged a greater role for the General Assembly (where all nations, whatever their size, have equal votes) in order to offset the impotence of the Security Council when, in the fall of 1950, it appeared essential to remobilize the capabilities of the United Nations for collective military action. American action since then has discouraged military risk taking by the Communists, and the Assembly's real role in this field is still not measurable. But as part of the same development, the Assembly has become a prime political forum for the nations which remain outside the East-West camps and pursue their own goals of political independence, economic improvement, and racial dignity. In this situation what might be called the North-South conflict cuts across the East-West issues and makes its own powerful demands on American diplomacy, at the same time offering frequent opportunities for the Soviets to seize the political initiative.

The membership of the United Nations at the beginning of 1960 was 82, consisting of 9 African states (excluding the Union of South Africa), 20 Asian, 20 Latin American, 16 Western European, 9 Soviet bloc, 2 North American, 3 additional "Old Commonwealth" nations, and 3 unaffiliated (Nationalist China, Israel, and Yugoslavia). With the acquisition of independence in 1960 by the French Cameroons, Togoland, Nigeria, Somalia, Congo, Cyprus, and eleven former French colonies, the membership of the United Nations exceeded 95. Over the next decade at least several more states, all similarly drawn from Africa, except for one or two from the Caribbean and Pacific areas, may be expected to become independent and apply for membership.[1] Thus in two or three years the United States may well be one out of close to 100 members. In ten years it could be one out of 105. In fifteen years, if the process goes on unchecked, at least 10 other African territories plus up to 10 more from the Indian Ocean, Pacific, and Caribbean regions could make the total 125 members (not even including the divided states of Germany, Korea, and Vietnam). It is a fair question to ask if the United States can really ever again expect the organization to conform to the American definition of the state of the world and the contours of the future, as it did at Dumbarton Oaks and San Francisco in the drafting process and in the Uniting for Peace Resolution of 1950. With the Afro-Asian group alone capable of commanding close to 50 per cent of the votes in an organiza-

[1] See the author's *The Future Course of International Organization During 1965-70*, General Electric Technical Military Planning Operation, Santa Barbara, 1958.

tion of 100 members, is the United States going to be submerged by sheer numbers alone?

On certain issues the trend is indeed from a majority to an actual or potential minority position for the United States. This has in fact already happened on a number of issues in the field of economic planning, such as the proposals for U.N. financing of economic development and in discussions of international pricing of primary commodities, as well as in the tendency to define self-determination in terms of the right to nationalize foreign-owned property with or without fair compensation. Some Americans, particularly those in private and public business and trade organizations who follow U.N. proceedings, have concluded from this evidence that the United Nations, far from serving American national interests, poses grave dangers to the free enterprise system.

Actually, the United States has sometimes found itself in a minority position in other than economic areas. As early as 1952 the proposal to include India in the anticipated Korean political conference, actively opposed by the United States, received a majority vote in the First Committee. In November of 1954 the Assembly by a vote of 33-12 overrode U.S. objections and asserted its own competence to decide if a territory had attained a full measure of self-government. By 1957 the United States was in a minority of 28 against a majority of 42 in the Political Committee's vote calling for new talks between the Netherlands and Indonesia over West New Guinea.

An American proposal to the Human Rights Commission in 1955 favoring an *ad hoc* commission to redefine the concept of self-determination was passed by the Economic and Social Council in July of that year but buried by the Assembly three years later by a vote of 48 against, only 16 for, and 18 abstentions. At one stage of the balloting in October 1959, the same size majority favored Poland over the American-backed candidacy of Turkey, supported by 33, for a contested seat on the Security Council. Such examples of numerical majorities consisting usually of Arab-Asians, the Soviet bloc, some Latin Americans, and occasionally European and Scandinavian members are becoming ever more abundant.

Since the increases in membership will continue to come exclusively from areas such as Africa, the Middle East, and the Caribbean rather than from North America and Western Europe, relative increases can be looked for in votes favoring U.N. financing of economic development, early independence for any colonial territory under Western control, international commodity stabilization, the seating of Communist China, self-determination as the right to national control of resources, and *détente* in the cold war. When the Western community interprets its own interests as in conflict with any of these, it is likely to find itself in a minority position in the United Nations.

The difficulties facing Western policy in the United Nations are thus important ones. They have affected the success of Western unity, and they color the prospects for the future. Seen through American eyes as complicating though not necessarily disabling factors in terms of the utility of the world organization, these difficulties have induced a decidedly negative attitude toward the United Nations in Western European policy-making and planning circles.

A favorite adjective in Western European comment about the changing United Nations and its new membership is "irresponsible." The representatives of newly created nations are not always in the tradition of Talleyrand, Metternich, and Castlereagh. The underlying grievance of European diplomats has been that the growing number of small, recently constituted non-Western states tend to gang up and pass judgment on their elders on issues regarding the tutelage of European countries over dependent territories without having responsibility comparable to that of the administrators. The Western slogan was neatly summed up by *The Economist* as "no representation without perspiration" (August 2, 1958).

There are modest signs that, making a virtue of necessity, the West might see considerable force in the educative value of the United Nations for these "uneducated" states. More to the point, the colonial issue is going to run its course in a relatively short number of years at the present pace of events, and there will be a clearer opportunity to test the real community of interests between West and, as it were, South. But at the moment it would be difficult to persuade our Western partners that this prospective pleasure outweighs the pain, and it is not much easier to convince ourselves that, without a significant reconsideration of certain American policies, the United States can avoid the anticipated minority position.

In the face of the apparent prospects, it can be expected that schemes for reorganization of the U.N. structure will be revived. Proposals to offset the growing minority position of the West would doubtless take the form of seeking to reverse the American-inspired trend toward greater authority for the General Assembly by "reviving the Security Council," or of curtailing the parliamentary strength of the majority of smaller and weaker nations by a scheme of weighted voting in the Assembly.

The Security Council may well be increasingly used where either the great powers seek speedy international action—as with the Congo—or when others choose to focus U.N. consideration on an issue of concern to them as a threat to the peace; for instance, the South African apartheid case of March 1960.

But to formalize a cut in the parliamentary power of the vast majority of states seems most unpromising as a panacea, requiring as it would the consent of the very states whose power would be thereby diminished. As long as the Assembly has no true legislative authority but only the power to recommend, the arguments for greater control by the more powerful states remain unconvincing. Weighted voting might become a real possibility in the case of a significant program of multilateral financing, such as for economic development or for a relatively large international force, on which the votes of the chief contributors would logically require greater weight (perhaps in a combination weighted and numerical vote). But the political obstacles seem formidable. More to the point, until the United States has a better idea of the role it wishes the United Nations to play in its national strategy, moves for limiting the activities of the numerous small powers merely irritate without serving any constructive purpose.

Actually, the apparent trend toward domination of the

United Nations by an unsympathetic majority is subject to important qualifications. A recent analysis of the American performance concluded that where this country has chosen to exert strong influence, the General Assembly has invariably acted in a way favorable to our interests:

> In propaganda battles, where its integrity and motives have been questioned, the United States has never lost a major vote. The same record holds for international disputes and threatening situations on which a firm stand has been taken.[2]
> . . . The United States has been a more successful advocate than any of the other Great Powers. Without exception political questions of vital concern to the United States have been decided in conformity with the major outlines of the American position. . . .[3]

One saving grace has of course been the two-thirds rule for voting on important matters in the General Assembly. But even without this constitutional protection, examples can be found of pro-Western majorities in recent times quite as large as the anti-Western majorities cited earlier. In the 1958 Assembly, 52 voted in favor of and 9 against the Western-sponsored resolution reiterating the United Nations' purposes with respect to Korea. In both the 1958 and 1959 sessions Asian-African resolutions calling for negotiations between France and Algeria, even after being highly diluted, failed to get a two-thirds majority. On October 21, 1959, 45 voted in favor of a critical resolution on the Tibetan situation with only 9 opposed (but with 26 abstaining), and at the same session 51 voted to debate the Hungarian issue, with only 10 opposing. In April 1960, the Asian-African group failed to muster the necessary 42 votes to convene a special Assembly session on apartheid.

The Arab-Asian bloc is by no means as solid as it sometimes appears.[4] At the 1956 Assembly as many of its members (10)

[2] Robert E. Riggs, *Politics in the United Nations,* University of Illinois, Urbana, 1958, p. 164.

[3] *Ibid.,* p. 175.

[4] For a detailed analysis of the performance of blocs, see the study commissioned by the United Nations project, Center for International Studies, Massachusetts Institute of Technology: *Bloc Politics in the United Nations,* by Thomas Hovet, Jr., Harvard University Press, Cambridge, 1960.

voted with the United States on the Chinese representation issue as voted against. None voted against the condemnation of the Soviet Union on the Hungarian issue at the 1956 Assembly. In 1959, 51 voted to debate the Hungarian issue, with only 10 opposing.

A recent writer has concluded that when the North Atlantic community members are not divided among themselves, the Assembly majority will go along with them in 4 out of 5 votes.[5] In the short run, this is reassuring, although the Western community has found itself divided both on issues of substance (Algeria) and of procedure (the Security Council elections in 1959).

But there can be no complacency about the future. Many thoughtful people in the West believe that, despite the success of the United States in having its way on vital political issues, a membership approaching 100 will by its predominantly non-Western complexion jeopardize important Western diplomatic positions.

The failure of the United Nations to affect significantly the present degree of world stability and well-being, combined with the projected trends, has led a number of observers to the conclusion that the United Nations represents essentially a drawback, an embarrassment, a hindrance, and even a menacing obstacle to Western security. All of these descriptions have been applied in recent times by some professional American diplomats and European political leaders in their private assessments of the situation.[6] Apart from certain overriding crises, when, in a manner of speaking, all signals were off, a case could be made that the fulsome and seemingly wholehearted statements by American leaders that participation in the United Nations is in our national interest have been contradicted by the facts.

Given the deadlocks, the frustrations, the intractable facts of life in and out of the United Nations, can anything genu-

[5] Waldo Chamberlin, "The North Atlantic Bloc in the U.N. General Assembly," I *Orbis* (1958), p. 466.

[6] See the author's *Western Europe and the U.N.—Trends and Prospects,* Center for International Studies, Massachusetts Institute of Technology, Cambridge, 1959 (mimeographed).

inely new be added to the common estimate of its actual worth? Given all these obstacles to creative planning about the uses of the United Nations, including the obstacles found in the planning process itself, is it really worth while to try to spell out afresh the framework for our U.N. policy?

NEW DIRECTIONS FOR PLANNING

The writer is reminded of the words of Alfred Duff Cooper when he pondered the fate of the League of Nations: "I have often thought that if the League had had some openly declared enemies it might have had a better chance of success, but when all pay lip-service and few have faith the cause is doomed."[7] If the United Nations has no undisclosed values for us, it really does not matter if our notions about it are accurate or not. It is not, however, entirely certain that we have recently been asking the right questions about the United Nations. Like the issue of numerical majorities, the questions commonly asked about the potential of the United Nations imply assumptions which are not necessarily valid. Can the United Nations prevent war? Can it bring about harmony between the Russians and ourselves? Can it replace governmental action in the financing of development programs? Or, the ultimate deception, can it replace governments themselves? The answer, for our times, is and must be, "No."

But are these indeed the vital operational questions? The crucial questions about the United Nations are those which proceed from the real rather than the supposed requirements of national strategy. Military strategy gives promise of revising its premises about the probability of all-out war as compared with limited war. Yet the traditional test for U.N. value has been either whether it achieved a U.S.-Soviet military combination—absurd from any present standpoint—or whether it can by itself somehow eliminate the threat of aggressive war. Because national strategy depended for some years on the notion that war with the Soviet Union must by definition be all-out, only that which was responsive to such a contingency had

[7] *Old Men Forget,* Dutton, New York, 1954, p. 158.

military value. Today, for familiar military and technical reasons, all-out war seems less likely than other more limited forms of military engagement. The questions to pose about the United Nations' security capabilities must consequently address themselves to the organization's capacity and limitations with respect not to the least likely but to the most likely contingencies: limited wars and brushfire situations starting in the non-Communist states. The questions would stem from the military situation of the 1960's, not the 1940's, and in the light of new military and technological data would address themselves afresh to the problem of political and military security.

Similarly, if the questions asked to test U.N. capabilities assume that the only choice is between world government or no world order at all, the cards are stacked very badly indeed against constructive action. A strategic doctrine for the United Nations that so escaped from realities would be no better than one that continued to underestimate its capabilities.

The temptation is always strong to wipe the slate clean and imagine into existence a different kind of world in which international relations partake of the qualities making for stability and mutual confidence in domestic societies. In response to the frustrations of the world we know, many proposals have been advanced that would utterly transform the nature of the United Nations by abandoning national sovereignty, drastically revising the Charter, and so forth. These suggestions are at best premature. At worst they are fantasies for evading the exigent problems that confront us. Of course, a global war could bring about a world government overnight. A series of trips to the brink might shake profoundly the rooted values and habit systems that place national sovereignty above virtually all else in today's world. But neither contingency furnishes a useful base for planning.

What follows does not assume that nation states as we presently know them are in their terminal state. It does, however, assume that there is a contemporary historical trend toward integration and limited forms of supranationalism, running parallel with the trend to ultranationalism and fragmentation of international society. This trend toward integration does not for the present era connote a tendency toward world government, but rather suggests a possible historical middle way between a world unified by force—the only presently available means—and a continuation of the international anarchy of the past. The alternatives of world government or of substantially reducing the present authority of the United Nations are thus not exhaustive. Other relevant policy questions have to do with the building of political, economic, cultural, and technical bases for new sectors of world community, and with ways of fulfilling the promise contained in existing movements for federation and integration.

The uses of the United Nations should be tested against its capacity to open up a middle ground where new territories and hitherto unclaimed realms might be neutralized, but without demanding that the concept of national sovereignty also be liquidated. Some new and acceptable form of international concern for emerging small and inexperienced countries needs to be developed to take the place of the imperial tutelage that lies in the past. We need an open mind toward means for attacking the baffling problem of raising standards of living in the face of population curves that are rising even faster. In posing all of these questions we require to know if action programs are possible—now, not in some unspecified utopia—that neither depend upon assent by the Communists nor close the door to their eventual participation.

The question remains before us as to whether a given step toward solution of these fundamental problems can better be taken in or outside of the United Nations. Put another way, how can the United States make the most effective use of the United Nations in achieving its paramount objectives in the years immediately ahead? In seeking realistic answers, there is only a seeming paradox in giving particular attention to the two things which above all else have made the United Nations seem an exercise in futility, frustration, and self-deception—its apparent lack of value in terms of the short-term security problem; and its seemingly remote prospects for bringing closer the kind of world order we can legitimately envisage without either having to solve all the short-run problems or having to attain a millennium in which the United States and the Communist states will have achieved an abiding consensus about basic values on which an organic world community, under law, can be based.

The working assumption is that there will be no all-out global, thermonuclear war in the period ahead. But the collateral assumption is that nonetheless we are not at peace but in a conflict whose stakes are the attitudes of mankind and the design of the political world. We would do well, in reformulating our national strategic doctrine with respect to the United Nations, to obey the advice Demosthenes gave to the Athenians in 351 B.C.: "In war one must not allow oneself to be at the command of events. One must forestall them."

CHAPTER TWO

Strategic Doctrine and National Interest
—A Guide for Planning

THE TASK we have undertaken is to evaluate the uses of the United Nations over the next few years from the standpoint of American national interests. This in turn requires that the potentialities and limitations of the United Nations be intimately connected to the real world of foreign policy in terms of national goals, objectives, and strategies which, wholly independent of the ideals of the U.N. Charter and the aspirations of the individual citizen, form the real substance of the national foreign policy setting.

The ensemble of goals and resources, of purpose and power, can be summed up in the phrase "strategic doctrine."

> Strategic doctrine translates power into policy. Whether the goals of a state are offensive or defensive, whether it seeks to achieve or prevent a change, its strategic doctrine must be able to define what objectives are worth contending for and to develop the appropriate force for achieving them. By establishing a pattern *in advance* of crisis situations, strategic doctrine permits a Power to act purposefully in the face of challenges. In its absence a Power will constantly be surprised by events. An adequate strategic doctrine is therefore the basic requirement of American security.[1]

[1] Henry A. Kissinger, "Strategy and Organization," 35 *Foreign Affairs* (1957), p. 380.

To develop a comparable doctrine that focusses on the possible uses of the United Nations, a more modest analytical effort is called for. It is an effort, nonetheless, that borrows from the larger picture some of its coordinates, and that seeks to place the United Nations in the perspective of the broad national enterprise. For either task—grand, or in this case specialized—the starting point must be located in relation to the determinative forces in the political world.

THE HISTORICAL SETTING

The contemporary international scene is dominated by three major forces which have the capacity to reshape the world. One is the force of the Communist movement, which disposes of the power, however reluctant, of one-third of the globe. The second is the force of nationalism powering the dynamic political and economic movements in Asia, Africa, the Middle East, and Latin America. The third is the force of Western civilization centered in Western Europe and North America and in outposts such as Australasia.

The strategic doctrine of communism is of course infinitely wider than a purely military strategy. It pursues its ultimate purpose of world communization with tactical self-consciousness at every level of operation. It is not necessarily overrating the future of the Communist movement to acknowledge its skill and the inner power conferred by its revolutionary and imperialistic frame of mind. John Stuart Mill perceived the enormous advantage of ideology over nonideology when he said, "One person with a belief is a social power equal to ninety-nine who have only interests." A contemporary writer elaborated this theme:

> All too naturally, by identifying himself with the *antithesis* of the Dialectic, that is, by professing a religious faith, the Marxist put himself into the state of mind of a man going upstairs on an escalator.[2]

As a comprehensive political movement, Communism has been operating with the extraordinary benefits conferred by

[2] Edmund Wilson, *To the Finland Station*, Harcourt, Brace, New York, 1956, p. 196.

two particular advantages. One is an unparalleled organizing capacity through which small and dedicated forces can apply immense leverage, by a sort of political judo, to overcome large, disorganized, and relatively inert masses of superior weight. The other advantage is the planning faculty summed up by Nathan Leites:

> The superior ability of the Party in diagnosis and prognosis is a major factor making for its victory. All appraisals must in principle be made on a world scale and with a long perspective. All details of the Party's policy must be part of an over-all plan. The Party must not permit itself to be dominated by the appearances of the moment, but rather derive all actions from a long-range plan based on long-run forecasts.[3]

To be sure, our own pragmatic approach to politics has given us a resiliency which the Communist approach lacks, and in the long run the dogmatism of communism will surely be among the internal contradictions causing its own downfall. But for the period under review the United States and the West as a whole are disadvantaged both by their failure to look sufficiently ahead and by their preference for improvised and essentially defensive reactions to crises which have mounted to the point where they cannot be ignored. The more our society is believed to be incapable of developing dynamic political, economic, and social doctrines over a protracted period of conflict, the greater success can attend Communist strategy, and the greater its opportunity to carry off its pose of the future incarnate.

The second prime contemporary force—nationalism in the world of nonwhite, economically underdeveloped, anticolonial, and politically neutralist countries and territories—also has a strategic doctrine, although a far less monolithic and coherent one than that of the Communists. The astounding strength of the newly energized nationalist movement does not arise from the clarity of its detailed program or from the possession of conventional attributes of national power. But the purposes of the nationalist movement are sufficiently explicit and potent in their appeal to have placed the Western powers

[3] Nathan Leites, *A Study of Bolshevism*, Free Press, Glencoe, 1953, p. 185.

on the defensive; and the Western powers have yielded up one territorial, economic, or political position after another while remaining still unable to substitute another image of themselves for the already outmoded "colonialist-imperialist-racist" image which continues to serve the revolutionaries as a target.

The third force—that represented by Western civilization—still counts for much in the balance scale of world power and influence; but with the explosive growth of the other two it has seemed by contrast to have become a latent rather than a dynamic force. Historically, the society which represents social and property values subjected to massive assault by new revolutionary forces labors under a handicap. Its paramount ideology is by definition a conservative one, representing an established position to be defended, a fixed terrain to be held. In the present age the Western world has been in such a position. It has predictably—and alarmingly—lagged behind communism and nationalism in the degree of its dynamism and in the impression conveyed to the rest of the world that it is still vigorous and still growing. Whether in terms of rate of economic growth, or in the quality of its contemporary political and economic ideas, or in the extent of its educational and technological expansion, the West has given the appearance of standing still while new movements armed with ambition, drive, and a dazzling sense of purpose seemed to be overhauling it.

Secular Western ideas of freedom, human dignity, and high living standards retain their intrinsic value, and have indeed been borrowed at will by other movements. But the West in recent times has not been able to derive satisfactory political profit as the evangelical force behind these ideas. They have become common property; their source of inspiration is virtually no more than an historical footnote. Where the West aids others in achieving these goals it is often regarded as recompense for past wrongs. Thus Western Europe has not developed a doctrine or ideology to take the place of three centuries of empire or even to account to itself for the harassed and often ignominious way in which European colonialism is ending. Caught between outgoing continental power and incoming hostility from the world to the South as well as that to the East, Europe has appeared suspended between two ages. Meanwhile, basic American strategy, whether expressed in political, economic, or military terms, has been defensive in nature. American tactics, which can flow only from its strategy, are incessantly vulnerable to transient domestic and international pressures. As a result, short-term goals have tended to dictate American policy, while long-term goals have remained unrealistic and inapplicable.

All of these truths have been sensed over and over again by Americans as the facts of life in the postwar world were pressed home to them. Yet the grounds for determined strategic actions have been insufficient, perhaps because the alternatives never could be portrayed in black and white as they can in a fighting war. The alternatives are rarely those of total destruction of the United States and its civilization, on the one hand, and the victory of the American Ideal in all the world, on the other. Defeat for America, if it ever came, would likely be slow and corrosive until the moment when, with the nation politically and spiritually isolated, the issue would at last be resolved in the one way doomed to fail—by force. A peaceful victory, however it might be defined—the spread of democratic institutions, greater international stability, a more predictable world order—would be unspectacular and perhaps imperceptible as all the components of the world equation—including ourselves—changed in the process. Because success and failure in this kind of process can hardly be conceived in sharp or simple terms, between them lies the tempting zone of indifference and inadequacy, where we find ourselves at this writing.

THE NATIONAL INTEREST

All attempts to formulate a suitable strategic political doctrine lead inexorably back to the same starting point: the identification of national goals, purposes, and objectives. National strategy is without meaning unless it points toward the accomplishment of a nation's larger purposes. And unless those purposes are sufficiently defined, there can be no end to improvisation, to the dominance of military over political objectives, and to the application of tactical rather than strategic principles to the use of instrumentalities such as the United Nations.

The inescapable precondition to a rational re-examination of the uses of the United Nations is the identification of the goals and objectives of American external policy. Without spelling them out we have nothing tangible against which to estimate the extent to which the use of U.N. machinery may advance or retard our cause. The utility of the United Nations, then, is tested in the light of what in political shorthand has come to be called the national interest. We have not always failed to recognize this interconnection. But we have found it uncommonly difficult to spell out precisely what our objectives actually are, and even what we mean by national interest.

THE MEANING OF NATIONAL INTEREST

Two classic definitions of national interest are clear and unambiguous. One—perhaps the only one not capable of a depressing number of alternatives—is the primordial interest of self-preservation, that which William Pitt once called "the first law of nature" for a sovereign state. The nation has a primary duty of preserving itself.

Much past analysis of the problem also centered around geographical factors summed up by Napolean when he stated: "The foreign policy of a country is determined by its geography." National interest as an expression of a country's physical location and topography is an obvious element of strategy. The British government was for several centuries explicit that its primary national interest was to prevent the creation of a preponderant combination of power on the European continent. Every detail of policy, from intrigues with France and Spain to the barrier policy favoring Belgian neutrality, flowed from the grand strategy defined by the national interest. The United States was also able for a time to define its prime national interest in geographical terms centering around its role as a dominant hemispheric power. Today this interest remains, but as one of a host of other more complex and diffuse interests.

Beyond self-preservation and geography the national interest becomes elusive. One analysis of the assertions of American Presidents and Secretaries of State during the postwar period concludes that the national interest has invariably been defined in the highly generalized terms of "Peace," "Security," "Freedom," "Justice," "Well-Being," and "Prosperity."[4]

As thus defined it does not tell us how we should act toward the Soviet Union in a given set of circumstances, nor whether disarmament poses greater dangers to our security than rearmament, nor what kind of objectives we should be striving for in our relationships with Asia and Africa. Above all, it does not tell us anything tangible about the uses of such diplomatic institutions as the United Nations.

The traditions out of which American idealism sprang and was nourished yield up the half dozen abstract ideals—Peace, Security, Freedom, Justice, Well-Being, and Prosperity. But their strength as reflections of our national morality is at the same time their weakness as descriptions of a program of external action. They convey great and serious meaning to men everywhere, in one fashion or another, but they are insufficient today either as vital ends of policy or as touchstones for selecting among alternative means of action.

Because excessively broad and abstract goals of foreign policy produce painful dilemmas for policy making when they are taken seriously and spelled out, the United States, wholly apart from its characteristically pragmatic style, understandably is inhibited from detailing its goals with greater precision. To act purposefully on our proclaimed objectives would at times be expensive, embarrassing, troublesome, and sometimes quite impossible.

But the situation in which this leaves the United States is

[4] Michael Brower, *The U.S. National Interest—Assertions and Definitions,* Center for International Studies, Massachusetts Institute of Technology, Cambridge, 1959 (mimeographed).

not merely one of moral ambiguity. No nation is free of this curse, and if that were the only issue we might be quite satisfied to continue as before. The real issue has to do rather with the prospects before us as a nation for dealing with the question of how to impose on the contemporary tides of history any effective design of our own, with the aim of helping our version of the ultimate end to prevail. By proclaiming broad goals but remaining unwilling or unable to implement them, we shall remain frustrated and in this sense impotent as a creative world force. Worse than that, we shall continue to mislead ourselves into believing that because platitudes cannot easily be made into reality, we are eternally limited to improvisation and sporadic counterpunching in our long-range planning and acting.

But it is not impossible to derive a more lucid and operationally meaningful interpretation of American external goals from our historical situation. The evidence suggests that the chief purpose for which our foreign policy operates is to develop an international environment in which we can enjoy our prosperity and cultivate our internal societal values without excessive disturbance or threat from the outside. To achieve this goal under present conditions we are required to take measures to protect the physical base of American society. This is the essential rationale of defense policy. The international posture that results from this goal is one of discouraging rather than fomenting or encouraging violent changes by war, revolution, or other dislocation or upheaval. As an entirely logical result, Western action policies are principally designed to stabilize, restore, and retain, as contrasted with the Communist purposes of unbalancing, revolutionizing, and seizing.

The logical consequences of such a policy preclude actions that would sharpen contemporary conflicts. They logically favor actions aimed at blunting and converting to acceptable and tolerable forms the thrusts of forces of revolution and change. In any overview of American policy today, all rhetoric aside, these are the basic contours. But because of the principles we feel to be at stake, and also because of emotional factors that reside in the process of domestic consensus and policy formulation, we have felt impelled to pursue at the same time unbalancing policies, at least at the verbal level, of "liberation" in Eastern Europe, reversal of the Chinese revolution, and other ends calculated to resharpen and intensify the conflict of forces. Because we *do* favor the restoration of self-government to the Eastern European satellites and of a friendly regime on the Chinese mainland, we cannot and will not formalize the present situation as the Communist leadership would have us do. But the embarrassing consequence is that we appear to be in favor of change in theory, but in favor of the *status quo* in fact.

We are rescued from this uncomfortable dilemma by the changing nature of the situation. We do not need to remain trapped between acceptance of the *status quo* or the fomenting of revolution in Eastern Europe and China, the price of which we are unwilling to pay. The *status quo* is never permanent, and our long-term program must actively collaborate with that eternal historical verity. But the short-term objective of stability is nonetheless of great validity. We run risks of involvement that sometimes verge on the intolerable on the occasion of any major threat to stability.

I would therefore formulate the grand strategy which follows logically from our fundamental national interests in the following way: For the Communist states we seek stability in the short run but change in the long run, exploiting the vulnerabilities in the Communist empire and encouraging the trends which seem to favor our long-term prospects. But our policy toward the forces of anticolonial, anti-Western nationalism logically is the other way around—in the short run to favor and to assist in the changes that are taking place anyway, with a view to long-term stability and the restoration of favorable relationships.

THE LARGER NATIONAL INTEREST

The nature of the world today is such that no great and powerful nation makes a decision that fails to take into account the interests of others. The revolution in technology and therefore in instruments of warfare may have already produced a situation where the interests of a single nation are almost indistinguishable from the interests of the whole community—even if the community does not behave like one. At the same time, no nation, including our own, will act in serious matters in a way that runs contrary to whatever clear sense it has of its own national interests. Superficially, this produces a paradox and encourages the belief that the concept of the United Nations—the prime symbol of internationalism and common interests—by definition clashes with the notion of national interest, with its traditional connotation of unilateralism and inevitably selfish and narrowly conceived national behavior.

But a nation's interest is not necessarily limited to the classic goals of seeking power and prestige. There is no automatic and self-regulating mechanism in history or politics which limits interests to a narrow rather than a broad spectrum. The broader concept of national interests represents the highest degree of self-interest for a nation in our circumstances in history, a nation which wishes to retain its power, if you will, but sees that to do so it must seek common interests with other nations. The overriding American interest in a more satisfactory and durable world in which to enjoy what it has leaves it little responsible choice between the political strategies that represent narrow and broad concepts of the national interest.

The significance of the United Nations to American foreign policy rests in great part on this insight. What cannot be done, however, is to disconnect the notion of national interest from the notion of common interest and to regard the United Nations as the natural enemy of one and friend of the other.

Common action through the United Nations rather than unilateral action is politically feasible on major political matters when the common interest involved has been made clear in terms not of its virtue as an abstract good but of an explicit national interest. The connection between the two is made when the national interest is defined in such a way that policies both in and out of the United Nations will more effectively serve its broad concerns. This process can take place only when national goals and objectives are more clearly perceived, and when policies necessary to move toward attainment of the goals are better matched with the capabilities and limitations of the international institution. It cannot succeed unless the sought-after ends are distinguished from the diplomatic and institutional means; and it cannot acquire meaning in terms of specific policy problems facing the nation until these in turn are sorted out, the short-term from the long-range, the military security issues from the nonmilitary issues of evolution and welfare, and the ideal of law and order from the preliminaries of community building.

The task is at once made easier and harder by the fact that both as an idea and as an institution the United Nations has the peculiar and perhaps unique quality of itself serving as an embodiment of long-range objectives. So far, the long-range goals embodied in the Charter have at best served as occasional moral guides, at worst as an excuse for complacently viewing history as a story with an inevitably happy ending. In this sense the United Nations has served to deepen frustrations and feed the human sense of futility. But if the United Nations is viewed not as an end in itself but as a means to socially desirable and politically valid ends, it may have a more significant role in working toward goals of our own choosing than we have so far attributed to it.

AMERICAN GOALS

There follows a suggested outline of America's external objectives, with the understanding that they represent a single student's attempt to spell out systematically the paramount goals of the United States in the world over the years immediately ahead. In effect, they represent in their totality a definition of the national interest as it grows out of the imperatives of the historical situation and the potentialities discernible at this point in history.

The paramount national interest is to secure a world environment in which the United States can cultivate its internal social values without excessive disturbance or threat from the outside. From this flow military policy, economic policy, and the ceaseless task of operating effectively on the political environment. From this interest can be derived four operational categories: Military Security, Political Security, Stability and Welfare, and World Order. These categories are not mutually exclusive. All have obvious implications for United States security in the broad sense. All of them are relevant to the East-West conflict, and, like it or not, many exist as goals only because of the motivation supplied by that conflict. All of them are related to the kind of world we wish to see emerge from the present dangerous and unstable period.

Each of the four categories represents a sector of the time spectrum, although the distinctions are not hard and fast. Short-range objectives represent goals of overriding urgency today, the achievement of which is essential to safeguard the existence of the nation itself. Reflecting the most basic national interest of all—survival and existence—the achievement of short-range goals automatically takes top priority. We cannot afford to wait until later to achieve them, and indeed may forego a long-range future if we do not give them their rightful priority. The military security problem for this reason properly belongs in the category of short-range (although it may well also constitute a long-range problem with which we must deal indefinitely).

Political and economic objectives are located in the middle range, but only because physical survival is possible without their immediate achievement, whereas it might not be if the short-run goals were not adequately met. We have sometimes tended to downgrade longer-term objectives in favor of short-run requirements with the excuse that the latter precluded significant action along broader fronts. This has been not only illogical but potentially destructive of opportunities for creative enterprise. Military policy, no less than U.N. policy, is a means to a larger end, not an end in itself, and can fulfill its true function only if regarded as a shield behind which political, economic, and social forces can play their more creative role. Target dates for significant fulfillment of the middle-range objectives would run approximately from three to ten years.

The last category—World Order—is assigned to the heading of long-range with a target of roughly five to twenty years for significant accomplishment. The danger in doing this is precisely the same as in locating other nonmilitary efforts in the middle range of policy goals. The long-range nature of the problem of world order has served to encourage the perpetuation of apathy and fatalism on our part. The near hopelessness of the current American philosophy of world order is illustrated by the all-too-common assumption that nothing can be done along these "futuristic" lines until the problem of communism is somehow "solved." It is also underscored by the absence of any real middle ground between apathy on the one hand and the framing of utopian blueprints for world government on the other. Such blueprints have so far not been helpful to us because they have had to assume that the problem of Communist imperialism and hostility would somehow vanish.

Between these two extremes are proposals and schemes for more limited forms of association, generally on a regional basis. But one seeks in vain for proposals that would significantly build today toward the kind of world order we have in mind and that are not dependent on some sort of magical transformation of the world political scene, or that do not limit themselves to primarily security objectives, or that are not confined to geographic regions, or that make use of the machinery of the United Nations insofar as that is possible.

The essential distinction between military security and world order is one of time only. World order, seen not as a utopia but as a process, has both relevance and immediacy, and constitutes a highly legitimate charge on planning resources here and now.

What follows, then, is an attempt to render a summary catalog of national foreign policy goals—of the national interest, that is—against which we can seek to test the present and future utility of the United Nations as an instrument of diplomacy and an agency of political action:

OVER-ALL OBJECTIVE: *To secure the kind of world environment in which our nation—and, by definition, other nations—can cultivate their societies without excessive insecurity and external threats of disruption.*

MILITARY SECURITY

BASIC OBJECTIVE: To preserve the zone of freedom and at the same time to minimize the chances of an all-out war.

Specific Objectives:

1. To discourage deliberate Communist military risk taking, by maintaining a consistently stable power relationship vis-à-vis the Soviet Union and Communist China, in order to neutralize Communist military capabilities of launching a successful military attack, surprise or other, on the United States or its free world allies, and in order to discourage Communist intentions to do so.

    a. To maintain an adequate deterrent in the form of military and technological strength.

    b. To back up the physical deterrent with maximum national will and determination.

    c. To make military adventure prohibitively costly, politically and morally as well as militarily.

2. To bring the arms race under control by safeguarded agreements, including the uses of outer space, before significant nuclear capabilities spread to additional countries and before the applications of outer space technology become even more threatening militarily; to minimize arms competition in the Near East and Latin America, and avert it in Africa.

3. To prevent accidental or inadvertent large-scale war from developing out of local hostilities either involving the Soviet Union or within the non-Communist states by improving military and diplomatic techniques of prevention and localization of dangerous situations.

    a. To prevent hostilities involving the great powers from leading automatically to all-out war, assuming a chance exists to localize them, by developing better military capabilities for limited warfare.

b. To create the maximum political deterrence to expansion of hostilities by developing the widest possible international support in the event of such hostilities.

c. To develop more effective means of dealing with smaller-scale breaches of peace involving non-Communist nations.

4. To find more effective ways of preventing and repulsing externally directed subversion and other aggression against political independence and territorial integrity.

5. To conduct hostilities, should they break out, in such a way as to attract maximum military and political support, limit the scope and aims of the hostilities, and terminate them as quickly as possible under the most satisfactory political conditions.

a. To ensure maximum international military and political support in the event of general war.

b. To hold war aims that permit reduction and liquidation of a given conflict rather than demand its enlargement.

6. To maintain the maximum political and military support and unity in the face of a continuing Communist threat.

POLITICAL SECURITY

BASIC OBJECTIVE: To ensure the survival and prosperity of our political and social values in an era of protracted international disequilibrium.

Specific Objectives:

1. To moderate the hostile quality of Sino-Soviet communism toward the non-Communist states.

a. To seek and cultivate common interests with the Soviet Union with a view to a protracted modus vivendi, including above all the common interest in reducing the threat of military aggression by the other side.

2. To encourage the evolution of the Soviet system into more internationally tolerable forms.

   a. To expose Soviet personnel, particularly the emerging élites, to the advantages of personal freedom and an international philosophy of live and let live.
   b. To offer alternatives to the Soviet government that involve collaborative relationships with other countries.
   c. To hold before the communized nations the alternatives of genuine coexistence rather than ultimate conflict.

3. To devise and exploit sources of division and internal tension within the Communist empire.

   a. To develop the means for effective application of appropriate pressures in situations where opportunities favorable to freedom may develop within the Communist empire.

4. To neutralize the ideological thrust of communism by improving the capacity of free societies to furnish human and social satisfactions, both material and nonmaterial.

   a. To demonstrate through political, economic, technological, social, cultural, and humanitarian policies that a free, open, and competitive society is capable of supplying acceptable leadership in these fields and can yield more ultimate satisfactions to the individual than a totalitarian system.
   b. To sustain the validity of our own form of society and government as a model by purposefully working to remove its blemishes.
   c. To give other peoples, particularly those in uncommitted countries, a demonstrable stake in freedom and cooperative relations with the West, as well as confidence in voluntaristic rather than coercive methods in the creation of their own social orders.
   d. To defend ourselves successfully against hostile propaganda, systematically revealing the fundamental fallacies of Communist doctrine.

STABILITY AND WELFARE

BASIC OBJECTIVE: To develop greater stability and less friction in international relationships.

Specific Objectives:

1. To find ways of minimizing resort to violence as a technique for settling international disputes.
    a. To reduce the present and potential sources of tension and political instability in the non-Communist states.
    b. To remove from future conflict such potential sources of dispute as Antarctica, international waterways, and outer space.
    c. To improve international capabilities, preventive and remedial, for resolving territorial and other disputes more effectively, predictably, and justly.

2. To achieve means of peaceful change with the aim of preventing dissatisfactions with the *status quo* from leading, as in the past, to war.

3. To create conditions of economic stability, with the particular goal of satisfactory and durable relationships with the underdeveloped countries, by fostering economic and social progress.
    a. To develop a more effective and predictable flow of capital to underdeveloped countries.
    b. To develop an international trading system in which the industrialized countries can survive and prosper, including arrangements in the field of trade, currency, and the price structure of internationally marketed commodities.
    c. To maintain international arrangements aimed at retaining free access to raw materials for the United States and other developed countries.
    d. To seek the solution of problems arising from conditions of excess population, and from the relation between population and available material resources and human opportunities.

4. To expedite liquidation of the remaining Western colonial-type holdings and the substitution of more durable and mutually satisfactory relationships.

5. To channel contemporary forces of nationalism toward constructive rather than destructive tasks and purposes.
   a. To design and help execute constructive tasks for under-developed countries.
   b. To foster the growth of loyalties to broader communities of common interest, both political and functional, through the processes of integration.
   c. To develop concepts of greater responsibility by states, particularly the newer ones, regardless of size or strength.

WORLD ORDER

Basic Objective: To build a more reliable, predictable, and tolerable world order based on values reflecting freedom and voluntarism rather than totalitarianism and coercion, and combining the values of unity with the values of individual dignity and social and political diversity.

Specific Objectives:

1. To substitute processes of cooperation, order, and eventually world law for the anarchy and narrow nationalism that continue to endanger world peace and stability.
   a. To make existing international political and legal institutions more effective by policy, by example, and by use, with the aim of world-wide participation and compliance but without waiting for all the conditions of universality and without endangering short-run security requirements.
   b. To foster the growth of international institutions that reflect common interests in solving scientific and technical problems that transcend national boundaries.
   c. To work steadily toward the concept of international participation as a universal obligation of all states rather than as a reward for good conduct.

d. To promote and encourage the expansion of human loyalties on a widening basis, preserving the values of the state, but steadily broadening the area of common responsibility.

e. To encourage the formation and realization of common interests among nations to form the bases for community that underlie law and order.

Part **II**   **THE UNITED NATIONS
AND NATIONAL SECURITY**

CHAPTER THREE

The Changing Setting for Military Strategy

IT IS STILL TRUE that national security conceived as a military problem is concerned primarily with the deterrence of armed attack on the United States from the outside and the maintenance of a capacity to defend the country successfully against such attack if it occurs. But it is also true that in the present time of new weapons and a shrinking world, aggression anywhere is a potential threat to our national security, and that contemporary American military strategy must prepare for contingencies not implied in any historical concept of continental defense.

The nation has been involved almost continuously since the war in trying to define the vastly extended area of military strategy. The national debate has focussed on the two basic components in the formulation of military strategy—the degree of likelihood to be assigned each of the many conceivable contingencies that might involve military action, and the priority to be given the creation of appropriate instrumentalities for dealing with those contingencies. An increasing number of observers have urged that we move from a strategy based almost wholly on the likelihood of all-out military aggression by the Soviet Union to one that accepts the equally great likelihood of limited Communist aggression and outbreaks of violence of the brushfire variety elsewhere in the world. In and out of the military services voices have been raised criticizing the obsessive emphasis on the creation of instrumentalities of massive retaliation and seeking recognition of the need for versatility and for a whole range of military means embraced in the concept of graduated deterrence. With the issue of national military strategy still only partially resolved, we are still struggling with the problem of the right balance—or "mix"—of strategic and tactical elements and the allocation of resources to create and support them.

Throughout the continuing debate the emphasis has been almost exclusively on the composition of American and Western strength. Even among those who advocate an improved capacity to deal with military situations of the less-than-total variety, little serious attention has been paid to the potentialities of the United Nations. On the contrary, its assumed limitations have generally excluded it from serious attention in the organization of national military strategy.

A recent survey revealed that in the minds of selected American military officers the United Nations is not usually considered in the same frame of reference as strictly national military doctrines, missions, or weapons systems. It appears in a separate category in which other emotions and intellectual processes tend to predominate. A fractional percentage of those interviewed did emphasize the value of the United Nations as a security instrumentality in the military sense. But all of them placed their emphasis on making greater use of the United Nations in the nonmilitary field.[1]

A recent study by the Rockefeller Brothers Fund on the subject of military security, after dealing with the various components of military security that might advance American strategic interests, turned to the United Nations. But, characteristically, the United Nations was not treated as a possible factor in military security; it was invoked primarily as the antithesis to military alliances and defense programs.[2]

[1] Richard W. Van Wagenen, *Some Views of American Defense Officials about the United Nations,* Center for International Studies, Massachusetts Institute of Technology, Cambridge, 1959 (mimeographed).

[2] *International Security—the Military Aspect,* Rockefeller Brothers Fund Special Studies Report II, Doubleday, Garden City, 1958, see p. 37.

Such views are not wholly surprising in the light of postwar history. In 1945, when the United Nations was founded, its *raison d'être* was to provide greater security for its member nations. As the basic conflict of interests between Soviet communism and the free nations unfolded, the cold war rapidly came to suffuse the entire organization like a sort of nerve gas, paralyzing but not killing. In a relatively short time the United Nations was seen to be incapable of resolving or even seriously affecting the dominant world conflict; and the United States and its principal allies were forced to conclude that, except as it provided a forum for counterpropaganda, the United Nations was irrelevant to their overriding short-term military and security problems.

The Korean War threw a new light on the capabilities of the United Nations as a political mechanism for organizing and demonstrating world-wide resistance to limited Communist aggression. But the disproportionately large contribution that the United States had to make to the conflict strengthened doubts that the United Nations could play a central role in the short-run protection of American national security. It continued to exercise a powerful attraction for the American people since it exemplified their great will for peace. But as the custodian of the peace it seemed to be in a fiduciary relationship not to us but to an unborn generation who might have a capacity for managing its affairs more harmoniously.

Besides the moral attraction of the Charter ideal, there was the possibility of using the United Nations selectively in the settlement of disputes within the free world, and there was the unquestioned merit of its "secondary" activities involving dependent areas, technical assistance, and the humanitarian achievements of the specialized agencies. Nevertheless, although those functions have turned out to be important enough to sustain American membership, no amount of enthusiasm for the potentialities of the organization under different circumstances has been able to overcome the conviction that at best the United Nations must be considered to be "on ice" so far as the profound and immediate American security problem is concerned.

Skepticism as to the value of the United Nations in the area of American military strategy is largely explained by the fact that the usefulness of the United Nations has usually been tested in only two ways. One was in terms of achieving a combination of Soviet-U.S. power, which will remain a fantasy until alliance grows out of a new mutual interest such as the need for common defense against Chinese power. The other touchstone was whether it eliminated the threat of total war. The answer of course had to be negative on both counts.

But military actions arising out of outbursts of violence within the non-Communist states have proven to contain a significant potential for menacing world peace, and the more likely contingency may be not premeditated all-out war but the spread of what are initially small-scale hostilities. The point is that we have progressively written off the relevance of the United Nations to our central problem of military security for reasons that may have seemed valid but which in fact have not proven to be so with the passage of time. It is short-sighted, to say the least, to be guided still by a first appraisal so obviously obsolete. As national strategy revises its premises about the kinds of military actions that may be fought in the foreseeable future, a process that cannot ignore the role of U.N. military and quasi-military capabilities in the over-all framework of national security, the U.N. military potential should be evaluated in terms of most likely rather than least likely contingency.

Let us consider some of the changes that dictate a new line of reasoning.

Experience is demonstrating once again the historical significance of military forces as makeweights in the realm of political action—military forces that may never be used for actual fighting. The policy of deterrence is the outstanding example of this relationship. But the presence of nonfighting international contingents in the Sinai Peninsula, the Gaza Strip, Sharm-al-Sheik, Lebanon, and the Congo has illustrated lesser degrees of deterrence that can be conceived. One of the crowning ironies of modern history is that, whereas in 1945 it was assumed that the maintenance of peace would depend on decisively involving the great powers, events such as the Congo and Suez suggest that world peace may be dependent upon keeping the United States and the Soviet Union out of military situations that initially do not involve them. If this is so, a vital problem for national as well as international security is to supply the capability for such non-great-power military intervention.

Another of the significant consequences of the revolution in military technology is that the objectives of warfare must be regarded as having changed. Mankind can no longer accept the risks implied in a doctrine of victory at all costs or of unconditional surrender. The pressing awareness that any purpose for which military action takes place will probably be furthered not by the extension but by the termination of hostilities suggests that war aims need to be formulated on a more complex and sophisticated basis than the conviction that there is no substitute for victory. This was the lesson—imperfectly learned—of the Korean War. It marks a change in the rationale of warfare which is particularly crucial in the light of the seemingly unlimited objectives of the Communist leadership and the countervailing spirit of crusade on our part, both reflections of the breadth and depth of the quasi-religious wars of this century.

Moreover, the revolution in military weaponry has changed not only the kind of war most likely to be fought but also the attitudes of the great powers toward war itself. The political *status quo* of the West is anathema to the Soviets, and the territorial *status quo* of world communism is unacceptable to us. Yet as general war becomes an increasingly unattractive proposition for both parties, the *de facto* truce line which in fact exists between the two worlds has hardened. When it is crossed in strength, as in Korea, the entire world appears to recognize such action as a manifest violation of the peace, and counteraction becomes politically feasible. Even India and Egypt voted initially to oppose the Communist aggression in Korea. On the other hand, as we saw in Hungary, a general military counteraction across the line is quite impossible politically even if we are willing to lead it.

The United States through its President and Secretary of State has specifically renounced force to resolve political differences.[3] There is no doubt that we would react vigorously to open Communist aggression; i.e., action across the line. But we explicitly avoid steps that could lead to general war. The policy of renouncing force and expecting others to do the same is a highly logical expression of a peaceable, prosperous, and relatively satisfied power which favors things as they are and foresees only problems for itself in situations of drastic change. In addition it is the policy of a power that feels the responsibility of leadership and is acutely aware of the possibility of large-scale involvement in possibly unmanageable and unlimitable hostilities.

We applied this self-denying ordinance to ourselves in respect to the 1948 Berlin blockade, the crossing of the Yalu, Indochina, Hungary, and the variety of provocations emanating from the Chinese mainland. We have also applied this policy to our friends, as in the Suez crisis of 1956. Some believe that the United States could and perhaps should have blocked the shipment of Soviet arms into the Middle East in 1955, with the aim of heading off the subsequent crises. But in 1956 the President was being entirely consistent in refusing to lend American support to a local military action that could lead directly to world war, however great the provocation to our allies. A significant result of the Suez fiasco is the realization that both the United States and the Soviet Union are likely to veto military action by third parties that might commit them to expanding potentially uncontrollable situations.

It would appear, then, that, barring a drastic change in Soviet estimates of Western power, the paraphernalia for all-out war may actually have more political than military significance in the period immediately ahead. In turn, lesser instruments for exerting power assume increasing importance. The United Nations is one of them.

---

[3] See President Eisenhower in letter to Soviet Premier Bulganin dated February 15, 1958: ". . . our national dedication to the international renunciation of force as an instrument of national policy . . .," *Department of State Bulletin,* March 10, 1958, p. 375.

Another change is in the larger significance of disputes that arise within the free world. In the catalog of political and territorial disputes at any given time it is impossible to distinguish the one that might "go critical." As Suez illustrated, a dispute which does not directly involve the two super powers can nevertheless quickly pose crucial issues of concern for the entire human family. Among the control rods of the Suez "pile," so to speak, was the one represented by an international brigade of troops contributed to the United Nations Emergency Force, enabling the world to buy time with the help of a variety of U.N. instrumentalities and functions in the area, including U.N.E.F., the U.N. Truce Supervisory Organization, and the activities of the U.N. Secretary General.

These then are some of the reasons why planners of national military strategy ought to review afresh the role of the United Nations in the broader strategic setting.

It may be wondered why nowhere have I used the term "collective security" in defining this general topic. This is a deliberate choice, made lest the discussion be complicated by a concept whose symbolic historical meanings weaken its utility as a tool of thought. For one thing, the notion of universal collective security evokes images of failure in the 1930's which becloud the issue of future prospects. More to the point, the notion of universal collective security based on an abstract commitment to fight anyone, anywhere, anytime on the call of a majority has not yet entered the realm of reality. In the absence of a true world community and given the wide variety of meanings ascribed to the concept of justice, it has never really been a legitimate expectation.

Yet this is not the whole story by any means. Both in and out of the United Nations many states have acted as though they had assumed an important general commitment and meant to take it seriously. To a degree which the League of Nations could never achieve, all states are involved in each successive crisis. This has obvious disadvantages in potentially widening an otherwise limited conflict, but it has reflected a realization of the collective nature of security. What is commonly called the "failure of collective security" is a failure in procedures rather than in the substantive result achieved. In the years since the Charter was drafted there has been no general war, and one of the chief reasons for this has been that the important operational principles of the Charter—collective action for security and avoidance of violence in resolving disputes—have been in *general* effect. It might be said that the San Francisco principle has failed in detail but has had general validity in the sense that it has been translated into regional and self-defense arrangements which, because the Charter existed, were able to borrow from its spirit and purpose.

Semantic difficulties can be avoided if we regard *universal* collective security as a highly valued ideal and long-term goal, and collective security as the process described above. With respect to the United Nations, we shall refer to the specific task to be accomplished rather than to the larger abstraction. The crucial issue is to utilize more effectively that which is actually in hand to meet needs that are either present or clearly foreseeable.

The issue will predictably be made more complex as the debate on disarmament unfolds. Soviet Premier Khrushchev's proposal to the 1959 General Assembly for "total" disarmament suggested to logical Western minds the obvious corollary of such a scheme: a world police force to fill the vacuum that would be left by the elimination of significant national forces. The American Secretary of State speculated on this prospect in a talk shortly after the Khrushchev speech:

> Then what, if any, force will there be, other than moral force, with which to maintain the peace as between nations insisting on going to war with each other, even with knives?

> Are we going to come to a point where we are going to develop some form of international police force of sufficient strength and subject to a controlled direction on which the nations of the world can agree which can be effective in maintaining the peace for all the world?[4]

4 Secretary Herter before United Nations Correspondents Association, September 22, 1959, *New York Times*, September 23, 1959.

The temptation to be bemused by distant possibilities was evident when the N.A.T.O. parliamentarians in November 1959 urged the establishment of an international police force to enforce settlement of disputes through international judicial decision.[5] The extraordinary difficulties attending the very concept of a preponderant international force are sufficient without insisting on the fallacy that essentially political disputes can be resolved by purely legal adjudication.

Analysis of the prospects for such a military force will also need to take account of the likelihood under present conditions that Soviet leadership will interpret such planning as designed to impose capitalism by force in the event of disarmament.[6] Whatever the motivation behind their disarmament proposals, the Soviets perceive clearly that schemes for a standing U.N. force to counter large-scale aggression call for a preponderance of power at the center, and that unless the center is controlled by Communists their movement would be subjected to unthinkable danger. Reinhold Niebuhr summed up the issue involved here:

> Where is the police force, loyal to a world state, to come from? The police power of a government cannot be a pure political artifact. It is an arm of the community's body. If the body is in pieces the arm cannot integrate it.[7]

The conditions for total disarmament involve mutual confidence and trust. The conditions for a real world police force, by definition superior to any single national force, similarly involve a powerful degree of mutual confidence and trust. Planning for disarmament should properly include planning for such international forces. But with present political forces basically in conflict over the inheritance of the earth itself and supported by violently contrasting ideologies, such planning cannot legitimately assume short-term prospects. The

[5] Washington, D.C., November 20, 1959, *New York Times,* November 21, 1959.

[6] As suggested by Georgi A. Zhukov, Chairman of State Committee for Cultural Relations with Foreign Countries, *Pravda,* October 2, 1959.

[7] *The World Crisis and American Responsibility,* Association Press, New York, 1958, p. 95.

prospects are remote for the sort of disarmament that would leave the task of security to the international community. For our purposes, excessive anticipation of such a development could actually become an obstacle to clear thinking about the present and foreseeable context for such international forces as the world community is willing to support. It would indeed be tragic if we allow the still utopian prospect of total disarmament and international armies to divert our attention from the pressing need to integrate more rationally into our strategic thinking the possible uses of limited and admittedly imperfect international machinery for specific tasks which confront us today. Once this limited step is achieved, it may encourage further progress toward larger international responsibilities in the future. For the task at hand, our approach here is to review U.N. machinery in terms not of what it might be under wholly different circumstances, but in terms of enhancing its usefulness under present and foreseeable conditions, and in the process to construct better foundations for its future development.

But before outlining such possibilities as appear constructive, the role of the United Nations in terms of the ultimate security problem must be dealt with.

CHAPTER FOUR

General War and Limited War

ONE IMPLICATION of present world tensions is that general war can arise not only as a result of a deliberate all-out assault which could be met only by the application of total counter-measures but also as a climax to an unplanned and undesired chain of events growing out of one of the interminable crises of our age. A revolt in Poland or East Germany, a Chinese probe toward Taiwan, another Suez—any of these would automatically pose the issue of great power engagement, and could lead to incalculable consequences in view of the military capacities of the United States and the Soviet Union. At the extreme, the consequences of either planned or accidental general war would be the same: a total military engagement between East and West, with all its unthinkable results.

The prime American objective since World War II has been to minimize the chances of the calculated, all-out assault. The prime strategy for achieving this objective has been a policy of military deterrence in the hands of the United States. Has the United Nations any role in this area?

DETERRENCE

The components of a deterrence policy involve both neutralizing Communist military capabilities to launch a successful military attack and affecting Communist intentions to

51

commit such an act. These have little relevance to the present-day United Nations. In the short run and under foreseeable conditions, both are tasks that can be performed only by the United States and its allies.

In order to play a significant role in this area of American and free world security, the United Nations would have to have an independent military capability of its own, something that only a drastic alteration of the situation could achieve. Although it is conceivable that in time sufficient disarmament will have taken place to make the creation of such a force a serious possibility, we cannot count now on such a revolution in political arrangements as a foundation for serious planning in the short range or even in the middle range of policy planning, i.e., the next three to ten years. This would seem to be true even of suggestions for limited world government, such as those advanced by Clark and Sohn.[1]

Thus, without any military force of its own, the United Nations would seem of little use in the objective of reducing Soviet military capabilities. At the most, it can affect those capabilities only indirectly, by furnishing a forum for negotiating the limitation and regulation of armaments and restricting the use of outer space to nonwarlike purposes. Agreement on either of these of course affects national military capabilities. Despite the essentially bilateral nature of such agreements, the wide choice of means of negotiation offered by the United Nations should not be undervalued, as was shown when the Soviet Union used its facilities in early 1949 to put Ambassador Malik in private contact with Ambassador Jessup with a view to liquidating the Berlin blockade. But the U.N. role is, at best, marginal; and so long as deterrence of all-out assault is conceived to be the number one issue for U.S. national security, a United Nations without military force of its own will remain at a distance from this prime national interest.

However, the relationship between military capabilities and deterrence is a shifting one. When the chances are high for a

[1] *World Peace through World Law,* Harvard University Press, Cambridge, 1958.

deliberate military assault, the military component of deterrence is paramount, and the significance of other instrumentalities such as the United Nations is low. This is to some extent the story of the postwar years when Western strategists rated as high the probability of Soviet attack.

But a successful deterrence policy by definition results in lowering the chances of such an attack, and this is essentially the present situation. If a favorable military balance is sustained, it will also be the future situation. Military deterrence, when it works, is a shield behind which the battles are fought out by primarily nonmilitary means. In other words, to the extent that the American defense program succeeds in its primary mission, nonmilitary strategies and nonmilitary weapons become increasingly operative; they and they alone determine the success of a foreign policy operating behind the shield of deterrence, and other objectives come to the fore in advancing the national interest.

Many strange things have already come to pass under the shield of deterrence to general war. The Communist political and economic offensive has replaced the Red Army as Moscow's primary agency for political and territorial change. Under the shield of great power deterrence relatively weak states such as the United Arab Republic and Cuba—and Communist China—exercise disproportionate influence in the world and get away with behavior which great powers in another age would not have permitted. It is not the United Nations that gives the small states the means for irresponsible national behavior today. It is their relative immunity under conditions of what is in fact *mutual* great power deterrence, as Egypt demonstrated to her own intense satisfaction in the fall of 1956.

Under these conditions neither the United Nations nor any other nonmilitary institution of international action can be measured solely in relation to its contribution to military deterrence. There are other components of the general prevention of war apart from needful military strength and making credible the will and determination to use it if necessary. There is, for instance, the objective of making military adventures prohibitively costly politically and morally as well as militarily. The real significance of the U.N. Charter commitment undertaken by U.N. member nations—including the Soviet Union—to refrain from the threat or use of force is obviously not in its juridical quality. It is because any warlike act will immediately be brought before all the other nations that the Soviet Union is faced with the fact that it must persuade an effective majority that it has not breached the existing line which neither side can properly cross, whatever it may be doing behind that line.

Such a deterrent is not comparable to the deterrent of our Strategic Air Command, but there have been too many examples of Soviet sensitivity to world public opinion for us to write it off as meaningless. It is not always remembered that the U.N. resolution condemning Soviet intervention in Hungary was supported by 15 Afro-Asian states, with none in opposition. The Soviets periodically stumble badly because of the difficulty of sustaining a soft line in the United Nations when their line outside hardens. Soviet troops remained in Hungary, but the Soviet Union's reputation in the uncommitted nations was gravely tarnished just when its efforts to woo them were at a peak.

Primary responsibility for implementing the commitment in the U.N. Charter to oppose aggression has, because of the nature of the United Nations, passed from that body and into the hands of the regional and collective self-defense arrangements which have constituted a strong element, both military and political, in the generalized deterrent. Such organizations might have developed without that governing principle, but there is no doubt that the negotiation and development of such a security system was made easier because of the already existing principles from which it could borrow and in whose name it could act. The relative strength and cohesion of these arrangements clearly affects the Communist estimate of the vulnerability of the non-Communist states.

To sum up, the principle of collective resistance to aggression embodied in the U.N. Charter has played a major role in the deterrent. The fact that the United Nations exists can be set down as a consideration affecting Soviet calculations about the profitability of military operations even though it hardly figures as a prime factor.

GENERAL WAR

We can deal briefly with the role of the United Nations in an all-out war that does take place, whether by calculation or by accident.

We are prone to believe that general war would mean the end of the United Nations, and this may be so. Yet as Korea illustrated at a less than all-out level, the United Nations can serve as a symbol under which the United States and other free nations can legitimize their military response to a Communist aggression at whatever level. It can arm our side with the banner of moral right—a force still very much alive beneath the surface of contemporary world politics. It can make neutral nations available for the imperative and still underrated tasks of disentangling the combatants. It might have great political significance in providing a legal and acceptable way of replacing Communist representatives with spokesmen for free and democratic regimes. Indeed, this seems far more sensible than trying to expel the Soviet Union, under Article 5 or 6 of the Charter, in a war situation, since such a step, while perhaps more emotionally satisfying, would deprive our side of one of the organization's most valuable symbolic uses.

It should not be forgotten that under present and foreseeable conditions no national objectives would be served in any major conflict by the traditional aim of destroying the enemy regardless of political consequences. If political war aims were to be defined by a U.N. majority rather than by any single nation, including our own, hostilities might be brought to an end more promptly than otherwise, and a chance bought to try again with the weapons of diplomacy.

The continued failure of Americans to absorb the Clausewitz dictum of the interrelation between war and peace, long a centerpiece of communist doctrine, has in the past made it almost impossible to plan rationally for a fully orchestrated political and military strategy in the event of war. It explains American resentment at the restraining influence of both our own policy makers and of the U.N. majority in the Korean War. But in some future conflict we might well take another view of the restraints that the majority of nations place on our own claims for the right of hot pursuit, for invading a privileged sanctuary, and for total victory. For the U.N. General Assembly, inconsistent and not itself carrying the defensive burden, might in fact make a greater contribution to our broad objectives than those who define our war aims by claiming primacy for military over political objectives. We should not be ashamed of planning which hedges against the possibility that unreason could again whisper to us that there is no substitute for victory and that we cannot be satisfied with anything less than unconditional surrender. The United Nations' very existence can protect us from taking an irrevocable course which no single nation is wise enough to handle.

Above all, the continued existence of the United Nations even in an all-out war would give the world a framework to which to return for the task of patching up the shattered peace and carrying on. Our planning must not ignore this possibility, and we must assume there will be a postwar world to organize.

LIMITED EAST-WEST HOSTILITIES

There are two possible avenues to limited war with the Communist states. The first is a calculated military move by the Soviet Union or Communist China which is clearly intended to achieve only a limited objective. Several means exist for them to convey such an intention: proxy aggression, such as that by North Korea in 1950; guerrilla warfare, as in Greece in 1947; or militarily ambiguous testing action, such as the 1948 Berlin blockade. The second is unplanned involvement resulting from the highly dangerous brand of crisis diplomacy increasingly practiced by Communist leadership as its military arsenal expands. The continuation of this hazardous policy should not be discounted, particularly as Communist leadership remains confident in the strength of its nerve and in its capacity to draw back before making a fatal commitment. Com munist ballistic diplomacy may accompany a move designec to be ambiguous or in any event not fatally provocative, e.g., a modest harassment of U.S. access to Taiwan or West Berlin, but miscalculating badly the reaction of the West, as in Korea. Another time an area may be involved where, unlike Korea, tactical defense forces are armed with atomic field weapons.

Whatever the event—the deliberate limited probe or the unplanned military encounter arising out of diplomacy at the brink—an objective of U.S. policy must be to keep such limited hostilities from spreading. The question that arises embraces both the possibility and the means of achieving that end.

One school would discount the possibility. "Another war," writes Walter Millis, "will have to be all or nothing." There can therefore be no more wars, "not even small ones."[2] Another view would hold that, although the time factor alone would almost automatically make such a fight all-out, an open conflict need not become general, for there would still exist a common interest between the combatants not to go all the way:

> If one believed that the Communist powers had no desire to pre-
> vent unlimited war, no aversion to setting off a nuclear holo-
> caust, then the situation would be quite hopeless. But the desire
> to avert unlimited war and the determination to hold the line
> against it are more likely to be common to us and them. There
> are even elements of a bond, here, between us.[3]

The latter view reflects the position that limited war is not only desirable as an alternative to all-out war but also possible as a practical matter.

I do not believe that U.S. policy can afford to subscribe to the first view, with its implication of the hopelessness of any attempt at preventive action. It is true that the ability of the West to take purposeful action to prevent a conflict from spreading will be entirely dependent on whether the Commu-

[2] "Ultimate Weapons—Ultimate Questions," *New York Times Magazine,* April 14, 1957, p. 68.
[3] Louis J. Halle, *Choice for Survival,* Harper, New York, 1958, p. 125.

nists share this goal, as they did in Korea. But the evidence indicates that with a sufficient deterrence—military, political, and moral—the West can expect the Communists to regard their interests as served by avoiding a general war; I think we must assume that this will be so while being always prepared for the contrary. Communist doctrine is explicit about the importance of retreat when its whole power base is threatened. Moreover, there is another factor in the equation, one over which we exercise rather more control: our own intentions and rationality in a highly charged situation. The decision to expand a war may actually rest less with the enemy and more with ourselves, the more powerful factor being not the enemy's actions but the Western response to those actions. Here certainly is a realm in which policy planning has direct relevance.

To an even greater extent than in a general war situation, the key to the matter of Western response in a limited war is in our war aims. Shall the purpose for which we fight be the repelling of aggression or the accomplishment of an otherwise unattainable political objective as with our momentary dream of unifying Korea in the early fall of 1950? Can we be satisfied with aims that go no further than the restoration of the *status quo ante,* as eventually happened in Korea?

Sir Anthony Buzzard, retired Chief of British Naval Intelligence, answered the last question affirmatively:

> The crucial problem in defense is that of limiting war . . . the aims of Western defense policy [are] preventing or limiting war . . . to suppress aggression or any fighting which may break out despite our deterrents . . . global war is only in danger of occurring if we fail to deter or should mishandle a limited war. . . . In our war aims it is essential that we limit these to no more than halting the aggressor, achieving a cease-fire, and returning to negotiations on the basis of the *status quo ante.*[4]

Another writer on strategy urges that we abandon the concept of punishing aggression:

[4] *Boston Herald,* May 19, 1957.

Limited war, admittedly, requires different attitudes and expectations than we have become accustomed to; but, despite its handicaps, we gain more freedom than we lose. True, we give up the concept of victory in its traditional meaning. We discard the idea of punishing aggression. We accept limits on our military and general policy objectives, and, in effect, we accept existing political and territorial arrangements. But, in return, we obtain a passage between the Scylla of nuclear holocaust and the Charybdis of interminable retreat.[5]

Former Canadian Foreign Minister Lester Pearson is unwilling to abandon the "police" concept but wishes the hostilities terminated as soon as the aggressor is "defeated":

Limited war must have limited, not total, political aims. Every effort must be made, if hostilities ever break out again, not only to prove that aggression does not pay by repelling and defeating the aggressor, but also to localize hostilities, to bring them to an end as soon as the limited objective is accomplished, and then to work for a peace which will be just but not savage—the kind of peace that will not bear the seeds of future war.[6]

The President of the United States has officially declared the intention of this country to subscribe to the aim of limiting war if it should break out:

To achieve this peace we seek to prevent war at any place and in any dimension. If, despite our best efforts, a local dispute should flare into armed hostilities, the next problem would be to keep the conflict from spreading, and so compromising freedom.[7]

This still does not answer the question of whether we, not to mention the enemy, will actually be able to live with such a doctrine of restraint in a limited fighting situation, and indeed this may be more difficult than in the incalculable general war situation. A strategy of restraint could enable the

[5] William W. Kaufmann, "Limited Warfare," in *Military Policy and National Security*, Princeton University Press, Princeton, 1956, p. 136.

[6] Lester B. Pearson, "A Measured Defense for the West," I *Orbis* (1958), p. 434.

[7] President Eisenhower, State of the Union Message, January 9, 1959, *New York Times*, January 10, 1959.

Communists to score additional unpunished successes, or at any rate to hold on to their Hungaries while the West looks on responsibly—and helplessly. A strategy of restraint involves keeping alive opportunities for settlement during hostilities. Diplomatic contacts must be maintained. The enemy's retaliatory forces must remain immune. Sanctuary areas must be preserved. These are of course the conditions that many Americans found it supremely difficult to accept during the Korean War (even though both sides were so bound).

This dilemma cannot be evaded, nor can it be resolved, for it sums up the grand conundrum of the age: the prospect of choices, none satisfying, all implying undesirable alternatives. But we can be sure that the classical notion of military victory can only reproduce Pyrrhus' lament: "Another such victory and we are undone." Military victory is no longer really possible and as a goal does not serve national or international ends.

We come, then, to a threefold proposition: that preventing the spread of limited East-West hostilities is not a hopeless objective; that a decisive factor in achieving that objective will be our response to enemy action; that the key to our response must be war aims short of military victory, aims which are summed up in bringing hostilities to an end as quickly as possible so that political processes can substitute for military action.

It is in the light of this proposition—connoting goals that are unsatisfactory, but nevertheless profoundly valid and rational—that we must consider the possible role of the United Nations in achieving the objective of limiting East-West hostilities if they should break out.

The first and major value of the United Nations in such a situation is purely psychological and symbolic. By turning to the United Nations we can communicate to our opponent that we do not wish the conflict to spread into a general war. The scope of hostilities would still be largely determined by the estimates each side made of the intentions and the capabilities of the other. But given the will of each to keep them limited, the United Nations can then offer the advantages it did when the United States made its decision to resist in Korea.

These advantages are several. First, the United Nations furnishes one means for us to secure maximum world-wide political support. This support is indispensable if we are not to lose the sense of legitimacy and moral right that we as a people need in order to sustain a military effort. The second advantage is the opportunity afforded by the commitment made by all U.N. members to assist the organization in any action it takes in accordance with the Charter. This does not have to mean "action" in the legal sense of Security Council enforcement. Marginal offers of bases, transit rights—even "a sharpshooter on a camel"—not only demonstrate the breadth of international disapproval of an act of aggression but can also pay important strategic dividends. Economic sanctions could have a world-wide impact on the aggressive party. Thirdly, the mere fact that the conflict is before the United Nations tends to discourage participants from expanding the scope of the war recklessly or setting extravagant war aims.

The Korean lesson has not really been assimilated, for the principal reason that the U.N. role in Korea has been judged solely by purely military criteria. It has been reiterated that sixteen countries may have fought on the side of the United Nations, but that the United States contributed 50.3 per cent of the ground forces of the U.N. Command, 85.89 per cent of its naval power, and 93.38 per cent of the air; that, in other words, the United States *was* the U.N. Command. It has been consistently overlooked that Korea did, nevertheless, illustrate the political capabilities of the United Nations.

As a primarily political demonstration, the Korean action was of chief utility to the American national interest by legitimizing and broadening the political and moral base of a military counterdemonstration the United States felt it imperative to make. The price of such broadening was to impose constraints on American policy making, some of which seemed at the time irksome. The General Assembly's will was quite broadly interpreted in the early fall of 1950 when MacArthur drove his seemingly victorious forces on toward the Yalu, and one suspects that there were many in that majority who were as glad as we to use the occasion of military victory over the North Korean forces to implement the previous U.N. resolutions calling for extension of U.N. supervised elections and, ultimately, democracy to North Korea. But this failing, if you will, of human nature only points up the difficulty of prescribing in advance rigid rules for transmitting political guidance to military commanders. When the Chinese Communists entered the conflict and drove the U.N. forces back to the south, the political guidance, particularly from those not involved, became far more pointed. It was then that the influence of the Assembly majority bore down hard on negotiation and limitation of the objective to restoration of the *status quo ante,* action which, in any realistic appraisal of the war in Korea as a reflection of the larger stalemate, was of great value to the United States and had its payoff when both sides came to share an interest in seeking a way out.

Another Korea-type situation might well bear out the conclusion of one student of the Korean action that the major weakness of the U.N. performance was "the failure to develop adequate organs and procedures for giving political guidance to the military measures taken."[8]

CONCLUSION

This discussion has emphasized the political role of the United Nations, specifically in the General Assembly, with the understanding that meaningful collective security in terms of military capabilities is not now or foreseeably a prime function of a global U.N. organization. The military capacity to resist aggression comes chiefly from the national forces of the United States and its allies, for which the United Nations offers no substitute. But neither do national military forces substitute for the political role of an essentially peace-favoring organization, with its peace-favoring majorities, in the paramount task

[8] Leland M. Goodrich, *Korea: Collective Measures against Aggression,* in *International Conciliation,* No. 494, p. 164.

of staying the hands of the antagonists in any fight that threatens the whole fabric of world peace, a task that conforms to the vital political objectives of the United States. The political role of the United Nations should be a prime consideration in making policy within the larger framework of limiting East-West conflicts.

CHAPTER FIVE

Lesser Conflicts and a U.N. Force

A CRUCIAL LESSON being taught by contemporary history is the possibility of involvement for us—and for the Soviet Union—in hostilities arising from situations in which a military outbreak does not originate as an East-West conflict but as a conflict in the non-Communist states. What is the potential role of the United Nations in this context?

In significant ways the political history of the United Nations is the history of conflicts in the non-Communist world which were aborted, stopped, suppressed, or in a few happy instances resolved. The U.N. machinery of investigation and conciliation, the calls for cease-fires, the detail of uniformed personnel to observe and report—all of these techniques have with a few exceptions (such as Greece and Laos) been applied chiefly to intra-free world disputes. Indonesia, Palestine, Kashmir, Suez, and Lebanon all involved U.N. machinery designed to moderate conflict and separate the parties long enough for them to cool off and resume a less violent dialogue. Each represented innovations in the techniques used, and each in its own way was a success in terms of suppressing overt violence.

Needless to say, the temporary suppression of violence serves not to solve the dispute but to buy time for its solution, and to open avenues other than the military one for the parties to travel. The processes of pacific settlement and peaceful change are in a larger sense the ultimately decisive factors. Nevertheless, in considering the security issues posed for the United States and the West by spontaneous outbreaks of violence, the first focus of policy must be on military and quasi-military measures required to deal with the immediate threat to peace posed by such outbreaks—that is, on the suppression, or limitation, of hostilities in order to open the approaches to peaceful settlement.

In terms of such measures, the need that recent experience has increasingly confirmed is for an international military force available for the enforcement of cease-fires, a force designed not primarily for combat but for the discouragement, through its presence, of continuing hostilities. The immediate call for and dispatch of a U.N. force to quell the strife in the newly independent Congo in July 1960 underlined the need for such a force to be available on a twelve-hour basis. Our question, then, is whether the United Nations can fill such a need on the continuing basis required.

In one respect the nature of the kind of military force needed requires little clarification. Although it can be argued that such a force can be exclusively national, i.e., American, the overwhelming evidence points to the importance of giving such a force a wholly international complexion. The point has been made by events, and it hardly seems worth demonstrating this conclusion anew in terms of international political acceptability, American budgetary and other political constraints, and above all the urgency of finding ways of dealing with brushfire situations of this order without magnifying them to the level of American-Soviet involvement.

The need about which we are speaking must be distinguished from the need for an international military force designed to repel or suppress by military counteraction acts of military aggression. Indeed, if the two become confused, the chances for attaining the lesser—but urgent—requirement are placed in real jeopardy. We are talking about a nonfighting force, prepared to defend itself if necessary, but insinuated into the scene at a break in the fighting and preferably before the fighting breaks out at all. Its function would be to separate real or potential combatants, to show the flag, figuratively and literally, of the concern of the rest of the international family, and to demonstrate international determination not to allow the peace to be further endangered by violence. Its role would be to observe, to report, and in general to tranquilize, pending constructive political action to attack the sources of conflict. It hardly needs to be pointed out that if creative political solutions are not developed in the lull which has been so purchased, suppressive action does not necessarily have lasting value or significance. It should finally be repeated that such a limited force could well serve as a pilot model and forerunner of international forces of a higher order when and if conditions become propitious for such a development.

A NONFIGHTING INTERNATIONAL FORCE

To a certain extent, proposals for an international force not dependent on disarmament and designed primarily for nonfighting tasks are subject to the same conditions as a fighting international force. Present concepts of national sovereignty, profound ideological conflict, and the innate conservatism of governments in the presence of innovation all combine to limit the lesser kind of force to a role that is primarily political rather than military. Actual military contributions raised through U.N. action, while welcome, have their prime significance on political grounds. That is to say, the forces which would *not* have been raised if it were purely an alliance action themselves represent a symbolic demonstration of the breadth and depth of international concern and of the mobilization of the forces of political legitimacy.

Once a cease-fire is agreed to by the parties, the value of an internationally recruited military presence is evident. Primarily it is the advantage of having such an international presence physically interposed between the parties, and in a position to report back to the rest of the world an impartial account of the real situation. Thus the chief political value is not primarily in its numbers and certainly not in its fire power. It lies in the international take-over of a bilateral fight, bringing into that fight the ground rules of the U.N. Charter, and making it politically difficult if not impossible for the United States and the Soviet Union to become militarily engaged in that particular fight.

By this logic it should exclude the great powers and in most of the foreseeable instances should be composed entirely of contingents from small and medium-size powers, including as many neutrals as possible. For if world peace was once thought to depend entirely on getting the United States and the Soviet Union involved, experience in the summer of 1960 with the U.N. force in the Congo, initially mobilized from six African states and ultimately including military contingents or advisers from over a dozen small countries, emphasized that the success of such forces may depend on keeping the great powers out.

Of course there have been and will continue to be situations in which, with no prospect at the time of a direct clash of Soviet and American interests, it is not only reasonable but essential to utilize American and other great power personnel. Military observers contributed by members of the United Nations are still at work in other parts of the Palestine area and in Kashmir, performing functions that no longer make the front page but are an indispensable part of the long, arduous and often boring task of maintaining conditions of military standstill until arrangements can be worked out for longer-term area stability. It can confidently be predicted that this experience will be repeated elsewhere.

In terms of a military *force,* however, and particularly with the growing involvement of the United States and the Soviet Union in areas such as the Middle East and Africa, the principle of utilizing relatively unattached nations for this task comes to be of growing utility. Recent evidence strongly supports the assumption that the smaller nations are not only able but also willing to contribute to this opportunity to serve the cause of peace.

By the time the 1956 General Assembly session had adjourned, 6063 men had been contributed to the U.N. Emergency Force in Egypt, consisting of contingents from ten countries: Brazil, Canada, Colombia, Denmark, Finland, India, Indonesia, Norway, Sweden, and Yugoslavia. In addition, offers to provide contingents had been received from Ceylon, Chile, Czechoslovakia, Ecuador, Laos, New Zealand, Pakistan, Peru, the Philippines, and Rumania, in addition to unspecified offers to participate in U.N.E.F. from Afghanistan, Belgium, Burma, Ethiopia, Greece, Iran, the Netherlands, and Uruguay.[1]

Two years later, when Lebanon charged that its territorial integrity was being undermined by infiltration of hostile elements under the control of the United Arab Republic, the U.N. Observation Group in Lebanon—U.N.O.G.I.L.—was created with 190 military observers contributed by fifteen countries, in addition to sixty pilots, technicians, and specialized personnel for air operations.[2] Had the emphasis remained on the international observers rather than on the unilateral American intervention in Lebanon, the U.N. group might well have expanded significantly. A post-Suez reaction had already taken place in some high governmental circles in Western Europe since 1956, and U.N. operations in Lebanon in 1958 were in general highly favored over renewed unilateral intervention.

The U.N. force for the Congo,[3] created on July 13, 1960, included in its first month of operation units totaling approximately 10,000 men drawn from Ethiopia, Ghana, Guinea, Ireland, Liberia, Mali, Morocco, Sweden, and Tunisia. In addition, military advisers were on duty from Canada, Denmark, Italy, New Zealand, Norway, and Sweden.

We should be encouraged by this evidence to attach a new order of importance to the availability of neutrals who do not wear the colors of either side in the cold war, a posture sometimes deplored in high American places. In other instances the same importance attaches to the role of small powers who are not necessarily uncommitted in East-West

[1] *U.S. Participation in the U.N.*, Report by the President to the Congress, 1956, State Department Publication 6577, 1957, p. 70.

[2] *United Nations Review*, September 1958, p. 76.

[3] The force was called "O.N.U.C." from its French name—*Force de l'Organisation des Nations Unies au Congo.*

terms but are neutral in regard to a local dispute. We can no longer afford to view small states as irresponsible irritants whose political influence should be curtailed by weighted voting schemes in the General Assembly.

A further implication of this logic is that, rather than continuing to present the United Nations as a club of like-minded states, all presumably prepared to take identical action, we should be suitably grateful that some of them may constitute the necessary "third party" available to be interposed in such situations. We ourselves have been the "third party" on occasion, as in the Indonesian Good Offices Committee, or in Tunisia, and might well play such a role again.

Under present conditions only the United Nations can develop and perfect the sort of limited and neutral force along the lines discussed. No collection of forces derived from N.A.T.O. or the South East Asia Treaty Organization or C.E.N.T.O.—the renamed Baghdad Pact—could satisfy the requirements of neutrality, particularly in the Middle East or Asia (although the Organization of American States may represent a special case). In general only the United Nations can provide the flexibility and range from among over four-score countries, many of them not affiliated with any regional or other collective defense organization.

Some sort of U.N. force, then, becomes a crucial component of the "spectrum of capabilities," the military "mix," which needs to be created to deal with the situations most likely to endanger world peace short of overt Soviet or Chinese Communist military aggression.

It follows that, in terms of the U.S. national interest, the creation of a U.N. force ranks with the development of local capabilities among our allies to resist military incursions, with the need for strategic air transport, and with the desirability of maintaining a mobile reserve in the United States equipped to fight a local nonnuclear action. It should be thought of in this way, not as a luxury or as an idealistic experiment. A nonfighting U.N. force could be a key component of the arsenal for peace in an age when limited wars are likely and the limitation of war is imperative.

THE DIFFICULTIES AND A PROPOSAL

There are some basic limitations on the scope of an international force of the type under discussion. One is the handicap of being useable only when both sides agree to stop fighting.

There does not at present appear to be any realistic way of getting around the acceptance of the contestants, however implicitly, of a cease-fire as a precondition of the use of U.N. forces. Without drastically altering the Charter and the regime of state sovereignty on which it rests, there is no presently foreseeable way of insinuating neutral troops between forces actually shooting at one another. Furthermore, as a practical matter, under foreseeable circumstances most neutral countries would be unwilling to subject their troops to such cross fire.

Yet even here we cannot foretell the future. Circumstances could well arise that pose such dangers to the peace that a wholly new order of approach would seem imperative. It is possible to contemplate a situation in which international forces would indeed be introduced before an agreement was achieved to cease fire. But such a contingency cannot be planned for at this stage of history when we are having sufficient difficulty agreeing even on minimum measures of international responsibility. We should keep an open mind to the possibility of further steps, but concentrate on achieving the immediately desirable.

Another built-in limitation reflecting the present relatively low level of world order is that if the force is to be used on the territory of one nation—as in the case of Egypt in 1956—that nation has a *de facto* veto power with respect to not only the use of the force but also its composition. Egypt vetoed some of the proposed components of U.N.E.F., for example rejecting Canadian troops because of the similarity of their uniforms to those of the invading British. (Canadian service components were eventually substituted.) As with the other obstacle, a change in this *de facto* veto power would represent a profound change in the very concept of sovereignty and of

the delegation of powers to agencies of the "community."
Again, unplanned circumstances which cannot now be foreseen may carry the world over this threshold into a new order
of authority—and risk—for the tenuous and embryonic international institution.

The theoretical considerations apart, however, as a practical
matter there are likely to be countries among the contributors
which, however neutral, are sympathetic to one party or in
any event unwilling to stay in the territory if the "host"
country raises objections to their presence. It was clear in the
case of U.N.E.F. that India and Indonesia, for example, would
probably have withdrawn their troops if they had been asked
by the United Nations to be party to any action inimical to
the Egyptian "host."

A final consequence of the present level of world order is
to suggest a clear preference for nationally contributed contingents rather than individual recruitment for an international force. An only remote precedent for individual recruitment is the U.N. Guard, which is now limited to essentially
custodial functions. But the imperative present task is to create
an international force in the short run to help fill a dangerous
gap in the world's short-run capabilities. It would be unwise
to confuse and prejudice the issue by centering the debate
on concepts of sovereignty, or on the long-term theoretical
consequences of supranational programing, or on the type
of personnel who would be most likely to volunteer for such
a force. Nothing would be more calculated than the latter to
confirm the suspicions of the Soviet Union that we were planning to raise an "emigré" army designed to start a counter-
revolution in Eastern Europe. For the short run we should
concentrate on minimizing the troublesome symbols involved
and concentrate on the practical need defined by our own
strategic objectives. Out of a modest start, organic growth can
well take place.

Wholly apart from the political obstacles, there are intrinsic
problems of organization and financing which so far have appeared to be insuperable. In his pioneering study of a possible
U.N. force, William Frye concluded that a reasonable size

might be 7,000 men, costing approximately $25 million when not in action. He ultimately reduced this to a planning operation, costing not more than "a few hundred thousand dollars," for a paper organization which could be brought into being with fair speed.[4]

I would suggest a variation on this proposal in the form of a training command located in a facility leased by the United Nations from a neutral nation such as Sweden or Switzerland or perhaps India. At this center a small permanent cadre would conduct six-month training exercises for national contingents furnished in rotation by member countries. The emphasis in training would be on the primary mission of a U.N. force: observation, patrol, and enforcement of cease-fires. It would emphasize the kinds of police-type duties that call for diplomacy, tact, and vigilance, by contrast with the tactical training such troops normally receive. On returning to their bases the units so trained could, if the country concerned agreed, be specially designated, perhaps by wearing a U.N. insignia; with the same qualification, they could conceivably remain available for a specified number of years for call by the United Nations. It is even possible to contemplate a stand-by wing of civilian or military transport planes and perhaps some surface transport craft, similarly earmarked and available on short notice to the U.N. forces. To be able to call upon its own transportation during acute crises would free the United Nations of dependence on individual great powers —including the Soviet Union, which supplied part of the airlift to Leopoldville in July of 1960.

Assignment of companies or battalions to the training center could be considered a high honor, competed for within national armies and other military services. The force itself might be called U.N.C.O.P.—U.N. Corps for Observation and Patrol; or, if U.N.C.O.P. seems too frivolous, perhaps U.N.-P.A.T.—U.N. Patrol. Over a period of time a sizable quantity of personnel could be trained. The costs would remain low, although there is little doubt that the United States would

---

[4] *A United Nations Peace Force,* Oceana, New York, 1957, pp. 78, 81-82. See also Lester Pearson, "Force for U.N.," 35 *Foreign Affairs* (1957).

have to contribute a minimum of thirty per cent—our present assessment to the regular U.N. budget—and probably a higher proportion if we wished to see the project succeed.

The financial burden, by contrast to current over-all military expenditures, would be miniscule. But given the inherent resistance of governments to additional costs for such an untraditional form of security, some new ideas on financing are needed. My suggestion would be to require that recipients of allocations for military support under the American mutual security program utilize a portion of the funds received for the express purpose of training and funding a unit designated for U.N. service.

Such a scheme could have larger consequences. There has been widespread criticism of the purely military component of American foreign aid as not particularly relevant to the gross military picture. In 1959 the President's Committee to Study the U.S. Military Assistance Program, the so-called Draper Committee, recommended an increase of $400 million in military assistance, primarily for N.A.T.O. The Senate Foreign Relations Committee responded by adding $233 million for the purpose but reducing by the same amount the proposed military assistance to non-N.A.T.O. countries. This clearly reflects a trend.[5]

Of the 40-odd countries receiving some form of military aid apart from the chief Far Eastern recipients—Korea, Taiwan, and Vietnam—are such non-N.A.T.O. countries as Ethiopia, Libya, Iran, Pakistan, Laos, and Japan. If such a dual purpose could be served over and above the support of purely indigenous forces, the rationale for continued defense assistance would be far more acceptable, both to the American people and to others. But more than that, the military assistance program would be geared to a positive and inspiring idea rather than to the sterile and sometimes meaningless military formula hitherto applied. There is a reasonable suspicion that the forces of at least some recipient countries are inadequate to oppose large-scale external aggression but quite large

[5] *The Mutual Security Act of 1959*, Report of Committee on Foreign Relations, 86th Congress, 1st Session, Senate Report 412, June 22, 1959, p. 5.

enough to be used for internal political purposes. So long as
no new rationale begins to emerge for the continued world-
wide build-up of forces, the military assistance program will
remain vulnerable to criticism as to its purposes and to proposals for drastic change year by year as estimates of Communist intentions vary.

But it would be quite another thing for the United States
to subsidize the armed forces of a small country *both* for purposes of its own self-defense and *also* in order that it might
make a genuine contribution to an international force, under
the United Nations, to be used in situations where it is in the
general interest that there be international action toward
pacification or the maintenance of a cease-fire but where
American forces clearly cannot be used. To be sure, this proposal calls for new strings to be attached. But they are the
kind of strings that could make sense even to a neutral country
which hitherto had rejected U.S. aid as designed solely to advantage U.S. military strategy.

It would be entirely consistent with existing mutual security legislation to require that military assistance funds be used
in part (or even in whole) for the purpose of raising, training,
and equipping for U.N. service and for the maintenance of
an earmarked force. Section 105 states that:

> Equipment and materials furnished under this chapter shall be
> made available solely to maintain the internal security and legiti-
> mate self-defense of the recipient nation, or to permit it to
> participate in the defense of its area or in collective security
> arrangements and measures consistent with the Charter of the
> United Nations.

If the financial burden were minimized through the device
suggested, one of the chief grounds for continuing opposition
and inertia would be eliminated. If Sweden, for example,
were willing to make a training facility available at nominal
cost, or even as her contribution to the scheme, the way
would be even more eased. But the chief obstacles to such
modest progress—Soviet opposition and uncertainty of the
American commitment—remain unsolved.

UNITED STATES POLICY

The United States has generally supported appropriate international steps after a crisis has fully erupted. The question for American policy is whether American interests would be better served by making far more definitive preparations for international action to prevent or suppress hostilities in the non-Communist states.

In the summer of 1958, at the height of the Lebanese crisis, President Eisenhower included among his proposals to the emergency session of the General Assembly the suggestion that it consider action looking toward the creation of a stand-by United Nations Peace Force as "a matter for urgent and positive action."[6] During the month of August 1958 both the American Senate and the House of Representatives by overwhelming majorities passed resolutions calling on the United Nations to consider at once the establishment of a permanent U.N. force available for observation and patrol where peace is threatened.

The United States subsequently requested only that the Assembly give the Secretary General a small planning staff for the purpose; and, apparently because Soviet opposition was privately made explicit and even menacing, Secretary General Hammarskjöld in October of 1958 reported to the General Assembly that it would be "inadvisable" at present to establish a stand-by force, whether modeled on U.N.E.F. or otherwise.[7] On November 5 the Special Political Committee shelved the United States request for planning machinery toward a U.N. force, which by then had become opposed by such key members as India and the United Arab Republic, doubtless because of Soviet opposition.

Presumably the Secretary General is going ahead with quiet work on his own drawingboard, utilizing existing staff, and meanwhile discouraging attempts to make the program in any way explicit or public. This is, from his standpoint, under-

[6] Address to Emergency Special Session of General Assembly, August 13, 1958, *New York Times*, August 14, 1958.

[7] *New York Times*, October 16, 1958.

standable. Mr. Hammarskjöld's recommendations represented an exercise in the art of the possible as he saw it, and they presumably aided him in establishing the Congo force in a relatively short time.

The implication of a Soviet veto power not only in the Security Council but in the General Assembly as well is portentous. It poses the dilemma of how to achieve constructive action now within the United Nations—which remains the most logical and perhaps even the only appropriate framework for thus supplementing our military facilities—without at the same time being dependent on the assent of the Soviet Union.

So long as the United States does not assign high priority to the establishment of a continuing U.N. force for the limited purpose of preventing the resumption of hostilities once halted, the Soviet attitude will dominate the possibilities. Thus two conditions would be necessary to alter the present circumstances. One is a change in the Soviet attitude. The other is a change in the priority which the United States assigns to this problem.

The Soviets are by no means immutable on such issues. When it suits their purposes they have blandly accepted and even themselves made use of such hitherto repugnant measures as the procedures under the Uniting for Peace Resolution providing for an emergency session of the General Assembly, which the Soviets sought to utilize in July, 1958, in the Lebanese crisis (although passage of a similar U.S. resolution made a vote on the Soviet resolution unnecessary). Indeed, the Soviet Union had supported the Yugoslav resolution of October 31, 1956, calling for an emergency Assembly session on Suez; and, while generally critical of U.N.E.F. to the point of refusing to pay their assessed share of the costs, the Soviets did not oppose the Swedish resolution of June 11, 1958, dispatching the U.N. Observer Group in Lebanon, and voted on July 13-14, 1960 in favor of a U.N. force in the Congo.

To translate present Soviet opposition into acceptance, or to proceed with determination without the Soviet Union as far as it is possible, the United States would have to reach the conclusion that this kind of U.N. force is vital for its security and for world peace, and apply its diplomatic resources toward that end. Determination of such magnitude can come only when American strategic doctrine deems a U.N. force as of parallel importance with the purely national elements in the military mix. The ultimate strategic argument was well stated by Mr. Frye in his study:

> If this force were strong enough to stamp out small wars, and if the courage and wisdom to use it were available, a great, gaping hole in the world's structure of security would be filled. The United States Government would be relieved of an agonizing problem which has hung over its policy planners for years: whether to gear the military establishment entirely to atomic war, or to maintain in addition, at great cost, a capacity to fight small wars with non-atomic weapons. If the anguish of the possible "small" war with all its consequences really could be lifted from Washington's shoulders, the savings in money alone would be enough to justify an investment of hundreds of millions of dollars in a U.N. force.[8]

Such logic was insufficient to move us in an earlier situation in which the United States took the leadership and failed to follow through, for reasons which can be understood if not entirely condoned. It will be recalled that under the Uniting for Peace Resolution, sponsored by the United States and passed by the U.N. General Assembly in the troubled fall of 1950, member governments were called upon to maintain within their

> . . . national armed forces elements so trained, organized and equipped, that they could promptly be made available, in accordance with . . . constitutional processes, for service as a United Nations unit or units . . .[9]

In replying to this resolution only four countries—Denmark, Norway, Greece, and Thailand—actually set aside any forces then in existence without a great many strings attached. (Uruguay also offered two destroyer escorts.) Perhaps the dismally poor response was due to the fact that the sponsor—the United States—replied to what amounted to its own call with a mes-

[8] *Op. cit.*, pp. 104-105.
[9] General Assembly Resolution 377 (V), 3 November 1950.

sage that has been called "a model of skillful obfuscation."
As one observer tells the story:

> Defense did not believe the U.N. could or should be relied upon,
> even in part, for United States security; was fearful that the
> United States might lose its friendly majority in the Assembly;
> wanted no action which could lead to de-emphasis of the United
> States' regional alliances; and did not want its hands tied, even
> morally, in respect to the future use of any specific element of the
> United States armed forces. . . . Washington found itself in the
> extraordinary position of having formally urged a course of
> action in the Assembly, won approval for it, and then been un-
> willing to take that action itself. The decision was reviewed in
> the government a year later, and reaffirmed.[10]

It is not easy to justify our inconsistency in reneging on a
presumably sound and important program of our own making.
But the program may not have been entirely sound. Many
political realities—some of them within our own bureaucratic
structure—militated against the secondment of U.S. forces, in
"peacetime," to a U.N. military formation.

Fortunately, this is no longer the point. The need today is
not for a force that includes the United States and, therefore,
the Soviet Union. It is, as I have sought to show, for a force
that explicitly *excludes* the great powers. Under these circumstances, it should be U.S. policy to advocate steadfastly and
with all the influence at its command the creation of a United
Nations force drawn exclusively from the smaller and neutral
nations.

The course of action that would follow from such a decision
would take several forms. In top-level negotiations with the
Soviet Union the chief American demand regarding the
United Nations has been for reduction of the existing veto
power in the Security Council in the settlement of disputes.
Although highly desirable, this proposal, implying an explicit
change in the power relationships of nations, must be rated as
unlikely of fulfillment at the present stage of international
relations. It would make far better sense to negotiate upon
something of proven relevance to our basic security objectives

[10] Frye, *op. cit.*, p. 60.

and to possible Soviet objectives as well, such as the modest beginnings of a U.N. force for exclusively pacific uses.

But diplomatic progress here should be no more dependent at the outset on Soviet concurrence than in the case of the Uniting for Peace Resolution, or the Atoms for Peace program, or the peaceful uses of outer space. The very priority assigned by the United States will give the effort a new order of political magnitude, and the prospects a new element of potential support.

To achieve its objectives, the United States would have to exert leadership in the United Nations equivalent to that exerted on such issues as the seating of Communist China, or the reduction of the American share in the U.N. budget, or, substantively, on such cases as Greece, Korea, and Suez. There is a reasonable chance that a majority could be secured to approve such a program if the United States were determined to have it and had arranged to minimize the financial burden falling on the poorer nations. The Soviet Union could and doubtless would denounce the force as illegal, refuse to pay its share, and seek to persuade a score of other countries to follow its unhelpful and mischievous lead. The Secretary General could in his wisdom make the most egregious show of reluctance, in order that his usefulness not end by his becoming *persona non grata* to the Soviets. Nonetheless, the force could be formed. Prediction is hazardous; but, as circumstances change, the time might well come when the Soviet representative, characteristically unconcerned with consistency, would call solemnly for the dispatch of the force to an area where Soviet interests were threatened. The United States should help him now to reach this historic stage, with the thought that our mission in shaping history makes far better sense than his.

CONCLUSION

American security requires the creation of a stand-by U.N. force; it should be, at least at the outset, envisaged as a nonfighting force composed of nationally contributed contingents from U.N. members other than the great powers; it should consist of a U.N. training facility leased from a neutral nation such as Sweden, Switzerland, or India, with national units rotated for six months of training and returned to an ear-marked—and honored—status in their national forces; the United States should apply its military assistance funds through the mutual security program to the financing of such units in recipient countries, thus supplying that program with a new and better rationale; the United States should give such a proposal priority in its bilateral negotiations with the Soviet Union over legalistic changes in the Charter and unattainable changes in the great power veto; and, despite Soviet opposition, the United States should devise a proposal that commends itself as sound and commit itself and its diplomatic resources to bringing the proposal to fruition, however arduous or lengthy the task.

CHAPTER SIX

Subversion and Indirect Aggression

IN A WORLD where ideologies are in conflict, yet resolution by force is increasingly debarred because of its disproportionate risks, the application of techniques of indirect rather than direct action toward attainment of strategic goals is increasing.

The Communist movement has long utilized techniques of indirection that favor both the need for concealment and the position of one who must operate from an initially inferior power position. Communist power has multiplied, but so have the risks of overt adventurism; and so long as an effective deterrent to such adventurism is maintained by the West, the process of change in the Communist states may do its work of draining away the movement's Messianic spirit and revolutionary élan. In the meantime, Communist penetration into new areas of political conquest will undoubtedly favor the techniques of subversion and indirect aggression. In addition, other lesser movements infused with an evangelical spirit, typified by Nasserism in Egypt, Castroism in Cuba, and Nkrumahism or Mboyaism in Africa, will for many of the same reasons probably employ the paths of indirection in their attempts to extend their influence beyond national frontiers.

There must therefore be included in the catalog of paramount American security objectives the need to find more effective ways of preventing and repulsing subversion externally directed against the political independence and territorial integrity of other nations.

It has been frequently asserted that subversion and indirect aggression must be effectively outlawed by the United Nations or that organization will perish. Such assertions reached a crescendo in the summer of 1958 as the Iraqi-Lebanese-Jordanian crises played themselves out against a background of multiple internal and external pressures on those countries chiefly directed from Moscow and Cairo. But on close inspection it is not at all certain that the United Nations either could or should be used indiscriminately in the type of case which, in its very ambiguity and its combination of internal and external elements, is the most likely to evade the classic description of the act of aggression.

One set of difficulties inherent in trying to draw up universally applicable rules in this area was acutely illustrated at the height of the 1958 crisis. During the early part of the summer, according to reports in the American press, discussions were taking place within the U.S. government as to whether the U.N. General Assembly, then about to meet in emergency session on the crisis, should be asked to do something tangible and dramatic about the general problem of indirect aggression. The specific issue from which general principles were to be inferred was the alleged infiltration of hostile personnel and arms into Lebanon from Syria under the political direction of the United Arab Republic authorities and to the accompaniment of hostile propaganda designed to undermine the stability of the Lebanese regime and encourage the rebellion then in progress.

In his speech to the emergency Assembly session, President Eisenhower called for "an end to the fomenting from without of civil strife."[1] His texts were two resolutions passed by the General Assembly in 1949 and 1950. The Essentials of Peace Resolution in 1949 called upon every nation

> to refrain from any threats or acts, direct or indirect, aimed at impairing the freedom, independence or integrity of any State,

[1] *New York Times,* August 14, 1958.

or at fomenting civil strife and subverting the will of the people in any State.[2]

The Peace through Deeds Resolution, passed on November 17, 1950 in the midst of the Korean action, reaffirmed that

> . . . whatever the weapons used, any aggression, whether committed openly, or by fomenting civil strife in the interest of a foreign Power, or otherwise, is the gravest of all crimes against peace and security throughout the world.[3]

But by the time the President actually appeared before the Assembly, the decision had apparently gone against the notion of making indirect aggression the central theme of the American presentation. The press attributed this change of heart to the realization that the United States might itself be vulnerable, at least in a legalistic way, to the charge of indirect aggression in, for example, Eastern Europe. Clandestine activities sponsored by the United States, however idealistically directed toward the end of national freedom and justice, might be subject to precisely the same strictures the United States had contemplated applying to Nasser's political and paramilitary activity, as well as to the larger problem of traditional Communist subversive tactics.

The distinction that emerged was a useful and instructive one. It was one thing to oppose external support for the Czechoslovak coup in 1948, for example, which by all the evidence was a plot against an unwilling and free people to install an authoritarian regime stage-managed by a foreign power. But the lessons of the Czechoslovak coup could not be applied unqualifiedly to the Lebanese civil war of 1958, or to the subversive aspects of the pan-Arab movement as a whole. Any government attempting to apply formulas developed to cope with traditional Communist methods of infiltration, subversion, and ultimate take-over would find itself facing a complex dilemma growing out of the generally "popular" nature of revolutionary movements that marched under the nationalist banner, however subversive their techniques. It was

[2] General Assembly Resolution 209 (IV), 1 December 1949.
[3] General Assembly Resolution 380 (V), 17 November 1950.

possible that in Iraq and even Lebanon in 1958 a numerical majority of the citizenry applauded or would applaud the overthrow of the existing regime in favor of one more unequivocally dedicated to the cause of Arab nationalism or Arab unity, or in any event to less dependence on the West.

The frustration inherent in having to define the issue of indirect aggression in an ambiguous political context was evident in the U.S. Representative's statement on July 16, 1958, before the Security Council:

> But we think there is a difference between normal aspirations of nationalism, which are proper and which are healthy and which can even be idealistic and forward-looking, and the subversion of the independence of small countries on the other hand.

> Mr. Sobolev creates the impression that Arab nationalism and subversion of independence are all one thing. Well, they are not one thing. They are two entirely different things. We are in favor of nationalism and we are against the subversion of the independence of small countries.[4]

The same dilemma pervades American foreign policy at large today: how to ensure stability in the world without bottling up popular forces whose political expression might in fact represent more genuine democracy than the autocratic or feudal or—in the case of the Soviet satellites—imperial regimes now in power. The United States is torn in several directions when it comes to formulating in concrete terms workable ground rules about subversion and indirect aggression.

Ideally speaking, we would presumably wish to see *all* feudal or imperial or internally undemocratic regimes discouraged, and popular and democratic rule enhanced. Thus we profoundly oppose aggression against friendly democratic regimes that is aimed at imposing undemocratic or tyrannical forms. We shall in such cases doubtless help to support the existing government in every way, as we are now doing around the world, and we shall oppose the forces of infiltration or subversion. On the other hand, we would certainly not agree in advance to support international sanctions against forces acting to support pro-freedom or pro-Western revolutionary

4 Henry Cabot Lodge, *New York Herald Tribune,* July 17, 1958.

movements. And finally, given the variety of circumstances that conceivably might prevail, we are not ourselves always prepared to intervene in any way at all or even to express an official view.

Indeed—and this is the hardest of all to acknowledge—it could be that we would for overriding security reasons discourage external assistance from any source to genuine forces of revolution; witness American self-restraint in East Germany in 1953, Poland and Hungary in 1956, and Tibet in 1959. In point of fact, for reasons of military strategy or political stability we have occasionally given aid and comfort to regimes repugnant to our democratic principles; for example, Tito's Yugoslavia, Franco's Spain, Gomulka's Poland, Trujillo's Dominican Republic, and Batista's Cuba. It is easy to condemn such inconsistency as immoral. It is less easy to weigh the values in a complex situation involving at best a choice of varying evils. There are obvious and excruciating difficulties in attempting to generalize a policy on this score on the basis of either simple-minded maxims or abstract rules of morality. The very ambiguity of the characteristic subversive situation has made even the defining of indirect aggression no easier than the effort to define aggression, itself a mire of semantic and political pitfalls.

If the United States cannot afford the luxury of a simple copybook morality on this subject, what alternative courses are open to it? Can it be selective in its approach to subversion and indirect aggression? This would mean closing an eye to externally caused disruption in the Communist empire and non-Communist regimes we do not favor, while insisting on the principle of nonintervention in areas chosen as targets by Communist and other forces as well as in countries with undemocratic regimes with which we find it convenient to deal. This position, which roughly approximates the present reality, is not particularly attractive either politically or morally.

Another alternative would be to act consistently on our announced principles. But to oppose all forms of outside assistance to revolutionary movements would carry us back to the worst excesses of the Holy Alliance and breed the same unsatisfactory reaction. It would retroactively put into moral question the substantial assistance given to the embryonic United States by France, for example, or the powerful indirect support afforded by England to revolutionary democracy in Greece in the 1820's, or by the West to Hungary in the mid-nineteenth century.

The final alternative in generalizing a consistent rule is unthinkable in view of our profound interest in world stability. Complete *laissez faire* with respect to subversive movements would encourage perpetual turmoil. More serious still, it would remove some important obstacles in the path of the antilibertarian activities of the Communist movement, frustrating our objective of preserving and, if possible, enlarging the present zone of freedom.

CONCLUSIONS

What conclusions can be drawn from this analysis? The first is that we cannot live by a hard-and-fast rule with respect to indirect aggression, a rule bearing equally on the just and unjust, and administered with blind impartiality like the law of the Medes and the Persians, regardless of whose ox is gored or which side wins out in the struggle. Our approach can only be a pragmatic one. We must be selective rather than general in our application of principles, precisely because there is neither any over-all political rule nor any unambiguous moral position which can be applied satisfactorily for all cases.

A second major conclusion is that, whatever action might be taken by multilateral agencies, the key to the problem of subversion lies within rather than without a nation's borders. The primary combination for sustaining the internal health of externally harassed regimes is widespread popular support, a stable yet adequately dynamic social and economic order, capable leadership, and, finally, the military and police facilities to maintain internal order and guard the borders. After almost four decades of unremitting propaganda, enmity, subversion, infiltration, espionage, and possibly sabotage, the Soviet Union, through the American Communist party and networks of Soviet agents, has made virtually no impression on the political, economic, or social fabric of the United States. The same has been true of every other Western democracy whose internal strength rests on solid foundations. But the non-Western societies which are the new targets of indirect aggression lack in varying degrees the conditions that make indirect aggression relatively profitless; and the development of their internal strength, in the final analysis their only sure protection against subversion, must be a self-generated process in which external assistance can be only marginal.

What is the implication of these conclusions for the role of the United Nations?

We should not look to the United Nations for *general* rules regarding externally generated pressures in situations primarily characterized by civil strife. As suggested, our interests would not necessarily be well served by such rules in the present political state of the world. There is also doubt whether others would find such strictures desirable either. The political atlas includes countries governed by regimes ranging from democratic to totalitarian; it includes stable governments and weak governments; it contains countries sympathetic to neighboring regimes, and countries implacably hostile. We could hardly expect widespread support of rules that would be examined by each country not in the abstract but, as we ourselves apparently did in the summer of 1958, in terms of the concrete policy problems facing a country now or in the foreseeable future.

But there is a role for the United Nations without imposing any such rules. The United Nations, along with other instruments of diplomacy and propaganda, can and should be used *ad hoc* where it would support our interests so to use it. A case in point would be a situation of blatant but nonovert interference from without, by means of infiltration, subversion, and propaganda of a tendentious and revolutionary nature, such as Egypt's pressures on Jordan in 1958. If our object is to curtail and discourage such activity, U.N. debate may be the most effective agency of bringing clandestine pressures to the widest possible public attention. Additionally, a U.N.

"presence," as it has come to be called, consisting of even only one man (such as Pier Spinelli in Amman in 1958 or S. S. Tuomioja in Laos in 1959) or, alternatively, a larger contingent of observers or conservators, also

> helps to deter indirect aggression by focusing public attention upon the foreign sources of subversion and the means used to incite violence.[5]

We should keep alive the awareness that multilateral action thus has its uses in the complex circumstances and subtleties of indirect aggression even though the United Nations is only the stage on which the act, in preparation elsewhere, comes to light and presents other governments with choices and decisions. To regard such cases individually and in the light of national interest may appear unpalatably Machiavellian. It is, nevertheless, the only course that reflects present political realities.

[5] Ernest A. Gross, "U.N. Record and U.N. Dilemma," *New York Times Magazine,* September 21, 1958, p. 69.

CHAPTER SEVEN

Disarmament

A DRASTIC general reduction in the level of all arms and armaments could conceivably come about if three basic political
preconditions were met: (1) a climate of significantly greater
world confidence; (2) the presence of international institutions
of a police nature which furnished adequate physical protection to all nations; and (3) a global political regime which, as
in any community whose members have laid down their arms,
supplied continuous and reliable justice to its members, including provisions for peaceful change through the process of
legislation. Thus the long-term goal of the United States
should be the creation of the bases for a genuine world community from which can come disarmament and world law.
There is no historical evidence that the process can work the
other way.

The discussions on disarmament in the League of Nations
covering almost its entire life span had, it will be recalled,
no effect whatever on the realities of the armaments problem.
Indeed, their only tangible effect was to soften the will and
the capacity of the democracies to survive as the latter came
to view weapons as villains rather than as sometimes the
tools of villains. The League debates never had any real-life
effect because France never received the guarantees she sought
from the United States and England against the possibility

of standing alone in the presence of a rearmed and hostile Germany. No amount of words in Geneva in the 1920's could overcome this obstacle.

By this logic, under conditions we can foresee over the years immediately ahead, resolution of the paramount problem of reducing capabilities for surprise attack remains first and foremost a function of the relationship between the United States and the Soviet Union and therefore at any given time subject to the nature of Communist ideology and Soviet foreign policy. The problem is further, and acutely, complicated in the longer-term future by the probability that Communist China will undergo an extended period of fanatical nationalism, expansion, and conceivably such hostility to the Western world—possibly including the Soviet Union—that even limited disarmament will long remain an impossibility. This prospect haunts our planning, for without inclusion of China there would be little hope for a durable agreement. We can therefore see no predictable end to present suspicions which will have to be significantly alleviated before even limited disarmament is possible.

In the face of these laws of political physics, so to speak, it is legitimate to wonder why present efforts to reverse or at least ignore the security-disarmament equation should have any brighter prospects than in the past. The answer lies of course in the awareness, which we hope to be general, that modern weapons make the irrationality of an arms race obvious to all.

Some have deduced from this logic that a real possibility exists for complete universal disarmament. I have suggested that the conditions for such disarmament are equivalent to those for world government, and thus are not priority topics of serious planning in terms of action in a reasonable future. As a practical matter the short-run problem of disarmament in the second half of the twentieth century is to reduce the possibility of widespread destruction or contamination by nuclear and other mass-type weapons. Even more specifically, the problem is to minimize the power of any given nation to mount a surprise attack sufficient to effectively eliminate the capacity to retaliate, a capacity that has so far deterred such risk taking. A crucial part of this problem is to limit the number of states possessing nuclear weapons.

In its most concrete terms, the aim of U.S. policy is to reduce the likelihood of a successful attack by the Soviet Union —or anyone else—on the United States and its allies. This is an interest that we presume to be mutual as long as the risks continue to be disproportionate to the possible gains. The task of diplomacy is thus to articulate and negotiate this common interest among the parties concerned.

But in political terms two events must precede genuine negotiations for arms control. The Soviet Union must come to the conclusion that success in its alleged historical mission will be possible without the military capacity to crush the capitalist world. Soviet leadership must certainly abandon Lenin's dictum that "only after the proletariat has disarmed the bourgeoisie will it . . . throw all armaments on the scrap-heap"[1] Furthermore, the United States must come to the conclusion that the dynamic nature of both Soviet and Chinese doctrine no longer carries an important threat to the West of overt military aggression to achieve political ends. In sum, both sides will have to agree to forego the kind of strategic advantage, insistence on which has helped to abort disarmament negotiations since time immemorial.

Let us first consider the prospects of Soviet willingness to forego the advantages it seeks. The popular Western assumption behind disarmament is that the new weaponry, like George III's generals, tends to menace its owners as much as it menaces others. If this assumption were genuinely accepted on all sides the prospects of agreement might be great. For a time it appeared that only we made such an assumption, and this perhaps more than anything else tended to unbalance the negotiating equation. Some Communists apparently still deceive themselves as to their ability to survive a global holocaust. Chinese Communist leadership has been quoted as anticipating with satisfaction that the 300 million Chinese sur-

[1] V. I. Lenin, "Military Program of the Proletarian Revolution," in *Collected Works,* International Publishers, New York, 1942, p. 366.

viving a thermonuclear war would inherit the earth, and expressing confidence that a superior civilization could be created "in the debris of a dead imperialism."[2] But Soviet doctrine has wavered uncertainly in recent years between confidence that communism will emerge triumphant from a war and acknowledgment that no one would win.

The more immediate difficulty in acknowledging a real mutuality of interests is quite a different one, bearing on the role of arms in the field not of battle but of diplomacy. Soviet leadership seems confident that its will and nerve are sufficiently superior to threaten nuclear warfare without much real risk in a variety of tactical situations. If others overreact, the threat can be readily withdrawn, a sequence that has recurred several times since November 1956. In short, Soviet brinkmanship has proven superior to our own variety. One of the most sobering facts in the political scene is the seeming confidence of Communist leadership in its ability to handle its own weapons rationally and self-consciously and not be controlled or panicked by them or by fear of them. Agreement is also inhibited by apparent Soviet confidence, despite its own doctrine, that the United States can be kept from launching a preventive or pre-emptive attack. The Soviets have demonstrated their ability to soothe us very quickly with the carrot when the stick becomes overly unpopular.

Thus an indispensable condition for even limited arms control would be a weakening of the Communists' confidence in their continued ability to manipulate American hostility. A genuine American willingness to put everything at stake might convince the Communists that the situation was not so manageable as they had thought, and that they would do well to reach an agreement before the Americans lost their heads. But this hardly seems likely as a prime motivation for serious Communist negotiation under present conditions. The acceptance by the Communist leadership of arms control as an interest-based policy must consequently depend on their willingness to forego the propaganda-diplomatic advantage conferred by

[2] See articles in *Hung Chi* and *Jenmin Jihpao,* both quoted in *New York Times,* April 23, 1960.

military power as well as their willingness to forego the capacity to repel capitalists who suddenly turn out as Lenin predicted they would.

But it is not only the Communists who approach disarmament negotiations with an *arrière-pensée*. The attitude of the American military community toward disarmament has been precisely that of any other nation's—and equally inhibiting to the prospects of agreement. Americans who are responsible for the nation's security tend, whether consciously or not, to ensure that any agreement will leave this country in a relatively favorable strategic position. Sometimes the quest for residual strategic advantage has been explicit, and sometimes so tacit as to be unrecognizable.

The changing technology of warfare may force an alteration in these traditional attitudes, particularly when a military establishment can no longer give assurances of its ability either to defend the nation successfully against attack or to attack the enemy in a way that will not invite annihilation in return. The central problem of disarmament, then, is how to exploit the basically altered situation by devising a scheme under which neither side would receive or even retain a net strategic advantage, a scheme which can convince military planners on both sides that their mission is no longer to secure that net advantage.

That problem is intensely complicated by the fact that twelve countries today are technically able to embark on a successful nuclear weapons program "in the near future" and eight more to a limited extent.[3] French production of nuclear weapons suggests that the Chinese Communists will develop nuclear weapons independently, or will exert pressure on the Soviet Union to enable them to acquire such weapons. The fifth-country problem will predictably become a multicountry problem, with incalculable ramifications for the task of avoiding nuclear war, not the least of which is the possibility of not being able to identify an incoming missile and making the wrong assumption about its source, with all that could follow.

[3] "The Nth Country Problem, A World-Wide Survey of Nuclear Weapons Capabilities," summarized in *Daedelus*, Summer, 1959, p. 395.

From this it is clear that prospects for even the kind of limited agreement most needed—minimizing the prospect of surprise attack—depend almost entirely on a bilateral American-Soviet decision, based on evaluations which both sides make of capabilities, intentions, and risks, including the risk in delaying agreement indefinitely.

In terms of the situation outlined above, what are the possible uses of the United Nations to achieve basic policy objectives in this field in the foreseeable future?

THE USES OF THE UNITED NATIONS

While in its initial stage the problem of arms control is essentially bilateral and the United Nations consequently has only marginal uses in that stage, the organization can supply useful means of negotiation; perhaps more importantly, it can act as a source of international pressure on the determinative powers to reach an agreement, in part by its capacity to develop impartial proposals; and it is the obvious framework for implementing an agreement.

The Russians boycotted the U.N. Disarmament Commission until their demand for parity in representation with the Western alliance was met by the device of making the Commission representative of the total U.N. membership. The parity theme poses difficult problems for the West, chiefly because of the derangement it implies across the board in multilateral diplomatic activity; but parity was soon granted in the form of a ten-nation group on disarmament established outside the United Nations by the Big Four Foreign Ministers in August of 1959. This in turn gave way again to U.N. debate after the Russian walkout from the 1960 Geneva talks.

But where and how agreement is reached is of no particular consequence so long as the nations now possessing or most likely to possess nuclear capabilities are involved in the proceedings. More to the point is that a bilateral or even ten-nation agreement will still leave the Nth country problem—the problem of other countries that have already developed or are on the verge of developing nuclear capabilities. By defini-

tion, the problem here becomes multilateral, and a wide multilateral forum would be the only appropriate basis for extending the agreement to all countries and binding them by it.

(The West will postpone as long as it can the issue posed
by the necessity of binding the Chinese to any agreement
reached. But it seems probable that the moment of agreement
will furnish the prime tactical opportunity for the Chinese
to insist on recognition and full participation in the United
Nations as a condition for inclusion in an agreement. If one
had to guess at what point in history the pressures will be
most acute to acquiesce in a formula for seating Peiping in
the United Nations, this would seem to be it, despite the
verbal formulas which assume that Peiping can be bound without an extravagantly stiff price.)

Another potential value of the United Nations in the initial
negotiating stage offers untried possibilities but would not be
easy for either of the dominant powers to accept.

We have seen that even if positive motivation exists on both
sides for an agreement limiting weapons or means of surprise
attack, it will still be necessary to overcome the built-in tendency of those responsible for military security on both sides
to seek a net advantage in any agreement. The most obvious
illustration is the Soviet Union's earlier insistence on "nuclear
disarmament" without significantly affecting Russian conventional armed strength. One can also cite the equally long-
time insistence of American military leaders on a high degree
of access to the interior of the Soviet Union. It is difficult to
see how any agreement involving inspection would not by its
very nature reveal more to us than to the Russians, and there
is no way we can avoid or minimize the necessity of some form
of inspection that is bound to have this effect. But because of
the frame of mind the protracted negotiations have created
on both sides, it might be instructive to turn to the middle
and small powers in the United Nations and charge them with
developing a disarmament plan to be considered by both sides
rather than continuing to have such plans developed exclusively by the chief antagonists. Such a plan might have the
virtue of being objective in the sense of denying any strategic

or tactical advantage to either side. Certainly it would be easy enough to discover if it afforded any net disadvantage.

Human nature being what it is, perhaps the situation has to become significantly more dangerous before we—or the Russians—could accept such a neutral proposal. As *The Economist* wryly—and sagely—remarked after the abortive disarmament talks in 1957, "The main lesson of the summer seems to be that there is still not enough fear about."[4] Still it might turn out to be the only way to surmount the inherent obstacle to agreement, assuming that other conditions were propitious. Logically we should welcome such third-party initiative in suggesting a fair and workable program under the aegis of the United Nations.

The uses of the United Nations seem even more decisive when it comes to the point of implementing whatever initial strategic decision the great powers are able to reach. At the root of its value is the need that will arise for an agency or system of agencies to police such an agreement.

The heart of the American position is the need for adequate inspection to ensure that clandestine violations do not go unremarked. If genuine negotiations are limited to the problem of surprise attack, inspection is even more crucial. The possibility exists of Soviet agreement to a limited form of inspection in connection with the cessation of nuclear tests, and one can hope for a progressive breakdown of the Soviet fear of penetration and espionage into the most sensitive installations in the Soviet security system.

Two factors enter planning for a suitable inspection system in the foreseeable future. One is the possible need for the availability of genuine neutrals, particularly if and when Communist China becomes a party to an agreement. The problem of execution may be markedly easier if genuinely impartial neutral nations are available and their nationals utilized to inspect, observe, and report. Since the United Nations is the only organization that includes the neutral nations, it should be the prime agency of implementation of any disarmament agreement. The experience of related U.N.

[4] *The Economist,* August 10, 1957, p. 442.

bodies will be of particular value in keeping up with both the technology and administration of control during a period when present possibilities appear to favor a limited agreement rather than a generalized lowering of military levels, and the problem of hidden stockpiles of nuclear weapons remains untouched.

But it is essential to plan ahead to the situation where a more general agreement becomes a possibility. The International Atomic Energy Agency, despite its disappointingly modest record so far, at least on paper enjoys important powers of inspection to ensure that none of the nuclear materials it dispenses are utilized for other than declared purposes. U.N. agreements on the peaceful uses of outer space, however limited, may also include provisions for control and guarantee. It is in the U.S. interest and in the general interest that the United Nations undertake such pilot operations. The combination of technical skills and administrative precedent and experience in both fields for possible future use in monitoring a system of international control for disarmament and outer space utilization makes it of vital urgency for the United States to encourage limited U.N. activity toward this end, whether agreements with the Russians are possible now or not. There are grounds for assuming that technical problems, while acute, do not constitute an absolute barrier to adequate inspection. A group of experts commissioned by Columbia University recently reported hopefully on this score:

> The main finding of this report is that it is possible to define systems of inspection which would ensure compliance with a wide variety of disarmament agreements.[5]

The fast-moving changes in the technological picture lead to the second factor in planning an inspection system. This is the prospect within the present planning period of bypassing at least some of the problems of penetration on the ground by utilization of inspection from spacecraft monitoring a disarmament agreement. Estimates as to the capabilities of

[5] Seymour Melman, Ed., *Inspection for Disarmament*, Columbia University Press, New York, 1958, p. 54.

observation anticipate that satellites with optical and television or photographic equipment can inspect objects on the ground with increasingly satisfactory definition and resolution.[6] Wernher von Braun estimates that a satellite moving in a two-hour orbit 1075 miles above the earth could detect all significant large-scale military activities or preparations through telescopic cameras. Other predictions are even more optimistic, and a reasonable assumption is that at its present rate the technology will continue to outstrip the limits of conservative planning.

All logic points to the operation of such a system by the United Nations rather than by individual parties to such an agreement. The U-2 plane episode in the spring of 1960 bespoke the dangers of unilateral inspection attempts. The evidence is still scanty as to the political acceptability of an international system of inspection from spacecraft, although Soviet scientists joined in recommending to the three-power Geneva conference regarding cessation of nuclear testing that satellites police a test ban in outer space.[7] The overwhelming rightness of the course proposed should continue to commend it to Western planning regardless of the variations in Soviet responsiveness at any given time.

A further use of the United Nations arises from the nature of the armaments problem when viewed apart from the confrontation of the super powers.

In the Western European Union agreement, a means has been found on a regional basis to limit West German arms production by assimilating it in a system of regional cooperation. Proposals have been from time to time made to limit the inflow of arms into the Near and Middle East. An opportunity existed for a time in late 1956 to at least try for agreement on the basis of language contained in the U.N. Assembly resolution on Suez asking states to "refrain from introducing military goods in the area of hostilities."[8] Potential problems of

[6] See forecast by A. A. Koepfer, Chief of Photo Reconnaissance Branch, Wright Air Development Center, Dayton, Ohio, *New York Times*, October 2, 1959.

[7] *New York Times*, July 11, 1959.

[8] General Assembly Resolution 997 (ES-I), 2 November 1956.

implementation were difficult, and they became temporarily insuperable in the light of Western commitments to supply arms to Lebanon, Jordan, Iraq, Iran, and Turkey. The dual objectives of stabilizing the area by keeping new arms races from developing and of erecting a framework to contain the Communist arms shipments were in fact vital ones. In early 1957 the Soviet Foreign Minister proposed agreement on banning arms shipments to the Middle East.[9] But even assuming he meant it, it would have required an initiative and a change of policy on our own part to achieve the desired end, and the forces of inertia were too great to overcome.

The possibility should be reconsidered, at a time when the Palestine area is *not* aflame, for an agreement limiting the inflow of arms to the most sensitive area in the region—Israel and its immediate neighbors. If it would be impossible to apply it to the region as a whole, there is a basis in the Palestine Armistice Agreements for regarding the parties thereto as under a special international mandate to refrain from warlike acts, including excessive arming. Those like Saudi Arabia and Iraq who were not parties to the Armistice could logically be assimilated for this purpose.

Ideally, such an agreement would be reached on a voluntary basis by the parties concerned, with a U.N. resolution underwriting it and providing appropriate facilities for inspection. Such a program might be urged on the parties by the United Nations, accompanied by the implicit guarantee of security and borders contained in the Charter. But the Arabs at this time are not likely to bind themselves to accepting Israel's current borders, and the likelihood of voluntary acceptance by any of the parties is remote. There remains, however, a third and more realistic possibility—a self-restraining ordinance by the great powers bilaterally or quadrilaterally arrived at, and a suitable ratification passed by the U.N. Assembly bringing all others into the agreement and possibly containing provisions for inspection of compliance by U.N. instrumentalities. The proposal for such an arrangement might well be a serious

[9] Dmitri Shepilov, reported in *Pravda*, February 13, 1957.

element in any Western negotiating package with the Soviet Union.

The same logic can be applied to the situation in Africa. One writer recently spelled out a proposal for a U.N. convention guaranteeing the African area against aggression and imposing a moratorium on the shipment of all arms other than those required to maintain internal order.[10] Such a moratorium could greatly facilitate African internal development and insulate it against potentially disastrous local arms races. Again, the best route to a U.N.-sponsored agreement would be in the first instance a great power agreement. Only an excessive sense of fatalism need prevent us from seeking serious negotiations along these lines as part of our policy objectives in a potential East-West *détente*.

CONCLUSION

With the understanding that in the first instance the general disarmament problem depends on the political environment and that the preliminary decisions are bilateral in nature, the United Nations supplies an alternative means of negotiation, a way of involving and using the talents of other nations who share concern with the problem, a source of international pressure on the great powers, and an agency for implementing agreements reached. To resolve the Nth country problem the final negotiations must be multilateral, including in some form the Communist Chinese. Given the built-in proclivity of the parties to seek advantage for themselves, it would be worth at least experimenting with having the small and medium powers in the United Nations draw up disarmament proposals with the thought that they might be more objectively conceived and thus more likely to secure mutual agreement.

The United Nations is the appropriate agency for implementing an agreement, first because of the availability of

[10] Arnold Rivkin, "Arms for Africa," *Foreign Affairs*, October 1959. For another regional approach to limitation of armaments, see Chile's initiative in 1960 to convene a Latin American conference on reducing regional arms spending.

neutrals, second because of the technical possibility of monitoring agreements from orbiting observation satellites in the not-too-distant future, satellites that logically should operate under international auspices. U.N. experience with limited controls and safeguards in the peaceful uses of atomic energy and, hopefully, of outer space, can supply valuable pilot models toward more comprehensive agreements.

Great power agreement should be sought on a priority basis to limit the inflow of arms into the Palestine area and also the continent of Africa. Such regional arms stabilization should be suitably guaranteed and inspected by an appropriate U.N. agency.

Part **III** **THE UNITED NATIONS
AND THE COLD WAR**

CHAPTER EIGHT

The Changing Soviet View
of the Changing United Nations

WE NOW TURN from military policy considerations to the realm of what might be called political security. Our analysis of policy objectives moves from the short run to the middle range of time and action. If our military security objectives fail to be met, it goes without saying that all else is in grave jeopardy. But assuming, as we must, that we can develop and maintain a comprehensive and versatile defense program, there is a good chance that the major battles will be fought out in the realm of politics.

Here it must be emphasized at the very outset that the West, and particularly the United States, must overcome the tendency to believe that, if the Soviet leaders temporarily rule out military means to achieve their goals, it follows that they are prepared to negotiate solutions in what we conceive to be rational terms. Peace and war, as Communist leaders have tirelessly proclaimed to their followers, are interchangeable phases of the basic conflict.[1] There can be no intelligent approach to policy making in the context of the cold war unless we accept the prospect of protracted political and ideological

[1] See Mao Tse-tung's *Collected Works*, International Publishers, New York, 1954.

conflict, a conflict in which by its very terms the Communists will be invariably taking the offensive.[2] There is no doubt that in the dedicated Communist mind the core battle between the United States and the Soviet Union is being fought for the prize of history itself, that all else depends on its outcome. De Tocqueville prophetically stated the case a century ago when he wrote:

> There are at present two great nations in the world, which started at different points, but seem to tend towards the same end. I allude to the Russians and the Americans. The principal instrument of the [latter] is freedom; of the [former] servitude. Their starting-point is different and their courses are not the same; yet each of them seems marked out by the will of Heaven to sway the destinies of half the globe.[3]

The United States possesses double political objectives—to ensure the survival and prosperity of our political and social values, and at the same time to find ways—and I use an oversimplified shorthand—of "liquidating the cold war" on better terms than those the Communists have in mind. It is with this double objective in mind that we inquire into the uses of the United Nations to achieve Western purposes in terms of what can conveniently be called political security.

Before considering the possible substance of U.S. planning, however, we must pause to consider two powerful conditioning factors: the basic view we hold as to the nature and prospects of the Communist system, and the Communist view of the United Nations.

THE U.S. VIEW OF THE COMMUNIST SYSTEM

There are two general and broadly contrasting American views as to what inner process the Communist movement is now undergoing and how we can affect that process in constructive ways.

---

[2] See the article entitled "Reappraisal of Capitalism: A Program for Soviet Ideologists," in *Mirovaya Ekonomika i Mezhdunarodnyye Otnosheniya*, No. 8, August 1959, pp. 3-14.

[3] Alexis de Tocqueville, *Democracy in America*, Volume I, Knopf, New York, 1945, p. 435.

One point of view sees the struggle with communism as fixed and essentially unchanging. Its proponents warn us against being seduced by the illusion that meaningful changes are taking place which justify altering our basic estimates of Soviet intentions.[4] The other and more widespread school of thought sees the Soviet system as in flux and moving toward a more acceptable international posture. This school urges us not to act as though communism were static, but to be prepared to respond flexibly to its dynamics, by abandoning the conditioned reflexes that the cold war has built into our responses to events in the Communist countries.

Those who fear that we may be taken in by superficial changes argue that Communist tactics characteristically make a virtue of necessity by using change to confuse and soften up the enemy while assimilating the changes into a renewed pattern of ideological strength. Thus Western strategy, unless it is to succumb to the disease of false optimism and wishful thinking, must sustain an attitude of unremitting skepticism toward apparent changes, and reject strategies that assume that such changes will significantly modify the profound hostility and implacable dedication of the Communist leadership.

There is much to commend this line of reasoning. The West in general, and Americans in particular, are at their most pitiful when they refuse to believe that the great dictators of the age—whether Lenin, Hitler, Stalin or Khrushchev—mean what they very clearly say. It would be gross negligence to proceed upon any other assumption but that the Soviet leadership today is still following the path defined by Lenin in 1920: "As soon as we are strong enough to strike down capitalism we shall seize it by the throat." Who is wise or prescient enough to guarantee that Nikita Khrushchev had something less harmful and more acceptable in mind when, thirty-six years later, he told the American Ambassador with a candor few world leaders permit themselves:

[4] A recent example is *Protracted Conflict* by Robert Strausz-Hupé *et al.*, Harper, New York, 1959, particularly Chapter 5, entitled "Deception and Distraction."

When we win this competition we shall also re-educate you. We
Bolsheviks are ravenous people. What we achieve through our
struggle in the past is not sufficient for us. We want more—
tomorrow.[5]

Certainly nothing could be more fatuous than our public
expectations that one more effort might "break the deadlock,"
or "eliminate tensions," or, in its most egregious form, "bring
peace."

But the advocates of "hold fast," despite the value of their
advice as a necessary corrective to wishful thinking, are not
entirely persuasive. They quite rightly warn us against entertaining false hopes for basic changes in the nature of Soviet
communism. But by accepting at face value the Communist
pretentions to consistency and to a fixed destiny, they themselves fall into the trap of historical absolutism which has
invalidated so much Communist doctrine.

Evidence of changes in the Soviet Union is multiplying.
The very foundation of security for the Soviet state—insulation
and isolation from the outside world—has been breached in
ways unthinkable a decade ago. Interpretations of this evidence may of course differ. The unprecedented exposure of
Soviet leaders to America, and of the Soviet people to Americans, may simply reflect a new confidence in Soviet power
and Russian immunity to Western influence. Considerable
internal reform in the judicial, penal, and administrative
environment of the Soviet Union has been reported since the
1953-1954 catharsis of de-Stalinization; but Communist leaders
are entirely capable of using these reforms, however genuine,
to delude us into believing that communism has abandoned its
élan vital along with some of its internal controls.

The prize exhibit for the theory of delusion is Mao Tse-
tung's "Let a hundred flowers bloom" campaign. Here, osten-
sible liberalization handily uncovered victim after victim for
renewed persecution. But we cannot be at all sure about the
inner sequence of motivation. Was the whole affair deliberately planned, or did the untoward reaction frighten Chinese
leaders into quick retreat? The same question remains un-

[5] Quoted in *New York Times*, April 22, 1958.

answered regarding Hungary. Were the Soviet withdrawal and the October 30, 1956, public statement on a more liberal satellite policy elements in a Machiavellian plot? Or was the trend suddenly and brutally reversed by the unanticipated reactions, accompanied by internal convulsions in the Soviet leadership? Evidence on both these counts would go a long way toward illuminating the interpretation of "liberalizing" trends in the Communist states.

The evidence of change resulting from the sociological processes within Soviet society has potent support from an authoritative source:

> Completely dominant, the ruling class has begun to abandon and lose the ideology, the dogma which brought it to power. The class has begun to split up into factions. At the top everything is peaceful and smooth, but below the top, in the depths, and even in the ranks, new thoughts, new ideas, are bubbling and future storms are brewing.[6]

> The world center of Communist ideology no longer exists; it is in the process of complete disintegration. The unity of the world Communist movement is incurably injured. There are no visible possibilities whatsoever that it can be restored.[7]

Perhaps the most impressive evidence of internal trends unfavorable to Communist dogma came in 1956 in Hungary. The lesson of Hungary was that, behind the monolithic façade, deep-seated processes are at work going contrary to the most basic assumptions and predictions of Marxism.

The only rational conclusion to be drawn from the conflicting evidence is that neither view is entirely persuasive, and that policy can therefore not safely rest exclusively on either. The truth is that we do not really know with any certainty what the trends are with respect to world communism. It is likely that the Communist leaders themselves are equally ignorant. It is this uncertainty that makes it impossible to accept as either intelligent or safe a fixed strategy based on traditional assumptions.

---

[6] Milovan Djilas, *The New Class,* Praeger, New York, 1957, p. 161.
[7] *Ibid.,* p. 183.

The acknowledgment of uncertainty furnishes an entirely proper basis for such policies as the exchange program. The validity of this program rests not on the sentimental hope that personal contact will somehow dissolve profound political differences at the governmental and societal level but on the deep breach it represents in the isolationism of the Soviet Union and the chance it offers to correct in some key Soviet minds dangerously inaccurate estimates of Western morale and capabilities. The great hazard of the exchange program is not that Americans will be corrupted by Communist ideas but that it will serve as an excuse for faulty reasoning and inadequate policies. One of the grossest errors on the part of top-level Western statesmanship in recent years has been to read into flimsy evidence proof that the Soviet system was on the verge of collapse, from which it was only a short step to the conclusion that the *coup de grâce* could be administered by purely verbal blows. Events soon revealed the fraudulence of this comforting view.

But we do not have to insist on the immediate collapse of the Soviet system in order to perceive changes of an evolutionary nature. The appropriate Western posture would combine two strands: open-mindedness to the notion that communism, like all other political movements, is subject to non-Marxian laws of growth, development, maturation, decline, and ultimate transformation; and the maintenance during this process of strong military and political defenses along with a purposeful policy designed to encourage the process of peaceful change.

The over-all strategy in such a posture involves four difficult but vital elements. To do more than hold our own in the political struggle, we must be less fastidious than we have been about finding better ways to exploit the vulnerabilities in the Communist system. We must cease to allow the political battles to be waged only on our own home grounds while accepting the Communist version of its own privileged political sanctuary. Second, we must continue to avoid sharpening the struggle by gratuitous provocation and by unrealistic cold war aims of our own. Third, we must encourage the process of change by acting on the assumption that communists, no less than capitalists, are creatures of history and subject to non-Marxian laws of historical development. We must prepare for transformations in the Communist system which today we cannot even begin to predict. Fourth, our objective in liquidating the cold war must be spelled out in better and more universally acceptable terms than the terms the Communists would impose.

It should be noted that, since there is an obvious difference in stages of development between the Soviet and Communist Chinese systems, and our focus here is on the possible values of the United Nations, for the present the problem of political strategy is limited to Western-Soviet relations. In that context we conclude that the Western interpretation of apparent evolution must be a dual one, combining a prudent skepticism with open-minded readiness not only to go along but indeed to help pave the way, by institutional and other means, for a more internationally tolerant and acceptable Soviet order.

THE SOVIET VIEW OF THE UNITED NATIONS

The second underlying factor in political strategy is equally fundamental. The potential of the United Nations in the achievement of political security objectives depends to a large extent on the place assigned to the United Nations in Soviet doctrine and planning.

Soviet leadership has consistently rejected the elements of imagery and symbolism regarding the United Nations that have been its strongest attraction to the United States. As one student of Soviet affairs put it, the Soviet view of the United Nations

> has followed with iron logic from the world view of the Communist leadership, which refuses to see in the United Nations . . . the budding parliament of man or the instrument of human brotherhood, but instead sees it as essentially another arena for the struggle between the two dialectic opposites of our age.[8]

The Soviet Union views the United Nations as a vehicle of

[8] Alexander Dallin, *The Soviet View of the United Nations*, Center for International Studies, Massachusetts Institute of Technology, Cambridge, 1959, p. 88 (mimeographed).

policy, not as a bridge or meeting-ground to compromise negotiable differences of ideology, social philosophy, or theories of interpersonal and international relations.[9]

Nevertheless, after sustaining with bitter rhetoric a consistent minority position in the United Nations for almost a decade, the Soviet Union in recent years has apparently become more optimistic about its prospects in the organization—which itself has changed drastically. The evidence suggests that since 1955 the Soviet Union has been endeavoring to transform the United Nations into a long-run serviceable instrument of the "Socialist Camp,"[10] Soviet reasoning being that the United Nations has shifted from the character of a security organization in which the majority tends to support the American side to that of a front organization in which, while avoiding direct confrontation with the enemy, the crucial gray areas can be concentrated on and exploited in harmony with the orchestrated world-wide Communist strategy. What better or more appropriate platform could be found for pressing the Soviet claim to stand for anticolonialism, anti-Westernism, and, more latterly, as the bellwether of technological and scientific progress? The 1955 "strategy of smiles" raised the curtain on the extraordinarily effective and portentous program devised in larger terms in the July 1955 plenum of the Central Committee. The line was quickly elaborated. Out of a meeting in Moscow in March 1956 came the decision to establish a United Nations Association in the Soviet Union. In September of the same year the Soviet Union joined the World Federation of United Nations Associations. By July, 1957, Soviet spokesmen were boasting about the role of the Soviet Union in establishing the United Nations.[11]

In the Security Council debate in the spring of 1958 over American bomber flights in the direction of Soviet borders, Mr. Sobolev made a statement which, while easily dismissed as characteristic hypocrisy and cant, nonetheless bore a stamp

[9] *Ibid.*, p. 99.

[10] *Ibid.*, p. 41. See also Alexander Dallin, "The Soviet Stake in Eastern Europe," *The Annals,* Vol. 317, May 1958, pp. 142-143.

[11] Dallin, *The Soviet View, op. cit.,* p. 45.

which distinguished it sharply from earlier Soviet evaluations
of the United Nations:

> We realize that there are forces which are not interested in hav-
> ing the United Nations and its Security Council condemn acts
> which threaten the peace. They pay lip service to the idea of
> strengthening the United Nations but in fact they make use of
> its forum to fan hatred among states. As soon as life puts a task
> before the United Nations, a task of taking measures to forestall
> the dangers of a new war, forces are to be found who paralyze
> the efforts of the United Nations designed to bring that aim
> about.
>
> The governments of some states prefer the United Nations to
> remain a feeble and impotent organization incapable of fulfilling
> its duty before the peoples. The interests of peace, the interests
> of the United Nations itself, demand that this be avoided on
> this occasion.
>
> The Soviet Union attaches great importance to the role of the
> United Nations in the struggle for the consolidation of peace.[12]

By the late fall of 1958, in summing up the results of the
13th General Assembly Session, the head of the Soviet delegation felt able to dismiss as "meaningless" what he and his
colleagues used to decry as "mechanical majorities." "The
United States," said Mr. Zorin, "has frequently lost votes and
there is not a single case where it gained votes." Soviet policy,
he continued, has met with "greater support and understanding on all continents, particularly in Asia and Africa." But the
United States, he continued, "aroused resentment and discontent by using its vote machine to drag through resolutions."[13] It was not entirely surprising, therefore, that in the
written and verbal debates between the Soviet Union and
West over the status of Berlin in 1958-1960 it was the Soviets
rather than the Americans (or French or British) who initially
introduced proposals for a possible role for the United
Nations.

It is unlikely that Premier Khrushchev really believed, as he
was quoted by a Cairo editor who interviewed him in late

---

12 *New York Times*, April 22, 1958.
13 *New York Times,* December 13, 1958.

1959, that a summit conference is only for an exchange of views, and lasting settlements would be made only by the United Nations.[14] Soviet leaders do seem to see events moving favorably for them in the world at large, and, because the world at large is reflected (as well as distorted) by the prism that is the United Nations, they appear to find in the United Nations an object of new value. They seem to assume that, since the United Nations acts out political dramas whose source generally lies elsewhere, any advantages accrued by the Soviet Union in outpointing the United States in economic programs or military capabilities, or in the effectiveness of propaganda stemming from these two, will carry over into the United Nations. The recent drive for "parity" reflected this relationship.

The Soviets, perceiving that the United States cannot use the United Nations as a purely national instrument of policy and must accept its neutrality in this sense, are now emboldened to press their demands for parity with the West. Parity in their sense means extending to the rest of the organization the equal position the Soviets have so far enjoyed in the Security Council through the veto. The United States opposed the parity drive on principle, on the grounds that "if conceded, [it] would give the Soviets a veto power in many functions of the General Assembly—enabling them to evade the will of the great majority and thus further to weaken the United Nations by, in important respects, importing into the General Assembly the same weaknesses that have crippled the Security Council."[15] The Soviet argument was, as usual, elliptical, but conveyed its meaning adequately: the Russians appraised their world position, and consequently their prestige position in the United Nations, as having improved to the point where the parity demand could be confidently raised.

> By acting in this way the United States Government continues to abuse its position in the United Nations . . . counting, as in

[14] Interview with Saleh Salem of *Al Goumhouria,* quoted in *New York Times,* November 11, 1959.

[15] John Foster Dulles, News Conference, March 25, 1958, *New York Times,* March 26, 1958.

the past, on an arithmetical majority of votes instead of attempts to bring about mutually acceptable agreement among the states concerned.[16]

In general, some degree of parity has increasingly become the pattern of negotiations outside the United Nations. Within the United Nations, where the arithmetic becomes explicit, we cannot and should not try to lay down any hard-and-fast rule to guide us. When it is important enough to us to give in to a procedural Soviet demand, as with the ten-nation disarmament conference outside the United Nations, we will concede parity. When it is important enough to the Soviets, they will quietly accept the old patterns. When it is important enough to both, as with the compromise over the composition of the Outer Space Committee voted at the 1959 General Assembly, both will compromise.

CONCLUSION

We can conclude from all this that the Soviet image of the United Nations is probably undergoing a process of change, based largely on the crucial place of the underdeveloped and neutralist nations in the United Nations in a period when Soviet strategy has shifted to political and economic warfare in the "gray areas" of the world. This is undoubtedly the paramount Communist interest in the United Nations today.

To return, then, to U.S. political strategy, and recognizing the bearing on it of the two basic factors outlined before, we can make two observations. First, U.S. planning must embrace a realistic view of the possibilities for change in Soviet communism, accepting both the likelihood of a protracted continuation of the cold war and the inevitable working of the laws of historical evolution. Second, in view of the current Soviet view of the United Nations, the United States faces the tactical task in the United Nations of recapturing from the Soviets the role of champion of the virtues prized by a growing majority of nations; and in this sense continued United Na-

---

[16] Arkady A. Sobolev, in United Nations Security Council, April 29, 1958, *New York Times*, April 30, 1958.

tions membership offers both a danger and an opportunity to develop a more constructive and politically profitable worldwide image of the United States and its values.

Having made these observations, and assuming a continued period of "competitive coexistence" which in the words of its author is an "economic, political and ideological struggle, but not military,"[17] we are bound to consider what influence, which would advance the U.S. interest, might be exerted by the United Nations in this struggle.

[17] Premier Khrushchev in a speech at Novosibirsk, October 10, 1959, reported in *New York Times,* October 14, 1959.

CHAPTER NINE

The U.N. Influence on Communism

THE ASSUMPTION is sometimes made that the United Nations, by exposing the Communist mentality to the values of the West, can help to modify its intransigent and dogmatic hostility. Some important possibilities exist under this heading, but they need to be separated from the common misconceptions that sometimes cling to them.

DIRECT INFLUENCE: ILLUSION AND REALITY

There is a temptation, for example, to take too literally the use of words such as "democratic" and "parliamentary" in referring to the processes that take place in the U.N. bodies. In the absence of a genuine constitutional order the appearance of a "democratic" process in international relations is so qualified as to be highly misleading. Likewise, the notion of the United Nations as a "parliament," while apt in a limited sense, tends to convey a homely image of a legislative body in which individual members act out of both interest and persuasion. The fact is that U.N. bodies have little if any genuine legislative powers; and nothing could be more fallacious than the widespread impression that parliamentary diplomacy in the United Nations has the primary function of persuading the individual delegates to adopt or reject certain positions.

It is true that on certain minor issues, or where delegates have been given full discretion, or, as in the case of some smaller countries, where delegates are completely uninstructed, persuasion *can* have a decisive effect on the individual delegate, resulting in a policy decision on his part that can be directly attributed to the debate itself. This has been known to happen within the United States delegation on some occasions. But in general, and particularly in dealing with delegates of the Soviet Union, the only legitimate assumption is that there is little or no connection between the delegates' personal roles in the United Nations and the policies of their governments. This is not to say that individuals are not influenced by what happens within the organization; they may be influenced profoundly. But such personal effect is generally, and specifically in the case of Communist delegates, unrelated either to basic governmental policy or to the development of genuine understanding between the countries concerned.

It is possible to conceive of a hypothetical situation in which a delegate from Israel and a delegate from an Arab state were so mutually stirred by the atmosphere of the debate and the logic of the arguments for reconciliation that in a transcendent moment they come to look harmoniously and sympathetically at the need for resolving their differences. But even if this unlikely event happened, there is little evidence from the diplomatic process as we know it at the United Nations—and elsewhere—that any change at all could be anticipated in the policies of the respective governments. It is far more likely, given the situation in the area, that the Arab government in question would repudiate its representative as a turncoat and traitor. If he happened to be a man of great influence at home, others might become individually influenced by his views. But however personally moved by logic or by the impulse to agree, a delegate representing a strong and self-disciplined government cannot normally be expected to commit his country to a course it is otherwise unwilling to take, or for which its public opinion is unprepared.

Recognizing this truth, deplorable as it may be to the

idealist, it would be logical to conclude that the proper target of U.N. influence is not the individual diplomat but public opinion in his country. In turn, world public opinion being a highly potent element in foreign policy today and for the foreseeable future, the most logical way to provide a genuine political foundation for international agreement would be to present the facts, neutrally and "internationally" interpreted, to all the peoples of the world. But it is unlikely that many governments involved in major international controversies would agree to have such an impartial—and potentially sub-versive—presentation directed to their people. The reluctance of governments—particularly the Communist governments—when it comes to proposals for even modestly increasing the efforts of the U.N. Department of Public Information[1] rests on more basic factors than the usual budgetary conservatism, and makes the success of such an effort essentially a long-range possibility. But as such, it is deserving of an important place on the agenda of planning. The United States, in the interest of promoting more rational international behavior, might well encourage greater propagation of neutrally oriented facts, looking toward the day when public opinion, even in the totalitarian countries, will demand as its right the privilege of access to unbiased information on international subjects.

The foreseeable development of communication satellites capable of broadcast-quality FM or television transmission simultaneously in several languages to the entire globe—so-called 24-hour satellites orbiting 22,000 miles over the equator—may accelerate the entire process, and U.S. planning should begin now to ensure that such potential propaganda and educational weapons are regulated and preferably operated by the United Nations rather than by any single government.

Another potentially deceptive and illusory aspect of the United Nations has to do with the passing of resolutions. It would be possible to arrive at highly misleading conclusions

[1] For details of a recent abortive attempt along these lines, see Richard Swift, "The United Nations and Its Public," *International Organization,* Winter, 1960.

about the common ground that actually exists if judgment were based on the increasing variety of unanimously passed U.N. resolutions on issues ranging, in the 1957 Assembly, for example, from Algeria and the credentials of the Hungarian representative to the establishment of an Economic Commission for Africa; in the 1958 Assembly, to continue the work of the committee on the effects of atomic radiation; and in the 1959 Assembly, favoring "general and complete disarmament." Highly dilute resolutions on controversial subjects, however unanimously passed, do not necessarily have significant influence on the course of East-West relations.

Dismissing the hopeful but generally misleading notions of the United Nations as a pervasive benign force that can alter Communist purposes simply because it exists and the Communist states partake in its processes, there still remains the simple but important fact that the United Nations is a place where the two opposing sides can keep contact.

The contribution of the United Nations to peace, Hans Morgenthau wrote in 1954, lies in taking advantage of the opportunity provided by the coexistence there of the two blocs for the unobtrusive resumption of the techniques of traditional diplomacy. The United Nations, he said, is "the new setting in which the old game of diplomacy is played again."[2] The famous corridor conversations between Ambassadors Jessup and Malik in February 1948, which led to negotiations on lifting the Berlin blockade, are frequently cited as evidence of the value of continuous contact. Indeed, during the airlift, contact had been informally maintained in one or another U.N. agency, providing a place where one side or the other could "bail out" if necessary. That episode and others that have followed have demonstrated the value of casually rubbing elbows at times when such unpublicized contacts would be next to impossible in more conventional diplomatic settings—corridor conversations in New York are not normally featured in sensational headlines in the same fashion as the

[2] Hans J. Morgenthau, "The New United Nations and the Revision of the Charter," 16 *Review of Politics* (1954), p. 15.

arrival of the Soviet Ambassador at the State Department at the height of an international crisis.

Secretary General Hammarskjöld went considerably beyond this in his evaluation of the effect of the United Nations on the structure of international conduct. He saw it as a genuine bridge:

> It is because world community does not exist at a time when world interdependence has become a reality that world organization has become a necessity as a bridge which may help us to pass safely over this period of transition. . . . A more effective and increasing use of the United Nations as a diplomatic instrument, in which the functions of debate and vote are used more frequently to further a diplomacy of reconciliation . . . rather than merely to score propaganda points, or to defend against them, offers the best hope . . . for a peaceful evolution . . . in the relationships of the West with the communist countries.[3]

Mr. Hammarskjöld founded his "diplomacy of reconciliation" not on the past record or even on present trends, but on a projection into the future. Another wise and prescient diplomat, Charles Malik of Lebanon, suggested perhaps the greatest value of the United Nations for these purposes when he characterized it as "a handy mechanism for disengagement or disembarrassment" of the great powers if and when they choose to be disengaged from their continuing and menacing encounter.[4] The limited but realistic view of the United Nations is as a neutral ground where the battle can be safely waged and, if possible, moderated, and where the two giants can be pulled apart when they grapple too closely.

The fact that the United Nations is a continuous point of contact between the Communist bloc and the West may acquire special significance. Its very existence can be helpful in giving the Soviet Union assurance of being readily accepted into the community of nations in its role of great power even while generally rejected as a Messianic force. The collapse of the 1960 summit conference suggested once again the desira-

---

[3] Dag Hammarskjöld, "The Vital Role of the United Nations in a Diplomacy of Reconciliation," *United Nations Review,* May 1958, pp. 6-7.
[4] *New York Times,* November 16, 1958.

bility of experimenting with the U.N. Security Council as a less fateful "summit" through the special "periodic" meetings envisaged in Article 28 of the Charter. The participants in such special meetings of the Council could be heads of state, heads of government, foreign ministers, or their deputies. A variation of this proposal would have the Secretary General, by agreement, be the host of meetings between top-level East and West statesmen and perhaps chair such conferences. Failures to achieve concrete results would not then be turned as acutely on one or the other power as on the impersonal United Nations—an organization with utility more than once in the past as a convenient shock absorber and even whipping boy.

United Nations membership can have the effect of sustaining and encouraging the independent identity of such satellites as Poland. There are not many places in the world where the outlines of the Soviet empire can be thrown into such sharp relief as in the United Nations. True, the public aspect of U.N. diplomacy has tended to portray that empire as a monolith, united and unanimous; but as change takes place and the seams strain, the collective diplomatic weight of the non-Communist states in the United Nations on one or another satellite could be telling. Value also attaches to the facility for communicating with bloc diplomats in a fairly uninhibited setting. With Albania, for example, we maintain no other relationship anywhere. If Communist China were ever seated the same might be true since, despite frequent assertions to the contrary, U.N. representation has nothing whatever to do with diplomatic recognition.

In the context of possible change in the Communist bloc, an interesting trend has been discerned by some Soviet specialists who attach significance to the increasing usage of the concept *sodruzhestvo sotsialisticheskikh strangosudarstv*—Commonwealth of Socialist Nations. There may exist a longer-term trend toward creation of new forms of association among the communized nations—forms that parody the British Commonwealth (or the French Community) but which might wind up giving greater emphasis to the autonomous nature of each state. Perhaps the Soviet leadership will once again find it expedient or even mandatory to pick up the radical theme of easement of the imperial ties enunciated on October 30, 1956, and quickly dropped when control had to be restored in Hungary. The continued representation of the satellites as ostensibly independent members of the United Nations could reinforce such a trend. In any case, the United Nations furnishes the best, if not the only, setting in which the West can encourage such representatives to play a more significant role in international affairs, as the Yugoslavs have in and out of the United Nations since the initial break with the Soviet Union.

To sum up, then, in terms of present realities, the influence that the United Nations can have directly on the Soviet attitude does not alter significantly the pattern of Communist hostility, but the United Nations provides a locus where aspects of it can be continuously discussed and even negotiated.

Taking the Soviet estimate of the United Nations at its face value—the only prudent course—one must assume that the Kremlin will continue to remain far less influenced by the processes of the United Nations than by its own strategic decisions arrived at on the basis of evidence regarding power relationships, internal stresses, and the like. A U.N. consensus condemnatory of Soviet action, as in Hungary, can embarrass the Soviet Union. But there is no reason for believing that the United Nations, either through a general influence on the tone of international morality or through actions which under present arrangements can be only hortatory, can have a significant effect of itself on the direction and quality of Soviet policy.

Nevertheless, the United Nations has a value that is particularly great at times of tension for bringing Communist and Western diplomats into continued casual contact, thus furnishing an important supplement to more traditional diplomatic channels. Moreover, the United Nations plays a politically crucial role both in offering constructive alternatives for international behavior to the Soviet Union and in assisting in keeping alive the prospect of more autonomous national identities on the part of the satellites. Looking further ahead, the influencing of peoples could take place meaningfully through a greater supply of "neutral" internationally sponsored factual information, such as might be assured, for instance, by U.N. operation of a broadcasting satellite when it becomes available.

COMMON INTERESTS

Direct influence is not the only measure of usefulness of the United Nations in terms of its possible effect on communism. Since the only real basis for international harmony lies in the realm of common interests, it is worth while to ask whether in the period ahead the United Nations can promote and institutionalize common interests among the great antagonists.

From one point of view, history is not very encouraging. Although the very existence of the United Nations bespeaks a common interest among the great powers in having available to them a place where action can be taken multilaterally rather than unilaterally or bilaterally in great areas of international relations, it was not long in the history of the United Nations before the difference in the way the Soviet Union and the United States viewed this interest became painfully apparent. The implicit symbolism of the United Nations carries to many the message of a more enduring and coherent future world order under law, but this symbolic connotation itself underscores the two profoundly different schools of thought as to how mankind should govern its affairs in the future. To the extent that the Western version, already written into the U.N. Charter, appears to prevail, we can anticipate bitter Communist hostility to the United Nations itself. Any programs developed in the spirit of the United Nations and leading to a world order that reflects Western political, economic, social, spiritual, or cultural values will be viewed by Communists as a threat to their version of the future. Thus it might appear that the only common interest between the two sides regarding the existence of the United Nations is the possibility of using it as a weapon in the political and propaganda warfare between the two. But this is not the whole story.

The Secretary General of the United Nations has perceived a gradual wearing away of fundamental differences:

> In spite of temporary developments in the opposite direction under the influence of acute tension, the tendency in the United Nations is to wear away, or break down, differences, thus helping toward solutions which approach the common interest and application of the principles of the Charter.[5]

The Secretary General cannot be expected to acknowledge the still unbridgeable nature of the gulf between East and West; he could not and would not say publicly that the differences are deliberately conceived and that on one side at any rate the motives include the extermination of the other side rather than the reconciliation of differences. But the fact that much of the problem stems from deliberate conflict has so far made it impossible to base world organization on the assumption that there really exists the community of values written into the Charter.

Yet even though it acknowledges no common interest in the formation of a world community based on Western "bourgeois" values, with the passage of time the Soviet Union has come to find a succession of partial and, to it, temporary common interests of a specific nature. This is a step-by-step process, as one or another topic opens up to common treatment by both sides. Frequently, as with the Atoms for Peace program, the limited program for the peaceful uses of outer space, and some of the specialized agency activities, the Soviets do not act until the international program is well under way. But experience argues powerfully for the possibility of creating areas of common interest, even if limited, by moving ahead with such international machinery and institutions as do not wholly depend on Soviet collaboration, without waiting for Soviet participation. In this way perhaps more than any other the United Nations, as Arnold Toynbee wrote in 1947, is "a political machine for putting into effect the

[5] Introduction to Secretary General's Annual Report, *New York Times,* September 5, 1957.

maximum possible amount of cooperation between the United States and the Soviet Union."[6]

What are some of the specific common interests that can be anticipated and planned for?

There is a self-evident interest in curbing the possibility of a catastrophic surprise attack by the other side, in eliminating the hazards arising out of nuclear testing, and, conceivably, in a significant reduction of the general level of armaments. A common interest may also exist in reducing the potential military dangers that could develop out of outer space technology, although here the advantages—military, propaganda, and political—of the Soviet lead militate against the possibility of early agreements on other than relatively low-level functional cooperation. The Soviet Union, at least for the present, might continue to object to a U.N. police force as setting a dangerous precedent for intervention, as well as detracting from Soviet controls in the United Nations via the Security Council; but, since a Soviet interest exists in avoiding unwanted involvement in small wars, we can seek to create such international machinery on the realistic assumption that, as in the other instances cited, the Soviets may well come to acknowledge their interest in participation.

One of the common interests we can reasonably postulate is the interest in being "taken off the hook" by the United Nations, in the sense that the French, British, and Israelis were in 1956 in Egypt, the Americans (and Russians) in Korea, the Americans and British in Lebanon and Jordan in 1958, and the Soviets on numerous occasions. The essence of this process was captured in the phrase Secretary General Hammarskjöld used in privately describing his efforts in "denaturing" the Syrian-Turkish crisis manufactured—and then repudiated— by the Soviets in the fall of 1947: "Operation Parachute." The object was to let everyone down softly and safely.

So long as both sides remain outside their overextended boundaries, so long as both have commitments with respect to territories not of prime strategic significance but of political

6 Arnold Toynbee, "The International Outlook," XXIII *International Affairs* (1947), p. 469.

importance, and so long as face must be saved when those interests are jeopardized and conflict seems possible or even unavoidable, the common interest in this species of "disengagement" may be very strong. There is at times a desperate need for a "third party" who can step in, mediate, disentangle, substitute neutral forces, and allow the temperature to return to normal. The United Nations in this sense constitutes a needful third party in the cold war. Third parties traditionally suffer abuse common to those who stop fights, and the United Nations can be expected to carry the onus of appeasement and the stigma of seeming to prevent nations from doing their "duty" as it disengages parties from situations unpromising for world peace. Nevertheless, where the common interest exists in having facilities available for this brand of "disengagement," the machinery of the United Nations has sustained value to U.S. strategy.

There is a school of thought which, accepting the political struggle as a given, sees the technical and nonpolitical areas of collaboration as the proper foci of concentration in the task of "building bridges" with the Soviet Union. Active common interests have been found in limited areas of everyday contact, such as safety at sea and in the air, and control of epidemics, development of agricultural and reforestation techniques, and so on. It is argued that so long as the ideological battle is unsolvable, efforts should be focussed on new areas of practical common interest which reflect the reality of interdependence and provide a basis for creating limited communities of interest and action.

There is much to respect in this point of view. New technologies may overtake political arrangemnts even more dramatically in the next decade. The field of science contains highly promising possibilities for cooperation between the scientific communities and perhaps between the governments as a consequence. Lloyd Berkner has testified that in the scientific field the Soviet attitude has been "softer"than in any other field in which Americans have dealt with them,[7] and

[7] Dr. Lloyd V. Berkner, President, Associated Universities, Hearings on H.R. 11881, 85th Congress, 2nd Session, p. 1037.

many would agree with him. Based on the extraordinary success of the International Geophysical Year in transcending political barriers and creating bonds of collaboration at the scientific level, a strong sentiment has developed for bypassing political obstacles by increased scientific collaboration. The 1959 Soviet-American agreements to engage in joint health research projects and for cooperative programs in nuclear research are illustrations of this trend.[8]

But this approach, promising as it is, has obvious limits. The effect of scientific collaboration on political decision making in the Soviet Union has to be measured in terms of the relative place of the Soviet scientific community and intelligentsia in the Soviet power hierarchy. A strategic choice made at the apex of political power can wash out all the bridges built at the professional and technical levels, as tragic experiences with German scientists prior to World War II showed. So long as the political atmosphere is poisoned by ideological hostility, the so-called functional areas are of secondary importance in the larger strategic scheme. Until a common interest in accepting the legitimacy of other societies materializes in Soviet doctrine, such collaboration will take place in a political climate whose essential danger to world peace and stability remains unbounded.

But recognition of this condition does not diminish the value of continuing to offer the Soviets alternative courses of political action that one day may appear realistic and attractive to them. With or without them, we should continue to work to institutionalize areas of common action and to create an international community that can compete success-fully with the barren Soviet variety. We have already led the way in nonpolitical programs such as health and technical assistance which the Soviets, for many reasons, ultimately have come to join. It is in our interest to urge greater experi-ments with multilateralism among those disposed to cooperate, and in this area of action there is no substitute for the good offices of the United Nations.

[8] *New York Times,* September 27, 1959, and November 29, 1959, re-spectively.

Finally, it can be speculated that with the passage of time a common interest may develop between the Soviet Union and the United States with respect to Communist China. It is possible that increasing strains between the two Communist giants will culminate in a collision of national and ideological interests comparable to that between Rome and Byzantium.[9] The way in which Western planners evaluate this prospect should be a major determinant in estimating the value of having China in or out of the United Nations.

In conclusion, the United Nations is not capable by itself of exerting primary influence on the course of events in the East-West conflict, but there are possibilities at the margin which U.S. policy would do well to consider attentively. In view of the dynamic historical process that Soviet communism is undergoing and the evaluation that Soviet strategy makes of the United Nations, American strategy is necessarily a strategy of uncertainty, hedging against alternative possibilities, encouraging with positive and purposeful action those alternatives favorable to our aims, but never staking all on any one interpretation of the unfolding future.

COMMUNIST VULNERABILITIES

What can or should the United Nations—that is, an effective majority of its members—do to exploit vulnerabilities in the Soviet system as they may appear?

The United Nations can and should focus world attention on iniquities and injustices in the Communist empire, with emphasis on the contrast between Communist pretentions and realities. As the vestiges of Western European colonialism disappear in Asia and Africa and the Middle East—as they surely will over the next decade—and as new arrangements are worked out between the European nations and their former possessions, such vigor as the idea of self-determination still possesses may well be focussed on its ancestral home—Europe. In the United Nations, the embarrassment to which

[9] See Harrison Salisbury's dispatch from Ulan Bator which describes the two countries as "competing in classic great power fashion for dominant influence in Outer Mongolia," *New York Times*, August 4, 1959.

our Western European friends were subjected—in part from us—probably accelerated their withdrawal from former colonial areas. The Communists have not in the past been as vulnerable to such embarrassment, but potentially they are prime targets.

Communist vulnerability arises in the first instance from the hypocrisy of its ideological pretentions. Bukharin wrote:

> We do not speak of the right of self-determination of nations (i.e., of their bourgeoisie and their workmen) but only of the right of the working classes.[10]

Communist literature contains ample evidence that its strategy includes the exploitative uses of the colonial movement. So far it has not been profitable for the United States to take the lead in emphasizing this discrepancy in the course of U.N. debates on colonial problems. The anticolonial nations generally have not wished to see Communist pretensions exposed publicly, however they may sometimes agree privately. One reason is that cold war issues interfere with concentration on their own colonial issues. In addition, of course, some neutralist countries frankly do not believe the Western portrayal of Soviet policy, and have sometimes been able to contrast Soviet action on racial matters with the slights and abuses traditionally practiced by the West. Lastly, there has been little firsthand contact with the imperialistic side of Communist rule. At present, pointing in the United Nations to the Soviet occupation of Eastern European countries either bores those who care only about the imperialism they know or creates resentment on the part of others for using the United Nations to sustain or even sharpen international tension.

Nevertheless, the Soviet Union and Communist China are essentially imperialistic in their foreign policies, specifically in the Eastern Europe satellites, in the Baltic states, with the Moslem minorities in Russia and China, in North Korea and North Vietnam, in Outer Mongolia, and most recently in Tibet. The experience of Asian states with Chinese imperialism in Tibet and Laos, plus Indian concern for her northern

[10] N. I. Bukharin, *The ABC of Communism,* Part 59, "Communism and Nationality."

borders, may open doors for a new international focus on the Communist problem. If the United States cannot suitably act as the sponsor of comparisons between Communist words and action, it is conceivable that Asian or African states may be encouraged to take such an initiative themselves, particularly if disillusionment with Communist aid practices should grow. Future insistence by world opinion on the right of self-determination for Poles, Czechs, Albanians, and perhaps even for Uzbeks, Khirgiz, Armenians, and other Central Asian Moslem and Christian minorities, might have an effect on Soviet planning and thinking which we are unable to predict today.

Western strategy can and should use the United Nations for purposes of embarrassing and if possible restraining the Communists when situations like those in Hungary and Tibet arise. In this connection, it is worth while here to look again at Hungary. To many, the touchstone of the value of the United Nations was "its" failure to redress the Soviet suppression of the Hungarian revolt in the fall of 1956. In fact, the capacity of the United Nations for action was directly dependent upon United States policy.

Significant counteraction was never seriously proposed by the one power that had the capacity to enforce an Assembly recommendation along these lines. The United States, torn in an agony of frustration and anxiety and powerfully diverted by the Suez crisis, decided to do nothing that might precipitate widespread hostilities in an area where they were bound to expand uncontrollably, given the instability of the rest of Eastern Europe and in particular East Germany. Public statements were actually made to reassure Soviet leaders that the United States had no intention of exploiting the situation.[11] The verbal policies of condemnation and disapprobation which were thenceforth pursued in the Assembly could be taken by the Kremlin as annoying but nonetheless reassuring messages about the extent to which interference from the outside need be feared.

[11] See Secretary Dulles' address to Dallas Council on World Affairs, October 27, 1956, *Department of State Bulletin,* November 5, 1956, p. 697.

American restraint was, in my opinion, justified. There were legitimate grounds for believing that nothing but disaster for the people of Hungary—and for the peace of the world—could come from attempts to intervene across the truce line, so to speak, and into the Russian preserve. The people of Hungary could not be forcibly freed from Soviet rule without having to fight a war of potentially disastrous dimensions. Certainly it is doubtful whether a United States call in early November 1956 for collective military action in Hungary could have secured a majority. But a majority might well have supported the designation as a U.N. presence of members of the Budapest diplomatic corps, while the Nagy government was still functioning, to investigate and report back to the United Nations. Although perhaps not staying the Soviet hand, it would have made even more explicit, particularly to neutral representatives and their states, the extent to which the Communists actually practice self-determination. The Hungarian tragedy dramatically exposed to a brief moment of light the breath-taking failure of the Communist system to brainwash, convert, or otherwise spiritually seduce most of the peoples it has forcibly embraced, particularly the youth. It is at least conceivable that, with powerful leadership, economic and other nonmilitary sanctions might also have commanded a majority. It is certainly easier to contemplate such measures in retrospect than it was at the time, for the dangers were great. The United States Representative to the United Nations the following autumn asserted that the consequence of the use of a U.N. force in Hungary along Korean lines "would have been World War III."[12] The Secretary of State in justifying his policy said:

> . . . I believe that certainly the handling of that situation by the United Nations has made it less likely that there will be a recurrence of such evil deeds as marked the suppresion of the . . . Hungarian people.[13]

[12] Henry Cabot Lodge, *New York Times*, September 9, 1957.
[13] John Foster Dulles on July 10, 1957, *Department of State Bulletin*, August 12, 1957, p. 274.

Other official spokesmen have used the argument that the United Nations actually took the same action toward Hungary as it had with respect to Suez, i.e., a recommendation to the parties to withdraw which in the one case was complied with, in the other not. By this reasoning the United Nations did all it could. But this rationale has been insufficient in the face of the profound emotions the Hungarian crisis aroused. Many Americans felt deeply that none of the rationalizations for inaction, logical as they were, compensated for the sense that we had failed ourselves and failed those we had promised to liberate. In our British and French allies that sense was compounded by the indignities they felt we had visited upon them in Egypt while leaving the Russian invaders of Budapest unmolested. So the United Nations has been both a convenient and a natural target for the irritation felt by the West at its own failure to do anything significant about the reassertion of Soviet rule in Hungary.

The lesson of Hungary is that without great power initiative or at least acquiescence, the United Nations is impotent as an agency for significant political action. Certainly on matters involving challenges to Soviet power it is nothing without the United States; and, having made its "hands off" decision, the United States had effectively removed any chance that the United Nations would take effective action in Hungary.

In the absence of American willingness to go beyond purely verbal protests, the United Nations probably did all it could in Hungary. To the extent that its resolutions of condemnation impressed people in areas where the facts are not readily come by, the United Nations even rendered a valuable service. The utility of embarrassing the Soviet leadership was politically significant despite its lack of effect on their actions. Conceivably it may have sensitized a good many nations, like an inoculation of antibodies, against Soviet propaganda on the workers' paradise.

But the conclusion from this tragic episode is a sobering one. We are by no means prepared to stand still for new Communist aggression, but until and unless we are prepared to crush the Soviet Union in order to alter the present territorial *status quo,* we are essentially onlookers, confined to the use of moral and political weapons, regarding what it does behind the truce lines. The larger dilemma remains: how can the United States and the West sustain the hope of those people for eventual freedom and self-determination and at the same time work toward greater international stability? How can vulnerabilities in the Soviet empire be exploited without, as it were, letting all the wild animals out of the cage?

I have no answer to this dilemma. What is clear, however, is that a policy of promoting unrest combined with a refusal to jeopardize the peace by exploiting such unrest when it breaks out is irrational as well as frustrating. The hope for the future rests on a combination of dynamic processes, aided where possible within the United Nations, leading to evolutions which we cannot now foresee but which we can consistently help to materialize.

Part **IV**   **TOWARD A MORE STABLE WORLD**

CHAPTER TEN

The Settlement of International Disputes

THE ISSUES dealt with so far—military and political security in the context of the basic Communist-Western conflict—have represented overriding priorities for American foreign policy in the postwar years. Policy planning has tended to make all else subordinate, and justifiable only insofar as it contributed to American objectives under these two headings. Yet even if the United States were to achieve all its objectives regarding these issues, the over-all national interest would remain only partly served.

American interests have become tied to the politics of every region, the economy of every nation, the social health of every people. They are particularly challenged by the unfolding development of new countries, new centers of population, new coalitions of political influence. The goals of American grand strategy take shape in the face of that set of problems no less than from the cold war. For the American objectives of a more stable world and a more reliable and predictable world order are the natural, logical, and rational response of a rich, powerful, and stable nation to a political environment characterized by chronic instability and a highly impermanent equilibrium.

Wholly apart, therefore, from the specific issues of the cold war, there are real and exigent issues with which American policy would have to deal regardless of the shape of the overshadowing conflict. It is obvious that these issues acquire particular urgency at least in part from the cold war. One crucial issue within the non-Communist states is the maintenance of unity in the face of the Communist threat; another is the acquisition by the peoples in the "discontented areas" of the world of a genuine stake in an international system which, while responsive to their particular needs and wants, is at the same time characterized by the values we prize. The issues that must be dealt with if such a strategy is to be successful would be difficult regardless of the cold war. So far as the United Nations is concerned, it is here above all that the organization has taken significant action, and it is therefore here that its present and future potential is most clearly measurable.

Within this general range of issues lie the deep-seated conflicts between the non-Communist nations, often about colonial problems; the aspirations of the newly articulate masses for the tangible economic and social benefits of political freedom; the peaceful evolution of world society toward a true community. The bulk of these issues fall within what I have elsewhere called the "North-South conflict"[1]—the generalized tension between the European West and the world of underdeveloped, anticolonial, and often neutralist areas of Asia, the Middle East, and Africa, and, to an extent, Latin America. It is these that are our present concern.

Within the non-Communist states one of the principal problems has to do with international disputes which, besides threatening the fabric of unity, sometimes lead to violence. The heart of the problem today is that if such violence is unqualifiedly suppressed, it can lead to even greater difficulties later; yet if not suppressed, it may involve the great powers in a war of unpredictable dimensions. One way or another, therefore, the peaceful settlement of international disputes occupies a high place in our catalog of national objectives. High priority attaches to ways of minimizing resort to violence, to devising better preventive measures in advance of such explosions, and to institutionalizing such measures as prove effective in order to construct a more durable interna-

[1] *Evolution or Revolution?*, Harvard University Press, Cambridge, 1957.

tional regime within which we can perfect our own society and advance the values we cherish.

Three factors have inhibited genuine steps in the direction of peaceful settlement of disputes. First, our interest in order and stability has been matched by an equally active interest on the part of the Soviet Union in fostering disorder and instability on which revolutionary forces could batten. The Communists have characteristically worked to exacerbate and worsen certain situations which the nations with a relatively greater interest in world stability sought to pacify, such as those in Palestine, Cyprus, and the Congo—wholly apart from disputes such as Iran, Greece, Korea, and Berlin and others to which the Soviet Union was itself a party.

Second, and regardless of cold war considerations, disputes in the non-Communist states have often contained elements of at least temporary irreconcilability (e.g., Palestine, Kashmir, and Algeria) which sometimes could not be overcome by the most meticulously even-handed justice; hardly ever can they be resolved by reversion to the *status quo ante*. The problem of pacific settlement thus invariably becomes the problem of peaceful change.

Third, one of the most historically popular means for settling an international dispute definitively—a military decision—has now been all but ruled out. It is no longer acceptable or tolerable, not necessarily because of a new degree of civilized virtue, but because of the drastically altered nature of general war and the consequent universal unwillingness to look tolerantly on local situations carrying the potential of dangerously involving the great powers and their disproportionately destructive military capacity.

This combination of circumstances has led to the present American policy of renouncing force in the settlement of disputes. As in Suez, this policy also rules out the use of force by others where our influence extends. But this policy has been cynically exploited by the Communists, who have sought to intimidate and extract concession by threats of violence which they knew Western governments would not be able or willing to match. The consequence of this dilemma is to underscore the vital necessity of developing more reliable means of preventing local disputes from reaching a point where East-West diplomacy could intervene with the contingent possibility of applying the military power which our strategy above all seeks to avoid invoking.

The United States has been in the forefront of those devoting time and diplomatic energy to the amelioration of dangerous international disputes. But when it comes to seeking institutional improvement in the international capabilities for preventive peace measures, the United States has recently been almost indifferent, apart from what has become a virtually ritualistic call for the removal of the veto on peaceful settlements, a change which is highly unlikely of agreement.

The decisive consideration in U.N. action to settle disputes has been not the veto but the climate of international relations, and in particular the power and will of a U.N. majority to stand back of its determination that force shall not be used in the settlement of disputes. A revision in the veto power could well follow a fundamental alteration in East-West relations accompanied by revisions in the present concept of national sovereignty. Here we shall examine the areas of action in which, in the years immediately ahead, more effective use might be made of the existing machinery of the United Nations to advance the objective recently expressed by the British Foreign Secretary as "fireproofing the world in which we live."[2]

THE UNITED NATIONS AS NEUTRAL GROUND

It might seem obvious that, of all the available or foreseeable diplomatic agencies, the United Nations is best qualified to furnish the needful neutral ground or third party in international disputes. There is, however, by no means general agreement with this proposition.

The view of the United Nations as a prime agency for the resolution of political disputes is not shared widely even within the Western alliance, primarily because the agenda of

2 Selwyn Lloyd in "How to Live with the Russians," *Reader's Digest*, April 1959, p. 39.

conflicts has been heavily weighted with quarrels between colonial metropoles in Western Europe and rebelling or newly independent territories. At least half of the pacific settlement issues before the United Nations have been of this variety, including Indonesia, Suez, and Algeria, to mention only a few of the major cases. Moreover, with the transfer of focus from the Security Council to the General Assembly, Western European nations have become even more reluctant to subject matters affecting their vital interests to a body that more and more sympathizes with the anticolonial side in any argument, whatever the particular merits or complications.

Thus France tended in the late 1950's to base her opinion of, and plans about, the United Nations exclusively on the attitude the organization took with respect to Algeria. The French delegation may have said from time to time that the Assembly debate on Algeria had been a "useful" step toward ending the revolt, and that "much groundwork has been laid" toward a cease-fire.[3] But the more common French reaction to debate in the United Nations, not just on Algeria but earlier on Tunisia and Morocco as well, was one of profound annoyance, leading to the French walkout in the 1955 Assembly and French nonparticipation in the debates on Algeria in subsequent Assembly sessions.

Western European diplomats and politicians are skeptical of the usefulness of the United Nations on other grounds as well. They tend to assume, often with reason, that public debates in the United Nations have an incendiary effect on the local situation. If they place any value on the United Nations in such cases it is usually on whatever facilities it offers for quiet diplomacy. The permanent head of the British Foreign Office wrote after his retirement:

> It is now generally recognized that the fashion in open diplomacy launched by President Wilson at Versailles in 1919 was ill-conceived and disastrous. Yet we still cling to it and in our hours of stress continue to clamor for the worthless panaceas of summit conferences and General Assemblies of the United Nations. Later

[3] Jacques Soustelles, speaking for the French delegation, reported in *New York Times*, February 13, 1957.

generations will marvel at the obstinacy with which we refused to
give ourselves the best chance of negotiating any international
agreement.[4]

Sir Harold Nicolson has often articulated this theme:

> These conferences do little to satisfy the vague desire for what
> is called 'open diplomacy'; but they do much to diminish the
> utility of professional diplomatists and, in that they entail much
> publicity, many rumors, and wide speculation,—in that they
> tempt politicians to achieve quick, spectacular and often ficti-
> tious results,—they tend to promote rather than allay suspicion,
> and to create those very states of uncertainty which it is the pur-
> pose of good diplomatic method to prevent. . . . Such nego-
> tiation as may occur in New York is not conducted within the
> walls of the tall building by the East River; it is carried out
> elsewhere, in accordance with those principles of courtesy, con-
> fidence and discretion which must forever remain the only prin-
> ciples conducive to the peaceful settlement of disputes.[5]

Indeed certain American diplomats, notably George Kennan,
have been similarly moved by what seemed to them a deterioration of the value of the trained diplomat.

The writer's experience with the operation of the United
Nations leads him to the conclusion that, on balance, these
critics are to a degree correct: the objectives of diplomacy
would often be better served by privacy and quiet rather than
by publicity and the clamor of the crowd. But, like the location of the United Nations in New York (which for the same
reasons could be considerably improved upon by removal to
Bermuda, or Hawaii, or Majorca) the new tradition of public
international debate cannot and will not be done away with.
Like the American Congress the United Nations does much of
its work in the smaller sessions, the cloakrooms, the private offices. But, also like the Congress, it has a public function as
well, which the membership, for varying reasons, cherishes and
would not readily see tampered with.

In retrospect it was perhaps a mistake to provide for open

---

[4] Sir Ivone Kirkpatrick, "As a Diplomat Sees the Art of Diplomacy,"
New York Times Magazine, March 22, 1959, p. 13.

[5] Harold Nicolson, *The Evolution of Diplomatic Method,* Constable,
London, 1954, pp. 89, 91.

meetings of the U.N. organs. But it was not a fatal mistake so long as the opportunities for negotiations and settlement that the U.N. environment elsewhere offers are fully exploited. It is a positive asset if the public facilities of the United Nations are used to set in motion constructive international actions that will bring the weight of world opinion to bear on parties to negotiate, to agree to cease-fires, or to submit disputes to arbitration or adjudication when that is appropriate; and, finally, to give its approval to agreements that contribute to the achievement of the primary objectives we and most other nations of the world share.

In its nearly universal membership the United Nations has a potential for the peaceful settlement of disputes that no regional or alliance organization can duplicate. The prime value of universalism is that parties to a dispute are committed to seek a peaceful solution, are present, and are necessarily involved. Negotiations rarely succeed without the presence of the parties. N.A.T.O. tried in December, 1957, to deal with the New Guinea problem, and at other times sought unsuccessfully to contribute to solutions in Cyprus and Algeria. But given its primary military role, N.A.T.O. is a symbol which, like the abortive Users' Association in the Suez Canal dispute, is not helpful to the conciliation of disputes involving non-N.A.T.O. and particularly anti-N.A.T.O. forces. The United Nations remains the only neutral ground where virtually all parties are present.

One interesting and little-noted characteristic of a third party operating from neutral ground is his ability to supply a financial lubricant or inducement to the settlement process. The International Bank for Reconstruction and Development in the late 1950's effectively acted as the third party in more than one thorny international political situation. The clearance and maintenance of the Suez Canal, in which officials of the I.B.R.D. played a significant role, and the negotiations conducted by Bank officials with India and Pakistan in the long-standing dispute over the waters of the Indus River Basin both represent political disputes with strong economic or financial aspects. It is not cynical but realistic to suggest that the largesse with which the Bank can implement negotiations may give it some advantage over purely political mediation processes. It, too, provides a third party when one is badly needed and thus adds to the means for resolving disputes which, however economically involved, are at the same time a source of major political tension and potential danger to the peace.

U.N. "PRESENCE"

A rule of thumb which was explicitly recognized by Article 33 of the U.N. Charter[6] is that everyone is better off when an international dispute is resolved quietly, with a minimum of fuss, and without involving the global machinery of the United Nations. There is every reason to encourage the settlement of disputes before they ever come before the United Nations. The United States has played a role of which it can be proud in privately seeking such settlements, and, if this proved unsuccessful, in working toward a settlement within the United Nations once a matter has gone that far.

However, in the light of our strategic goals this has not been an entirely adequate policy for three reasons. One is that purely American or Western or N.A.T.O. efforts are not always welcomed by the parties involved. Another is that we have been selective in our diplomatic efforts, tending to avoid settlement processes in some disputes in which our own national prestige has become involved. The third is that the tempo of events has favored the approach of the fire brigade, putting out fires after they have started, but not so often the efforts of the fire marshal in preventing their outbreak.

In the face of the obvious limitations of purely national diplomacy, one of the insights of the postwar years is that mul-

[6] "1. The parties to any dispute, the continuance of which is likely to endanger the maintenance of international peace and security, shall, first of all, seek a solution by negotiation, enquiry, mediation, conciliation, arbitration, judicial settlement, resort to regional agencies or arrangements, or other peaceful means of their own choice.

2. The Security Council shall, when it deems necessary, call upon the parties to settle their dispute by such means."

tilateral instruments have developed a role in the settlement of disputes that goes beyond the original concept of a group of governments publicly debating, investigating, and, in effect, judging. One such innovation is what has come to be called a U.N. "presence." Looking back on the procession of crises and outbursts in the postwar years, a U.N. "presence" has increasingly shown itself as being among the most effective instruments available to the world today in the realm of preventive peace.

This is an area in which Western policy has not always acted on a clear sense of Western interests. For since the late 1940's, when the Interim Committee studies on peaceful settlement were initiated by this country, there has been little to suggest that American planners have given it the attention it deserves. Our European allies, generally deploring the part played by the United Nations in facilitating the demise of their colonial empires, have not done any better. The innovative efforts in this field of Lester Pearson of Canada and a few others have been almost unique.

If a government is actively using its good offices or otherwise seeking solutions, such independence is justified. Certain situations cannot be helped by public exposure and debate. Once entangled on the "U.N. flypaper," governments lose some of their freedom of action, and if this prejudices an eventual settlement it is to be deplored. The problem, however, is not the situation that is being constructively dealt with elsewhere. The problem is the situation that remains unimproved between recurrent crises—the Chinese offshore islands, for example; and the situation that cannot be handled constructively by "vest-pocket diplomacy"—Suez in the summer of 1956. Despite the exigent nature of situations of this order, the United States and its chief partners have usually been reluctant to use international preventive facilities, choosing instead to rely on bilateral diplomatic activity or, more often, on the wait-and-see principle.

The Suez case is a classic illustration of how we have become prisoners of outmoded ways of thinking about the capabilities of the United Nations for preventive peace. Throughout the intense and futile negotiations in the summer of 1956 the United States and its partners rigidly shunned any positive use of U.N. instrumentalities. One American motive was to avoid the possibility of a public discussion of the Panama Canal, by association, as it were. Consequently we relied exclusively on the so-called London group. This forum was unacceptable to Egypt. At the same time we failed to avail ourselves of a wide range of possible actions through the United Nations, including appointment of a U.N. mediator, or of a U.N. agent-general to operate the Canal in the interim without prejudice, or the establishment of a joint regime, or, at a minimum, recognition through a U.N. resolution that the Canal was international in character. Reasonable proposals that enlisted heavy U.N. support could conceivably have altered Egypt's intransigence. We now see that when the British and French finally went to the United Nations in early October it was to clear the way for unilateral action. Only when fighting broke out did we ourselves turn to the United Nations to stop it. This was of course the one thing the United Nations was unable to do apart from its exertion of purely moral force and apart from whatever outside pressure individual members such as the United States and the Soviet Union could apply.

Western statesmen have spoken for years, quite correctly, about the great value of the United Nations in getting the parties to a dispute around the table, substituting talk and mediation and conciliation, however endless and frustrating, for bullets, and offering a variety of institutional means for limiting the conflict and facilitating peaceful change. In the case of Suez we underestimated the preventive capacity of the United Nations before the crisis became acute, overestimated its capabilities when the crisis arrived, and again lost interest when the crisis had passed.

Our attention immediately wandered to another dimension of the problem—the possibility of overt Russian military aggression. The resolutions regarding a peace settlement for Palestine and the refugee problem which we introduced in the early hectic nights of the crisis were never again referred to, and instead we brought forth the Eisenhower Doctrine for the

Middle East. This is not to deny the possible value of posting a U.S. keep-out sign in the area, however belatedly and even though the possibility of overt aggression was comparatively slight. The trouble was that this was our only real move to remedy a whole array of critical local problems which did not primarily involve the Communist bloc but which instead reflected the basic sources of conflict in the area.

Other factors have inhibited the avowed American determination to wage preventive peace. The number of crises alone has been sufficient to distract attention within the government from longer-range approaches to the general problem of disputes and the means of dealing with them. In a period when the highest American decision makers were involved in personal negotiation of one current crisis after another, there was a powerful bureaucratic disincentive to planning and action in forefending future crises by timely and decisive action, with the use of such available tools as U.N. machinery provides.

The plainly discernible result has been the decreasing use that we have made of U.N. facilities in settling potentially dangerous international disputes. The United States in obvious embarrassment discouraged proposals to use the Peace Observation Commission in the situation in Burma in 1954 involving the alleged activities of Chinese Nationalist elements along Burma's northern frontiers; it attempted bilateral good offices along with Great Britain in the situation between France and Tunisia in 1957, with unimpressive results; and it has minimized the possibility of using the United Nations to forestall new incidents in both the recurrent Formosa Straits crises and the contingent situation regarding both Berlin and the access routes from West Germany.

The fate of the Peace Observation Commission is a revealing indication of the preference of nations like our own for do-it-yourself diplomacy in the realm of prevention, by contrast with their instinctive flight to the United Nations after a situation gets out of hand. The P.O.C., established under the Uniting for Peace Resolution in 1950, was designed to "observe and report on the situation in any area where there exists international tension the continuance of which is likely to en-

danger the maintenance of international peace and security."[7]
The P.O.C. was used exactly once, in Greece.[8] P.O.C. machinery has been allowed to languish as though there were no
problems for it to deal with and no areas sufficiently com-
bustible to warrant a neutral international presence before the
flash point is reached.

But there is in fact a wide and versatile range in which a
U.N. presence can manifest itself. It can take the form of a
civil field commission with a political function but able also to
observe and report, as the U.N. Commission for Korea did to
our great advantage on the night of June 24, 1950; or it may
be a body of military personnel such as the U.N. Truce Supervisory Organization in Palestine. It may be a subcommittee of
the Security Council, bypassing the veto by, at least technically, making no "recommendations," as in Laos in 1959, or a
single individual who speaks and acts in the name of the U.N.
Secretary General, as Mr. Pier Spinelli did in Amman, Jordan,
in the tense summer of 1958.

The Korean precedent is doubly significant. Without the report from the U.N. Commission for Korea at the time of the
1950 attack there would still be doubts on the part of many
nations as to who actually attacked whom. That Commission,
in Korea with the responsibility of using its good offices to
bring about the unification of Korea, was on the scene at the
time of the attack, and the reports submitted in the name of its
Indian Chairman gave immediate authenticity to U.S. charges
based on our own reporting.

The function of international observation need not be explicit. The vital point is the international presence itself,
which by its very nature is capable of the kind of double duty
performed by the U.N. Commission for Korea, a function for

---

7 General Assembly Resolution 377 (V) Part B, 3 November 1950.

8 A P.O.C. subcommission, replacing the former U.N. Special Committee on the Balkans, conducted observation of Greece's northern frontiers;
at the latter's suggestion, it was discontinued on August 1, 1954. On May
29, 1954, Thailand brought the Indochinese situation to the Security
Council as a threat to her own security, requesting that the P.O.C. establish a subcommission which would dispatch observers. On June 18, 1954,
the Soviet Union vetoed the proposal, and there have been no other
serious attempts to utilize the P.O.C. machinery.

which no national diplomatic presence can provide a substitute.

The United States should make a far more conscious and determined effort to place international personnel on troubled frontiers to make impartial observations in the case of charges of external aggression or infiltration which ought to be reported back to the entire world community. Greater use of this technique, whether through the machinery of the P.O.C. or not, could serve our interests in the majority of disputes that involve such charges of threatened aggression or of other forms of externally directed penetration. Propaganda could be revealed for what it is, and U.N. machinery should be elaborated to monitor and report on belligerent radio and other programs beamed to foreign countries. The moral influence of the General Assembly could be better utilized by giving it greater opportunity to act on the reports of its own agents.

The invoking of U.N. presence is a use of the United Nations that does not depend on a change in the complexion of world politics or of international life in general. The means are already at hand to improve our capacity to deal with international disputes as they arise. Only American leadership will make this possibility a reality; i.e., American insistence, as a matter of fixed policy, that an early rather than a desperate last step be the dispatch of a U.N. presence to the scene for observation, reporting, and whatever other neutral functions seem desirable.

THE U.N. SECRETARIAT AND INTERNATIONAL DISPUTES

In the development of the indispensable third-party function in the peaceful settlement of disputes we have identified three vital ingredients: the availability of neutral ground, supplied by the existence of the universal organization itself; the U.N. presence in areas of international tension, preferably placed there in advance of hostilities; and an independent source of funds.

A fourth ingredient is the availability of personnel to carry out the functions described. We have noted that the U.N.

presence can assume a variety of shapes. Most often it takes
the form of sub-bodies of the appropriate U.N. organs—the
Security Council and the General Assembly—which national
governments themselves staff with diplomatic and military
personnel. But still another avenue for carrying out the third-
party function has been increasingly opening out, particularly
as the veto disabled much of the working of the Security Council, and the qualities of unwieldiness and public passion
limited the use of the Assembly in some instances. That avenue involves the peculiarly neutral personnel available in the
form of the Secretary General and, more recently, other elements of the U.N. Secretariat.

"The problem now before the United Nations," Elmore
Jackson has written, "is how to increase the number of experienced, trusted, and available persons."[9] This same need has of
course existed in connection with proposals to strengthen the
more traditional instruments of investigation, mediation, conciliation, and good offices traditionally supplied by governments on the call of the U.N. organs. The greatest need is for
a standing mechanism, in being, which can be invoked without
having to invent it afresh each time. It is precisely here that
the traditional means have been least responsive to the need.
Little success has accrued from schemes to make national personnel available on a standing basis, such as the Panel for In-
quiry and Conciliation established by the Assembly in April
1949,[10] or the United Nations Panel of Field Observers created
later the same year.[11] (Perhaps more promise attaches to the
recommendation made at the same time that greater use be
made of the technique of appointing a *rapporteur* to exercise
conciliatory qualities with the parties to a dispute, a technique
employed with some success by the League of Nations and so
far relatively neglected by the United Nations.)

But these suggestions for standing groups of national personnel do not seem to get to the heart of the problem. As

[9] Elmore Jackson, "Mediation and Conciliation in International Law,"
International Social Science Bulletin on "Techniques of Mediation and
Conciliation," Vol. X, No. 4 (1958), p. 543.
[10] General Assembly Resolution 268 (III) Part D, 28 April 1949.
[11] General Assembly Resolution 297 (IV) Part B, 22 November 1949.

things now stand, the parties to a dispute come to the United Nations not as to a court where impartial judgments are passed, but as a place where the processes of diplomacy in various forms can be applied to the amelioration of situations and disputes. In terms of its readiness for compulsory measures for settlement of disputes, the world is somewhere midway between the primitive stage of self-judgment and the compulsory submission to legal processes. At the present stage, essentially political disputes seem to yield best to a facility that is international and nonpartisan in nature but at the same time utilizes the process of diplomacy rather than law. While the panels of mediation and similar proposals have gathered dust, the potentialities of the diplomatic role of the Secretary General and his staff have been increasingly revealed.

For perhaps the first time in history, the Secretary General has begun to furnish to parties to a dispute a truly third party, not judicial but political, not representing any government but at the same time not bound by rules of law or by preference for the *status quo*. The Secretary General has acted in Middle East diplomacy as perhaps the only world agent able to deal confidentially, authoritatively, and acceptably with the various parties to the several disputes and situations in that region. The growing disinclination of numerically outnumbered Western European members to rely on the judgments of unfriendly majorities reinforces the conviction that in a variety of foreseeable instances the desirable third party can be better supplied from the Secretariat side than from the political organs.

Predictions are already being made that the enlarged General Assembly will by its very nature encourage the development of the "executive arm" of the United Nations. The inevitable consequence is that the Assembly will turn increasingly to the Secretary General in periods of crisis.[12] There has already been considerable acceptance of the notion that he has come "to have the accepted right to deal directly in the name of the U.N., representing this earth as a whole and no single

[12] Elmore Jackson, "The Developing Role of the Secretary-General," XI *International Organization* (1957), pp. 444-445.

individual nation."[13] The U.N. Congo action was on his initiative.

The question, therefore, is how this highly significant and
promising development can be encouraged and if possible
regularized. The United States, in consulting its interests in
this matter, must necessarily look beyond Mr. Hammarskjöld's
tenure and seek whatever institutional or other long-term
means will enhance the prospects for a third-party political
element removed from national governments yet operated on
a diplomatic rather than a juridical basis.

It is argued by some admirers of Secretary General Hammarskjöld that the extraordinary role he has played has been a
function of his personal qualities and not necessarily of his
office. According to this argument, it would be a mistake to try
to institutionalize that role for fear both of straitjacketing his
ineffable qualities and of impairing his flexibility. We should
respect these arguments without necessarily accepting all their
detailed implications. Certainly, because of the highly individual nature of the Secretary General's role, it is not easy to
prescribe realistic ways to institutionalize his developing position; but the United States could well seek to exploit a related
development—the extension of Mr. Hammarskjöld's third-
party role to other officers and agencies of the U.N. Secretariat.

A notable example was the little noticed but historically mo-
mentous Beck-Friis Mission to Cambodia and Thailand in
1957-1958, a successful mission of conciliation organized and
dispatched by the Secretary General at the request of the parties to a dispute without specific reference to the political organs of the United Nations. Another highly significant example was the dispatch of Mr. Sakari S. Tuomioja, Executive
Secretary of the U.N. Economic Commission for Europe, to
Laos as the Secretary General's personal representative in mid-
November, 1959, despite the public displeasure of the Soviet
Union. The purpose was to supply a continued U.N. presence
even after the departure of the Security Council subcommittee
on Laos. Other high officials of the Secretariat have been asked
to supplement the efforts of the Secretary General in supplying

13 C. L. Sulzberger in *New York Times*, July 12, 1958.

good offices, not only in current cases before the United Nations but also on questions in chronic dispute.

These precedents represent a new philosophy of the uses of intergovernmental machinery, preserving impartiality and eschewing publicity but far advanced beyond the self-effacing role of an international servant typified by Sir Eric Drummond as Secretary General of the League of Nations. In the Security Council debate on the Lebanese situation in July, 1958, Mr. Hammarskjöld, justifying his intention to enlarge, on his own authority, the U.N. Observer Group in Lebanon, said:

> I believe that it is in keeping with the philosophy of the Charter also that the Secretary General should be expected to act without guidance from the Assembly or the Security Council should this appear to him necessary toward helping to fill any vacuums that may appear in the systems which the Charter and traditional diplomacy provide for the safeguarding of peace and security. . . . Were you to disapprove of the way in which these intentions are translated by me into practical steps, I would, of course, accept the consequences of your judgment.[14]

Mr. Hammarskjöld was not unmindful of the jealously guarded prerogatives of governments. In his speech in Copenhagen a year later on the potential uses of the United Nations in the Berlin crisis, he drew the line sharply between what he called "the imposition . . . of executive authority on the United Nations for administrative tasks which require political decisions," which he excluded, and "the right [of the Secretary General] to take a stand in these conflicts to the extent that such stands can be firmly based on the Charter and its principles and thus express what may be called the independent judgment of the organization."[15]

But he went on to say:

> Something like an independent position for the Organization as such has found expression both in words and deeds . . . [The Beck-Friis Mission] is an example of what I should like to call active preventive diplomacy, which may be conducted by the United Nations, through the Secretary-General or in other forms,

14 *New York Times,* July 23, 1958.
15 May 2, 1959. U.N. Press Release SG/812, 1 May 1959.

in many situations where no government or group of governments and no regional organization would be able to act in the same way. That such interventions are possible for the United Nations is explained by the fact that in the manner I have indicated, the Organization has begun to gain a certain independent position, and that this tendency has led to the acceptance of an independent political and diplomatic activity on the part of the Secretary-General as the "neutral" representative of the Organization.[16]

Action to strengthen the Secretariat will predictably encounter sharp objections, two in particular. For one thing, national governments, particularly strong ones, do not like to see authority exercised by international civil servants in realms that impinge on areas traditionally the exclusive preserve of states. The second objection, which reinforces the first one, is that some individuals in international secretariats are not really impartial, and that in fact some are actively working toward the results desired by one or another government. It is difficult here to distinguish between the legitimate concern over suborned or unduly officious or hostile Secretariat employees and the less justifiable concern over the influence or beliefs of an individual which may run counter to a given nation's wishes. The principal remedies for such abuses as exist lie in proper Secretariat supervision (and also in higher caliber delegations from small governments, whose policy vacuums are often willingly filled by politically ambitious Secretariat personnel).

Such objections, while compelling in the individual instances which have occurred particularly in the economic and social field, are secondary in the light of the larger objective, which clearly points to the need for a vigorous and consistent American policy of supporting and strengthening the third-party capabilities of the U.N. Secretariat.

To execute such a policy, a major alteration in the American attitude toward international service will be necessary. In the postwar years, despite frequent proposals and a number of modest administrative efforts, there has never been any concerted effort by the U.S. government to place top-flight Ameri-

16 *Ibid.*

cans in the U.N. Secretariat. This is in part explained (and justified) by the desire not to influence the Secretary General. But unlike many other governments, the United States has never encouraged such service as an honor or, in the case of government officials, as a basis for continued advancement in the national service. On the contrary, because of the publicity attached to the exposure of alleged American Communists in the U.N. Secretariat in 1952-1953, the stigma of working for the United Nations became positive rather than passive. In the period that followed, the Department of State made a modest effort to develop rosters of Americans for U.N. service, but the effort remained unreal in view of the general climate in which many senior levels of American public life regarded service on the U.N. Secretariat.

Perhaps one reason for relative American indifference to the staffing of the U.N. Secretariat was that there was no real element of competition with the Soviet Union. For years the Soviet Union neglected to fill the quota of positions assigned to it and seemed disinterested in the Secretariat (below the top level) except perhaps as a means of espionage. But the Soviet attitude has changed. In recent years Moscow has made a serious effort to fill vacancies, and it has complained of discrimination against Soviet candidates.[17] A development of more than passing interest was the Soviet placement of 25 of its nationals in the Secretariat of the International Atomic Energy Agency —18 more than American officials had earlier predicted.

Two specific steps would produce more significant progress toward the achievement of revised American objectives regarding the U.N. Secretariat.

1. The United States government should overhaul its own system for recruitment, along with the accompanying frame of mind that has in the past effectively excluded the most able and effective diplomatic and administrative American personnel from service with the United Nations. More is needed than simply the preparation of a new roster of names and improved

---

[17] See Alexander Dallin, *The Soviet View of the United Nations,* Center for International Studies, Massachusetts Institute of Technology, Cambridge, 1959, p. 81 (mimeographed).

machinery for secondment or leaves of absence. Until a tour of duty in the U.N. Secretariat is made appealing to the most able of our career officials—the Robert Murphys and also the younger men of promise—no administrative arrangements will effectively change the picture. Service with the United Nations must be made a matter of both professional honor and national interest rather than, as it is now, tacitly if not openly stigmatized. This in turn can only be advanced by a rational acceptance of the interest this country has in the goal, and its diffusion by responsible leaders to the agencies they direct.

2. But it is only part of the answer to encourage top-flight Americans to serve. Americans occupy many key positions, but openings are few. The Secretary General will need top-flight alternates and other staff members to carry out the growing third-party function, and these must necessarily come from countries other than the United States and other great powers. In view of the kinds of cases that can be anticipated, there will be a growing need for trained nationals of Asia and Africa, supplementing such traditional Western sources of mediators as Sweden. Steps should therefore be taken to improve the qualifications of personnel from the areas concerned. One way would be by creating a service academy for the United Nations, in which personnel from all member countries would be trained for service as Secretariat officials, by analogy to specialized training for a national diplomatic corps, but with the realization that an even more specialized need may exist for training a corps of international civil servants, particularly from countries with limited higher educational facilities. Alternatively, such training could be supplied on a contract basis by qualified private universities. An incidental by-product of such a secretariat training program would be as an outlet for surplus trained and educated personnel in underdeveloped countries who constitute a focus of discontent and instability in the period before their own national economy can usefully absorb their talents and energies.

CHAPTER ELEVEN

Peaceful Change

DISPUTED AREAS

The cease-fire, the standstill, the buying of time, while preserving the peace, offer no guarantees that a dispute will be settled or its basic causes even dealt with. Such was the case in the Suez crisis of 1956. None of the substantive proposals made during the feverish days and nights of late October and early November 1956 for international cognizance of the canal or for political settlements or for arms embargoes ever came to anything. The action sponsored by the United Nations and amplified by pressure on the part of the United States and the Soviet Union took the form of a cease-fire. This action was an indispensable prerequisite to restoration of stability, and should by no means be minimized:

> Here we have a record of strong, swift action which, without doubt in my mind, headed off a third world war. If the United Nations had done only this one thing in its short life, it would have more than justified its existence.[1]

But a call for a cease-fire or political standstill, however successful, may carry no promise whatever of actually settling the dispute, and is at best only a partial and incomplete answer to the problem of pacific settlement.

[1] Ambassador James J. Wadsworth, July 15, 1957, *Department of State Bulletin*, August 5, 1957, p. 238.

157

Thus, while all the present factors—the great-power standoff, the renunciation-of-force doctrine, and the growing capabilities of the United Nations itself—contribute to a remarkable development of responsible international action when shooting starts, a great and still unsolved problem of international organization has to do with the time before and the time after the actual shooting. We have considered the need for greater preventive activity. But plugging up the remaining loopholes to violent settlement of conflict by such means as a permanent U.N. force will only further compress the pressures for change by closing off one of the last places where the *status quo* can be changed by traditional means. Here the question is how to take advantage of cease-fires and truces and renunciations of force to bring about durable settlements.

Some writers continue to press for greater use of international juridical machinery—the International Court of Justice, arbitration tribunals, and the like—to bring about such definitive settlements. Yet the very issues that do not seem to lend themselves to easy political settlement are also the ones that are not often justiciable, for the reason that they generally seek a significant change in the existing political or legal order.[2] There is a special intractability in disputes such as Palestine, Kashmir, Berlin, Suez, Algeria, even Hungary, disputes involving the attempted or successful—but resisted—change of a territory or international regime from one basic status to another. Although they often contain legal issues that can and should be isolated and adjudicated, the basic problem is a political one, and it can be effectively met only by political methods.

The heart of such disputes, simply stated, is the desire to alter the *status quo* in a way that existing law is traditionally unable to accommodate or resolve. As George Kennan has pointed out:

There is hardly a national state in this world community, including our own, whose ultimate origins did not lie in acts of violence. . . . The task of international politics is not to inhibit

[2] This problem is analyzed in more detail in Chapter 17.

change but to find means to permit change to proceed without repeatedly shaking the peace of the world. This task will be best approached not through the establishment of rigid legal norms but rather by the traditional devices of political expediency.[3]

This holds for the United Nations at its present stage of development. President Eisenhower said in 1958 that the United Nations "reflects a healthy appreciation of the necessity for peaceful change leading to a more orderly and productive future for mankind."[4] This is generally true, in that Article 14 of the Charter is based on the premise that peaceful change is desirable; and in that it can actually happen—as with the creation of new states such as Indonesia, Israel, South Korea, and the former Italian colonies—when the majority in a given case may favor a proposed change in status. But the United Nations is incapable of legislating changes in the accepted sense of the word, and in any event is incapable of enforcing such changes when it does recommend them, as the Palestine and Korean cases also illustrated. In the Palestine dispute Israel did its own implementing; but in Korea no agency existed to execute the "mandate" to unify the country, even though a war was fought in the area by U.N. forces. What the United Nations can do is bring into focus pressures for change that a majority considers to be legitimate, and apply a whole variety of measures to bring it about.

No single rule applies in disputed areas. In some areas such pressure contributes to ultimate transformation, as in Indonesia, North Africa, Palestine, and various of the trust territories. In others it would be most improper to bring about change simply because there was pressure to do so, as with West Berlin. A third category, however, is perhaps most depressingly familiar. Here no serious attempt is made to adjust a *status quo,* even when it is patently unsatisfactory on both sides.

Quemoy and the other offshore Chinese islands are a striking

[3] Quoted by James Reston, *New York Times,* September 10, 1958.
[4] *New York Times,* March 10, 1958.

example of the last. In the available periods between crises there has been little evidence of serious activity aimed at working out an acceptable formula for the future. Although there exist alternate solutions for which a change in the status of these islands might be the price, the tactical initiative has remained with our opponents; in a future trip to the brink which is well coordinated between Peiping and Moscow it is possible that in order to sustain an admittedly indefensible position the United States would either have to make war on Communist China or evacuate the Nationalists from the Quemoy position, thus surrendering to enemy pressure. It is consistent with American interest to find a peaceful evolution for the offshore islands which represents neither a surrender to the Communists nor something for which a world war would have to be fought.

There are other present or potential situations in which both the *status quo* and the change desired by one party are inherently undesirable. In the colonial world West New Guinea—West Irian to the Indonesians—is a case in point. Foreseeably, West Berlin may be another in which the present alternatives may become intolerable but where holding on appears to be the only acceptable and honorable course for us.

It goes without saying that such disputed area situations are explosive—and that some kind of change is inevitable. Clearly, it is incumbent on the United States, in view of its grand strategy of seeking durable and stable situations created by a process of peaceful change, to seek new alternatives. How can peaceful change be facilitated in situations such as these? What part can the United Nations play in inducing or aiding the process of peaceful change in disputed areas?

One means of removing an area or territory from contention between two disputants is of course to give it to one or the other of them (or for one or the other to take it). This rarely produces peaceful solutions, for a whole variety of reasons ranging from ethnic to economic. The plebescite solution is a useful one in relatively advanced regions such as the Saar, as well as in fairly advanced colonial areas. Partition has been increasingly resorted to in recent decades. The "political partition" of Cyprus may have implications for such an area as Algeria.

In the face of the inevitable succession of conflicting claims which do not lend themselves to traditional solutions, new attention should be paid to the possibility of a third-party solution in the sense that the world community, such as it is, constitutes a neutral third-party alternative to possession or rule by one nation or another.

The most obvious kind of neutral solution would be to place the area in question under international administration for a specified time, or pending final settlement. The analogy to the trusteeship concept is apparent, but trusteeship involves dependent peoples. One pending dispute does lend itself to trusteeship in this sense, but not by any single government. This is West New Guinea. The United Nations itself has never been designated the administering authority over a trust territory, but the machinery provided by Article 81 of the Charter, which states that the administering authority of trust territories "may be one or more states or the Organization itself," offers evident possibilities. The Netherlands might welcome a solution in West New Guinea not involving an Indonesian take-over; the Indonesian case rests in part on dissatisfaction with continued Dutch rule in the area rather than on any well-grounded territorial claim. A U.N.-administered trusteeship would be a sensible solution which the United States should strongly consider sponsoring.

But a new concept is needed for more advanced territories which require international disposition, but where the real need is to put them on ice, so to speak, rather than to advance the inhabitants "toward self-government or independence." Given strong motivation to find formulas that conform both to the goal of stability and to common sense as well, means for doing this can be sought within the framework of the United Nations, probably within the General Assembly rather than the Security Council, which for some years failed to choose a governor for the proposed free territory of Trieste and thus was unable ever to administer the territory as contemplated. Here again the availability of neutral nations to oversee the integrity of the territory in the name of the United Nations, and of U.N. personnel qualified to administer the operation in the interests of the inhabitants, underscores the value of an organization with neutral members and served by a corps of impartial civil and military servants. A territory with strong traditions and capacity for self-government might merely require the formal designation of an international status, the symbolism of a U.N. presence, and strong guarantees on the part of at least a significant and effective U.N. majority.

A thoughtful study of the possible uses of the United Nations in the Berlin crisis suggested that ample legal ground exists for creating a new legal status for nondependent "U.N. territories":

> Rather than attempt to squeeze Berlin into the established trusteeship patterns, it might be possible to create for it a special status under the aegis of the U.N. If there is no explicit authorization in the Charter for such a step, neither is there any express prohibition. And the broad powers of both the Security Council and of the General Assembly to deal with matters which affect international peace and security should provide ample authority for a new type of U.N. status for Berlin.[5]

The United States might well have proposed a U.N. protectorate for the whole of Berlin which would accomplish the purposes mentioned of international status, symbolic U.N. presence, and guarantees by the United States along with a U.N. majority. It is even possible that under some conditions such a regime for West Berlin would become desirable if it would not jeopardize the continued freedom of the inhabitants.

Another possibility for a U.N. protectorate would be Taiwan after the demise of Chiang Kai-shek. In this case the territory would, like West Berlin, be capable of self-rule—if not total viability—but the operative problem would be to devise an interim status, internationally underwritten, to carry

[5] Louis Henkin, *The Berlin Crisis and the United Nations,* Carnegie Endowment, New York, 1959, p. 18.

over through an unstable interim period until satisfactory permanent arrangements were devised.

Given continued intractability of the problem, other candidates for a form of interim U.N. territorial status of a nondependent nature might be Algeria, Kashmir, and the Chinese offshore islands.

With the passage of time, political solutions might be found that permit such a territory to be peacefully and logically incorporated in a neighboring state, or partitioned, or absorbed in a larger unit; as a final possibility, the territory conceivably could remain under international administration indefinitely on the ground that it cannot be fitted into traditional patterns of state sovereignty without endangering the peace. For the chief factor in the pacific settlement of international disputes is not always machinery or techniques or institutions or diplomacy, or even a will to settle, important as these are. It is sometimes the passage of time leading to new foci of international attention, or until enemies become friends and vice versa, or until the problem simply disappears or alters unrecognizably as conditions change.

It is thus not necessary to be able to forecast in detail the ultimate disposition of territories under U.N. protection. It is sufficient that a new dimension be added to the present two-dimensional world of national states in those cases where the international atmosphere is poisoned by tensions generated by unresolved territorial disputes.

Granted, the problems this proposal suggests are almost as numerous as the difficulties that prompt it. For the United Nations in its own name to administer or protect a territory means that the Soviet Union automatically has a voice in the process. For another thing, it is doubtful if either the Peiping or Taipei regimes would at this time gracefully accept U.N. administration of Quemoy or Matsu or ultimately Taiwan. India would not be likely to favor international administration of Kashmir, although it might be offered for a limited time—say, five years—as a way of buying additional time until the parties could agree on a final solution. West Berlin and the Federal Republic of Germany could be expected to disfavor any arrangement that removed the symbolic presence of Western troops—although the time may come when mutual withdrawals of Soviet and American forces would leave West Berlin as an exposed enclave of freedom and Western orientation within East German territory, and such a situation would require a new form of international guarantee for continued survival in freedom, a contingency which should be planned for now.

But the essence of the proposal is that the test of a scheme for international administration would be whether it promised reduction in present tensions and creation of greater international stability, along with justice for the inhabitants of the area and assurances to the disputing parties that neither will gain an unfair advantage. Such conditions are not beyond human ingenuity or inventiveness to supply, and the United States can most constructively work toward the goal of removing from conflict present and future territorial sources of instability and possible belligerence by actively studying the possibilities of such a form of international administration, with the aim of developing a concrete plan for presentation to the United Nations.

INTERNATIONAL WATERWAYS

The principle of international administration should also be seriously contemplated for international waterways vital to international maritime commerce, with the aim of taking preventive steps before another Suez-type crisis is upon us. The reactions to the premature and essentially vindictive Egyptian nationalization of the Suez Canal in July, 1956, revealed the intensity with which other nations can be expected to respond to unilateral changes in the status of such internationally vital facilities.

It is too late to begin an internationalization scheme with the Suez Canal, but none too early to take steps that might one day add up to irresistible pressures to broaden its management to satisfy the interests of the users, utilizing the universal agency supplied by the United Nations. When one examines the Turkish Straits or the Panama Canal, for example, it appears that the chief obstacle to a broadened and more internationally acceptable base of sovereignty is the fear of the dominant power that its interests will suffer if its control is diluted. Turkey has learned with good reason to fear Russian initiatives to alter the Straits regime. Increasing Panamanian discontent with U.S. control of the Panama Canal Zone has produced short-term American concessions but little evident planning designed to anticipate future possibilities. In both cases the fears that discourage such planning might under new circumstances encourage the trend to far worse possibilities, as Britain learned to her dismay in 1956 in the Nile delta.

Modern nationalism, as it continues to run its course into and through the Western Hemisphere, will undoubtedly increase the already active Panamanian impulse to recapture the soil of the Canal Zone. The Egyptian example will not be forgotten. "In the long run," as two recent observers pointed out, "the United States will confront a situation not unlike that faced by the British in Suez";[6] if this is so, it is incumbent upon us not to let events run their course until the United States is faced with unacceptable alternatives. If we ourselves initiate the planning rather than leave it to others, we could doubtless develop a proposal which, while broadening the basis of legal sovereignty and inviting the participation of others, would safeguard fully our special security requirements and financial investment. Suggestions have been made that control of the Panama Canal be vested in the Organization of American States. Given the universality of usership of the Canal, a U.N. agency would seem the more appropriate body to participate in a regime designed to serve the interests of the users while removing the wholly bilateral nature of the issue between Panama and the United States.

International waterways such as the Panama Canal involve powerful traditions and strong, if debatable, strategic interests. Attempts to create an international status for the Straits

6 Martin B. Travis and James T. Watkins, "Control of the Panama Canal: An Obsolete Shibboleth?", 37 *Foreign Affairs* (1959), p. 417.

of Tiran leading into the Gulf of Aqaba, to take another example, would present formidable obstacles involving the entire Palestine complex. But the paramount fact is that the process of change in such areas works today to maximize the possibility of future disasters. The *status quo* power tends to hang on until it is directly challenged, as Britain was in Egypt in 1956, and as the United States may soon be in the Isthmus of Panama. Then, because under present ground rules violent redress of political wrongs is discouraged by the world community, the action turns out to be irreversible. It is very much in the interest of the United States and better for the world as a whole for the peaceful change process to take place in the general interest, rather than always in the interest of the challenger to the *status quo*.

ANTARCTICA AND OUTER SPACE

The problems of disputed areas and international waterways loom large in the foreground of the current international political scene. There are already present the forces and omens to urge the United States as a matter of calculated policy to make every effort to bring them into the category of urgent international business. Equally important in their own way in considering the long-range prospects for peaceful change are the remaining unoccupied territory of the earth—Antarctica—and the emergent realm of outer space.

Antarctica is at a suspenseful stage in history. Claims to portions of it have been made by Britain, New Zealand, Australia, France, Norway, Argentina, and Chile. These claims have been rejected by the United States and the Soviet Union, who reserve the right to make their own claims. On December 1, 1959, a highly significant treaty was signed reserving Antarctica for peaceful purposes only and opening it up for unrestricted scientific activity by all the signatories.

The present treaty is essentially only a truce, although the obvious hope is that it will establish a durable pattern which may outmode the territorial claims, all of which remain in force. The Soviet Union has claimed to discover a region in

Antarctica rich in valuable minerals including mica, graphite, iron, and apatite. If technological developments materialize that significantly affect military or economic strategy, political considerations may come to be predominant again for Antarctica. The present situation is a frozen *status quo* in a so-far frozen continent. The ultimate issues, however—the future administration of Antarctica and the inevitable question of sovereignty—have still to be faced.

The next step to be planned for should involve irrevocable removal of the sovereignty of Antarctica from the reach of any single nation, thus converting the truce into a permanent situation. The need is not so much for a form of organization as for an assertion by the community of nations that Antarctica represents, in the language of international law, *res communis,* rather than a *res nullius* always open to claim and occupation. Such an assertion should be made by resolution or convention under the sponsorship of the United Nations, with the organization itself acting as the repository of the sovereignty of the territory and the guarantor of its continued international status and of free access of all for peaceful purposes. An incidental benefit would be to place agreement on a broad basis rather than limit it to those who by geographic accident or political design have a connection with the problem today. It would be shortsighted to exclude the possibility that a nation remote from Antarctica—Communist China, for example—could take a profound interest in its strategic possibilities or economic potential. A U.N. assertion would be presumed to affect all rather than only the signatory nations.

The cislunar and interplanetary spaces, the moon and planets, and perhaps ultimately the interstellar regions, constitute a new dimension into which the nations of the earth have begun to project themselves. In so doing they are also projecting their political conflicts and antagonisms. Unless new rules are devised, the possibility remains that they will project their traditional concepts of sovereignty as well, with predictably unhappy results.

The first effort of the U.N. Ad Hoc Committee on the Peaceful Uses of Outer Space was indeed modest, doubtless

because of the absence of the Soviet Union; the terms of
reference of the body established by the Assembly in 1959
after the Soviet Union rejoined the effort were even less ambitious. What is in store is a modest program of exchange of
information and coordination by U.N. agencies of technical
cooperation in technical and legal fields related to space
technology. These are entirely sensible and proper steps to
take. But when we think ahead to the next decade or so, the
steps proposed are inadequate to establish the needed framework for a realm where political innovation is not only desirable but imperative.

Prudence may well dictate a step-by-step approach so long
as it augurs continued Soviet cooperation. But the danger is
that because of the Soviet technological lead and American
political conservatism in formulating an international space
doctrine, it will be the Soviet Union rather than the United
States that decides the possibilities and limits of a regime for
outer space.

Because it is in the highest American interest to give clearer
definition to the shape of the political world, the cautious
and legalistic policy followed so far does not adequately serve
our strategic purposes. It is essential both to our strategy and
to our ability to maintain some control over a situation of
temporary weakness that we set our sights higher and aim
steadily at a regime under which the passage and activity of
man-made objects in space and on celestial bodies is controlled by no one single nation.

The corollary would be establishment of the rule that
national air space terminates at a fixed limit—100 kilometers
appears to be the most generally agreed arbitrary definition
for these purposes—and that the space beyond, with the possible exception of a contiguous zone of another 200-300 kilometers, by analogy to the law of the seas be considered *res
communis,* including all planetary bodies.

It may be momentarily convenient to find ourselves in
agreement with the Soviet Union that we both reserve all our
rights to make territorial claims in regard to outer space (as
with Antarctica) while recognizing no one else's. Such a

formula invariably satisfies the foreign office lawyer. But it does no credit to the imagination or purpose of the United States, and in fact deprives us of a clear ideological advantage over the Soviet Union by foregoing the opportunity to sponsor a constructive position. Thus the very problem our diplomacy has preferred to evade—the question of sovereignty and ownership, and of organizational forms of control—can be transformed into reflections of American purpose, and recognition can be given to the conviction that one of the prime meanings of outer space to America in the 1960's is as a demonstration of our version of how nations can better conduct their affairs, and of our intention to dedicate our national power and purpose to that demonstration.

Once such an attitude comes to govern our strategy, the questions of mechanics become less forbidding.

The difficulties in accomplishing these desirable ends with respect both to Antarctica and outer space are fundamentally political and strategic, not legal. Indeed, a group of eminent scholars in this field asserts unqualifiedly that

> . . . the United Nations has authority to internationalize those zones which have not been recognized as falling within the domain of states, and implied power to take the necessary legislative action for their effective administration. This authority derives from the status of the United Nations as the agency of the general community of nations and its mandate to create the conditions of order in that community.[7]

If it became an explicit and priority object of national strategy to denationalize outer space, the moon, and such planets as man may land upon, there is no dearth of formulas and instrumentalities that can be advanced to spell out the proposal in detail. The current literature includes ample suggestions which, while seemingly fantastic today, could be deadly serious tomorrow, ranging from a variation of the trusteeship system to manage any newly discovered planetary territories, as well as interplanetary operations, in the name

[7] *Organizing Peace in the Nuclear Age,* Eleventh Report of the Commission to Study the Organization of Peace, Arthur N. Holcombe, Chairman, New York University Press, New York, 1959, p. 9.

of the United Nations[8] to a series of realistic and sophisticated alternatives and stages for internationalizing outer space activity.[9]

A pattern for a treaty on outer space already exists in the encouraging Antarctica treaty, which becomes startlingly applicable by the simple substitution of the words "extraterrestrial bodies" for "Antarctica."[10] Organizational forms suggest themselves in abundance. Long before any agreement becomes possible on regulating or eliminating the use of outer space for military purposes, a design for the management of this region, under the auspices of the United Nations, could be set before world opinion, with the psychological and ideological benefits inevitably redounding thereto. The crucial point is neither the immediate feasibility of a given scheme nor the willingness of the Soviet Union to agree to it. The crucial point is that the United States, alongside its step-by-step actions, decide upon and publicly spell out the design for the future which it is prepared to sponsor, in specific organic terms and not simply in vague generalities.

CONCLUSION

To give concrete meaning to the concept of peaceful change —still more a slogan than a reality—we have ranged from territorial disputes through international waterways to the future status of Antarctica and outer space. With a clearly enunciated goal of developing greater international tranquility and a more rational world order, a political strategy can be developed to strive toward this goal without waiting for the world of nation states somehow to dissolve into something else. Such a strategy can be programed with the theoretical concepts and institutional means already available. The

---

[8] Proposed by C. E. X. Horsford, "The Law of Space," in *Space Law,* A Symposium, Special Senate Committee on Space and Astronautics, December 31, 1958, p. 80.

[9] Philip C. Jessup and Howard J. Taubenfeld, *Controls for Outer Space,* Columbia University Press, New York, 1959.

[10] I am indebted to one of my students, Mr. H. Roberts Coward, Jr., for this suggestion.

United States has the capacity to open a new chapter in international relations by devoting its planning and its diplomacy seriously and purposefully to the end of increased world stability through imaginative and determined uses of the United Nations.

CHAPTER TWELVE

The Underdeveloped Countries

AMERICAN INTEREST in the over-all health and welfare of the rest of the world is neither a purely charitable impulse nor is it limited to diplomatic arrangements for dealing with incipient conflicts. True, we are sensitive as a people to the fact that if there is widespread privation, human suffering, and social unrest in the world, the United States, try as it may, cannot comfortably enjoy its own prosperity. But wholly apart from any humane consideration there is also the pressing realization that the very future of our American society has come to depend increasingly on the health of the other societies which make up the world environment in which we must live.

The chief problem area toward which American economic and social strategies are directed today and in the foreseeable future is the portion of the world commonly denominated underdeveloped—that segment that includes almost half of the earth's land areas, 1.35 out of its 2.9 billion people, and which in 1959 had a gross product averaging $120 per capita compared with $1400 in the developed countries. This is the home base of neutralist sentiment in the cold war and anti-colonial agitation in the continued North-South battles; and, for obvious reasons, it is the prime target of Communist strategy. As one after another of its component regions and subregions awakens to the possibilities of technological and sociological transformation, it has moved from the bottom of the list to first place among Western concerns. The peoples of the underdeveloped areas, who already far outnumber the rest of the world, will inevitably have a decisive impact on the world environment of the future.

The general American purpose can be simply stated. In broad terms, the American objective of a more stable world environment calls for finding ways of influencing the course of the social revolution sweeping the underdeveloped areas so that when it has run its course we shall find ourselves not isolated in a hostile world of communist or other totalitarian societies, but in a world where democratic values can flourish and our own society prosper. This is the long-range aim, but the battle is now. The very center of the political warfare of today and tomorrow between the Communists and the West is in the regions of Asia, the Middle East, Africa, and increasingly the Caribbean area and Latin America. The stakes for the Communists are denial of this great gray zone to the West in terms of both military strategy and economic resources, and in the long run its engulfment in the Communist bloc. For the West the stakes are, at a minimum, denial of additional areas to Communist rule and, at a maximum, the development of new and more acceptable long-range relationships between the peoples there and the white Western world.

What is taking place in the underdeveloped countries cannot be solved in any one fiscal year or by any one heroic step; it is a process—the process of modernization. Where the process of modernization is in its early stages, political democracy as we know it seems distant. Even in its more advanced stages the economic, social, and educational preconditions for genuine democratic institutions do not always exist in full measure.[1] The task for those who cherish freedom is to develop

---

[1] In 1960 the following non-Communist countries were living under regimes which in one way or another have been described as "military": Republic of China, Thailand, Pakistan, Iraq, Lebanon, Sudan, United Arab Republic, Portugal, Spain, Cuba, Dominican Republic, El Salvador, Guatemala, Paraguay, and Laos.

the capabilities of these societies for democracy, and to see that the possibility of enjoying their economic progress in freedom is left open to them.

ECONOMIC DEVELOPMENT AND THE UNITED NATIONS

The United Nations has been heavily engaged in programs aimed at bettering economic and social conditions in the underdeveloped countries. The technical assistance programs, the Special Fund, the specialized agency programs of health and welfare, all have made a significant contribution to the American goals, shared by virtually all other nations, of helping the underdeveloped countries to acquire more of the material benefits of twentieth-century civilization.

Still unresolved, however, is the question of the extent, if any, to which the United Nations should be employed as a significant instrument in the flow of capital to underdeveloped lands. The pros and cons of this issue have been debated in a fairly desultory way for some years, but actually the basic American policy was set in the mid-1950's, a period when the broad contours of our foreign economic policy were often fixed by the Treasury rather than the State Department.

In 1956 the Secretary of State indicated that new thought was being given to the "question of whether or not more [foreign aid] should be given through international agencies like the United Nations or whether they should be done wholly on a bilateral basis or done through regional organizations."[2] A week later the President said, "I would be in favor of seeing the United Nations take a more active interest in this business."[3] Two years later the President said at his news conference:

In the economic field we have dealt completely on a bilateral . . . nationalistic basis, and I think that possibly there is coming about a reason, like the Mideast and others, where we might be

[2] John Foster Dulles, News Conference, April 17, 1956, *Department of State Bulletin,* April 30, 1956, p. 715.

[3] President Eisenhower, News Conference, April 25, 1956, *New York Times,* April 26, 1956.

better advised to use some . . . collective organization with which to agree—to argue.[4]

Meanwhile, private supporters of the United Nations asserted the desirability of "channeling more aid through the U.N.," and serious professional groups such as the Rockefeller Brothers Fund Special Panel on foreign economic policy recommended that:

> The United States should be anxious, in particular, to make additional use of the United Nations in its approach to economic aid. International agencies for economic and technical assistance and training can bring dividends far more significant than the gratitude which a single contributor of economic aid may expect—but rarely gets—from the recipient country. Participation by the Soviet Union in these activities may make a real contribution toward bridging over the chasm which separates the two ideological systems.[5]

But, apart from indifference to a problem that can be put off, there persisted the widespread belief in government circles that the Congress could be expected to look with disfavor on placing in the hands of an uncontrollable third party (including Communists) the significant funds that would be involved in a U.N. program for financing economic development. American policy in the 1950's was thus set squarely against the concept of a Special U.N. Fund for Economic Development (S.U.N.F.E.D.) annually proposed in the United Nations but defeated when its principal potential contributor, the United States, insisted that no such contribution would be possible until the cold war were ended, swords turned into plowshares, and "savings from disarmament" directed to a U.N. capital program of economic development.

In an apparent effort to head off the developing sentiment of S.U.N.F.E.D., the United States in the fall of 1957 sponsored a proposal for an additional U.N. technical assistance fund that would concentrate on surveying resources for capital financing from other sources such as the International Bank.

---

4 President Eisenhower, News Conference, August 20, 1958, *New York Times,* August 21, 1958.

5 *New York Times,* December 8, 1959.

The fund was proposed in terms of a total of $100 million. It was established by the 1958 General Assembly by a vote of 77 in favor and no one in opposition, but by the fall of 1959 only $15 million had been pledged by 51 member governments other than the United States, and the fund actually totaled $27 million. By then it had also become clear that the proposal would not succeed in permanently heading off the longer-range drive for a capital investment program through the United Nations, which had been the hope of the sponsors. (Indeed, the director of the Special Fund, Paul Hoffman, was himself proposing a ten-year program involving a total outlay of $70 billion.)[6]

The arguments for and against a substantial U.N.-financed program are too familiar to recite in detail. One reason American policy has not moved in this direction is a natural resentment with nations that refuse to contribute more than a fraction of our share but insist that we be far more generous. With little to lose and everything to gain, they demand a role for the United Nations that goes well beyond that envisaged by the principal powers:

> The United Nations must assume the responsibility for seeing to it that living standards in the poorer countries gradually reach those of more prosperous states.[7]

The United States is torn in two directions by its own sense of national interest. It prefers to carry out its economic policies through means that keep control and administration in its own hands; but apparently a growing majority of nations, not all of them underdeveloped countries (the Netherlands, for example, has been a staunch supporter of—and potential contributor to—S.U.N.F.E.D.), wish to see the United Nations given a major responsibility.

One of the elements in resolving the American dilemma here is the availability of various means of "multilateralizing," so to speak, what began as a unilateral effort. There seems

6 *Washington Post and Times Herald,* April 5, 1959.
7 Manuel Barrau Pelaez (Bolivia), in General Debate, 12th Assembly, *United Nations Review,* November 1957, p. 72.

little likelihood that such limited-purpose collective defense agencies as N.A.T.O. can be used for significant aid programs to underdeveloped countries. Occasional French attempts to convince others that N.A.T.O. could be a useful instrument for aid to African countries have generally fallen on barren soil. The probabilities are, as a Dutch delegate told the Atlantic Congress in June of 1959, that the principal beneficiary countries would either have to refuse aid from what they persist in regarding as a *machine de guerre* or accept it and then accept aid also from the Soviet side.[8]

A far more reasonable means is through the banking machinery of the U.N. system. In its 1959 report, the Draper Committee made this recommendation:

> The United States should increase its emphasis on a multilateral approach to development assistance and specifically should support the proposed international development association.[9]

The International Development Authority, established by 68 member nations of the World Bank and Fund on October 1, 1959, either alone or in combination with the International Bank might conceivably supply adequate multilateral facilities to do the jobs which, for political or other reasons, cannot be done as well unilaterally. It is even possible that before it is too late the oil companies and the oil-producing countries of the Near and Middle East will allocate a generous share of the profits of the one and the royalties of the other to a common development fund for the benefit of the people of the region. (In a regional variation of this, a Lebanese publicist has proposed that the two parties should lend 5 per cent of their annual profit to an Arab development bank at 2.5 per cent interest.[10])

Perhaps equally promising as a way of broadening the framework of economic assistance without losing control to

[8] *New York Times,* June 9, 1959.

[9] From a letter of transmittal accompanying third interim report of President's Committee to Study the United States Military Assistance Program, *New York Times,* July 24, 1959.

[10] Émile Bustani, *New York Times,* April 21, 1959.

either Communists or recipients is an association of the non-Communist industrialized states of the world—essentially the O.E.E.C. members and the United States and Canada (and conceivably one day Japan), as proposed by the United States in early 1960. Still, the pressure to do at least part of the job cooperatively with the underdeveloped countries can be expected to continue. Moreover, the political consequences of not doing so could profoundly affect the success of our purpose in extending aid in the first place.

A comprehensive survey of the American national interest in using the United Nations as an instrument of foreign economic policy concludes that, on balance, American interests would be furthered by considerably greater use of U.N. bodies for both technical and capital assistance to underdeveloped countries.[11]

Professor Higgins' analysis indicates that the underdeveloped countries generally favor capital assistance that is international in nature rather than purely American, and he suggests that those countries which share this feeling can best be assisted through multilateral agencies. He also believes that international agencies in some instances could allocate available funds more efficiently than, for example, the American Congress. Another virtue would be that a good deal of capital assistance could be separated from the military variety, which would demonstrate that such aid was without the kinds of strings to which the recipient countries are most sensitive. Professor Higgins thus sees a multilateral program as a kind of insurance policy for the United States, guaranteeing that its economic objectives can be achieved and thus favoring its broad political goals.

His recommendation is that the International Development Authority become the center for a new international consortium-type of financing operation, with the U.N. regional economic commissions acting in the capacity of regional subdivisions of the International Development Authority. A

---

[11] Benjamin Higgins, *The United Nations as an Instrument of United States Foreign Economic Policy*, Center for International Studies, Massachusetts Institute of Technology, Cambridge, 1960 (mimeographed).

weighted voting scheme would be obviously essential, but Professor Higgins wisely suggests limiting the U.S. share to 40 per cent in order to avoid undesirable majority control by one country.

Professor Higgins believes that the "boomerang effect" of American aid can be minimized by having an international agency review development programs as a whole as a basis for capital assistance. In this connection, U.N. agencies, as with so many other functions, can perform a unique service by serving as a "forum in which donors and borrowers can get together . . . , exchange complaints, and make commitments to be worked out in detail."[12]

In reappraising the possible value of the United Nations in giving expression to American interests in the economic development of underdeveloped countries, it will be necessary to balance out the values of efficiency in administration and absolute control over funds against the value of connecting American interests in the most intimate way possible with the interests of those countries as their most responsible leaders conceive those interests. At the same time, the value of efficiency could be itself well served, regardless of the capital investment, if U.N. agencies were more actively utilized to coordinate, in a clearing-house capacity, the many various international programs now operating.

IDEOLOGY AND ECONOMIC POLICY

In the protracted competition between the ideologies of freedom and authoritarianism it is useful to have a place where the values of the modern free enterprise system—what some are coming to call "peoples' capitalism"—can be publicly expounded and demonstrated in action. The United Nations at least in theory offers a forum in which both to demonstrate the virtues of our system in detail and to defend it publicly against attack.

12 *Economic, Social, and Political Change in the Underdeveloped Countries*, study prepared by Center for International Studies, Massachusetts Institute of Technology, for the Committee on Foreign Relations, United States Senate, March 30, 1960, p. 89.

But there are serious disabilities in this process. If the majority of nations is not in fact going to be living under, or even striving toward, the American type of economic system, the United Nations may become an increasing embarrassment to us. The developments in the General Assembly's Economic Committee in recent years have disturbed some American business interests far more than the trends in the political sectors. After the 1952 session—which in many ways marked the beginnings of a continuing trend—the U.N. observer representing the New York Stock Exchange, in his report to the President of the Exchange, noted:

> The debates in the Second Committee and in the plenary meetings indicated strong Marxist-Leninist-Stalinist influences and made clear that most underdeveloped countries desire the fruits of capitalism without displaying a willingness to accept capitalist disciplines or to adopt a capitalist mode of production.[13]

The fear that the American economic philosophy will be engulfed by alien ideas and practices arises primarily in the context of two issues: the fluctuating prices of internationally traded primary commodities, and the insistence by some states that the right to nationalize property should be written into the concept of "self-determination."

On the first of these issues, the United States started out with a position rigidly based on abstract doctrine. With a growing realization that a genuine problem exists for countries dependent on the world market price for often a single commodity, the United States, after boycotting the United Nations International Commodity Trade Commission for a number of years, took its seat and agreed to talk—but not to negotiate. The problem came to a head with the worldwide price disturbances caused by the American recession in 1957, and the representative of Malaya spoke for several countries when he said that all the foreign aid his country received was not equal to its losses due to the drop in world tin and rubber prices.

One of the prime American objectives in the international

13 Report dated January 20, 1953.

economic field is the support and encouragement of the American system of free enterprise and—within limits—free markets. But in a world that may be increasingly characterized by forms of state trading systems, American trade overseas will increasingly have to cope with systems of state capitalism which sometimes reflect socialist principles of government ownership of both productive facilities and distribution channels as well. Although the United States should make every effort in the United Nations to demonstrate the superiority of free methods of organizing production and distribution, it must be prepared to cope with a trend toward regulated systems. The makers of U.S. policy may have to find compromises between the orthodoxy of the free market and the concern of other countries in stabilizing the range of international prices as protection against economic disaster. Our dislike for governmental interference must be balanced against the fear of dissipating our efforts to build new and durable relationships with the countries producing raw materials. Here if anywhere is a case for pragmatism rather than rigid theoretical stands in the American attitude, particularly when it is considered that within the generally free American economy safeguards against disastrous price fluctuations, similar to those sought by Brazilian coffee producers, for example, have long been afforded to domestic agricultural interests.

Professor Higgins, in his study cited earlier, recommends an international program of commodity stabilization, the central feature of which would be loans by the International Monetary Fund made against stockpiles accumulated by governments of underdeveloped countries, valued at prices agreed upon in advance. Under his proposal, an organization of all the governments concerned would be set up within the U.N. framework, to provide for consultation and agreement on measures for such commodity stabilization, on the basis of the Fund's studies.

Professor Higgins also recommends measures for continuing the surplus agricultural program, hitherto administered bilaterally by the United States under P.L. 480, under international auspices. His reasoning is that while the program is substantively meritorious, American sponsorship has alienated other producing nations without commensurate benefits to the United States. He therefore proposes that the U.N. Food and Agricultural Organization make this a major function, with the F.A.O. Committee on Commodity Problems as a convenient starting point for the organization of a more extensive body. The U.N. organization of governments concerned, mentioned above in connection with commodity stabilization issues, would also serve to coordinate international activities regarding surplus commodity disposal on the basis of studies conducted by F.A.O.[14]

The United States should consider renewed experiments in the creation of a general international organization in the field of international trade. The dismal fate of earlier efforts —the abortive International Trade Organization and the Organization for Trade Cooperation—suggests that a comprehensive revision of the earlier program is in order before presenting the United States Congress and public, as well as other countries, with a new plan. But the development of a revised plan to establish an international trade organization should now be on the government drawing board, taking its guidelines from, first, the political failure of the International Trade Organization and Organization for Trade Cooperation, second, the inadequacy of the General Agreement on Tariffs and Trade, and, third, the new phenomenon of regional economic integration characterized by the European Economic Community.

The other issue, which I have denominated primarily ideological—the pressure to include in the concept of self-determination the right to nationalize property—has somewhat less real substance, but no less political significance. Quite correctly, the United States has insisted that nationalization could be made acceptable only by simultaneous recognition of the right to compensation under international law, and this ultimately became the agreed formula. But actually, if foreign property is nationalized, provisions for fair

14 Higgins, *op. cit.*

compensation will be offered according to the political situation between the parties and not because of a resolution on this subject by the Economic and Social Council or General Assembly. The significance of the U.N. debates and resolutions on this subject has so far been largely symbolic, and what they have symbolized is that somewhere under the surface is a very real force endowed with deep political passions.

Nasser's nationalization of the Suez Canal, ultimately followed as it was by internationally negotiated compensation, was, according to the U.N. compromise formula, "legal." But the Suez military action was fought on completely different strategic and political grounds. The nationalization by the Bolsheviks of American property at the time of the Russian revolution, still uncompensated, was entirely illegal under international law, but there is no sign that this fact by itself significantly affects the course of political and military relationships between the two nations.

In this sense, the United Nations is a proving ground for abstractions about economic and political theories but without particularly affecting the course of events. The ideological debates are useful only to demonstrate to one's own constituency the fidelity with which the home team is being defended. Others can be expected to use these debates for their own purposes. The Soviet Union will continue to utilize the United Nations to undermine and discredit the American economic system. More than this, the Communists may be looking around for something to counter the continuing successes of the movement for European economic integration. A straw in the wind was the Soviet proposal to the U.N. Economic Commission for Europe in the spring of 1959 for the creation of an all-European trade organization to "counteract the trends toward the dividing of Europe into closed economic groups."[15] The time may well come when the Soviet leaders decide that the United Nations could be molded into a prime counter to such Western-sponsored designs as the European economic movement. The United States faces a serious problem of balancing its own economic principles against the need for

15 *New York Times,* April 10, 1959.

an international stance that would be of maximum attractiveness to the majority of nations.

THE POPULATION PROBLEM

Of many remaining economic and social activities and potentialities of the United Nations which lack of space and technical competence require me to forego in this analysis, there is one that cannot be evaded.

Overshadowing the entire picture of economic development is the population problem. "The gap in wealth and power as between the rich and poor nations," wrote one analyst, "is becoming wider." On the basis of present trends, "the gap between the industrial and non-industrial countries will not be narrowed."[16] United Nations statistics forecast a tenfold increase in the populations of Latin America between the years 1900 and 2000, contrasted with an approximate doubling of the population of Europe. With the population of Communist China rapidly approaching the staggering total of one billion, the U.N. report concluded:

> The growth of world population during the next twenty-five years . . . has an importance which transcends economic and social considerations. It is at the very heart of the problem of our existence.[17]

Since the predictable increase of population in the presently underdeveloped areas has the capacity of nullifying the effects of the aid program, the problem of population must be approached seriously and comprehensively. Birth control has religious implications that make it a sensitive issue politically, and American politicians tend to shrink in horror from the prospect of governmental action to further the dissemination of population control information and techniques to the underdeveloped and overpopulated countries. Yet the huge American investment in the narrowing of the explosive gap between living standards may be frustrated by the inexorable

[16] Kingsley Davis, "The Political Impact of New Population Trends," 36 *Foreign Affairs* (1958), pp. 294-295.

[17] *The Future Growth of World Population,* U.N. Department of Economic and Social Affairs, Population Studies No. 28, 1958, p. v.

multiplication of populations as death rates continue to drop. All logic points to quietly encouraging a more decisive technical and educational effort by the United Nations, particularly the World Health Organization, an effort that we can stimulate others to sponsor, and that we can firmly support with a minimum of divisive and rancorous domestic debate. One can scarcely imagine a clearer case of utilizing the most logical and acceptable means—the technical and functional agencies of the United Nations—to accomplish an end important for American policy but which the United States finds itself helpless to implement.

CONCLUSION

In the broad context of welfare and evolution as they relate to U.S. interests in the underdeveloped areas, several principles suggest themselves regarding the uses of the United Nations.

First, there probably exist important advantages for American political purposes in utilizing the United Nations more decisively for action programs such as financing of large-scale economic development projects; in doing so the United States must be prepared to abandon total control over funds, and perhaps a degree of efficiency in the programs (although U.N. allocations might be more efficient than Congress'), in order better to serve our broader goal of aiding the underdeveloped countries to achieve relatively stable and less vulnerable economic and social orders and, hopefully, democratic forms of political organization. The United Nations can usefully bring together lender and borrower, and also act as clearing house and coordinator for the many international assistance programs.

Second, the problem of commodity prices should be approached from the same standpoint, and not as a test of the validity of classical economic theory. The I.M.F. and F.A.O. should both be used for action programs in the fields respectively of commodity stabilization and surplus disposal.

Third, the largely symbolic debates on the right to nationalize should be taken for what they are—reflections of the intense spirit of nationalism and identity in the affected areas, and of a rejected heritage of subservience to foreign ownership and rule. The United States can afford to be entirely sympathetic to this feeling, while working to perfect fair and more equitable arrangements for its foreign investment so that the *status quo* is not given a chance to explode into violent acts of expropriation.

Fourth, the population problem, which shows no signs of going away in the face of American domestic political embarrassment, can best be tackled by using the broader and more diffuse machinery of the United Nations to assist those countries desiring technical and educational assistance.

CHAPTER THIRTEEN

The Liquidation of Western Colonial Rule

THE MOST LIVELY process of political change in our age has been the liquidation of Western colonial rule over dependent peoples in Asia, the Southwest Pacific, Africa, the Middle East, and the Caribbean. At the beginning of the 1960's the process was nearing completion. Of the eleven territories placed under the trusteeship system, only six remained: Tanganyika, Ruanda-Urundi, British Cameroons, Nauru, New Guinea, and the Trust Territory of the Pacific. The first three were slated for early independence, leaving only three Pacific territories which present a special case. The powers that administer other non-self-governing territories have increasingly ceased the transmission of information concerning them to the United Nations as self-government in one form or another has been achieved.

In the face of such a process, history teaches that ultimate stability is achieved not by attempting to suppress changes in the established order, but by understanding the underlying forces and imprinting upon the process itself the outlines of the desirable outcome. Marxism adopted these premises, but among the reasons it has failed as a philosophy of history is that it has sought to superimpose on the process of change an end to change itself. The task for the West is to give purposeful direction to the process of change instead of either

187

leaving it to random fortune or attempting to prevent it. For whatever resistance the Western powers may put up or however long they may hold out, the only prediction supportable by evidence is that the process will continue to its completion. Nothing in sight could stop or even stem it. Only an enlightened and constructive attitude toward it can contribute to the larger Western goal of creating a new and durable pattern of relationships with the former colonial areas.

Having recognized the inevitability of the process, however, the United States and, as they cease to occupy defensive positions, other Western nations face multiple choices as to the way in which the recently colonial world can be seen through the present period of dislocation and emerge free and committed to democratic values.

Because of the provisions of its Charter and the fact that its parliamentary arrangements have given increasing political leverage to the champions of anticolonialism, the United Nations has played a key role in altering the status of dependent peoples and territories. The United Nations has been relatively impotent in resolving the issues growing out of the cold war, but it has acted with enthusiasm, and, in the eyes of some of the Western nations, abandon, in its concentration on what still remained of an earlier age of Western colonial rule in the great transequatorial arc from West Africa eastward to Polynesia. In fact, the colonial issue has been the centerpiece of U.N. deliberations even on the most unrelated subjects.

The issue for American strategy needs to be viewed against this background, and also in the light of the special problems and dilemmas United States policy faces as it confronts the last chapter of the colonial drama.

COLONIALISM AND FREE WORLD UNITY

Among the paramount objectives of American world strategy is the maintenance of a high degree of unity among the Western nations.

Arguments about the place of the United Nations in the grand strategy of the United States and the free world have often revolved around this issue. For perhaps the central problem for American diplomacy in the United Nations has been the difficulty in holding together the Western coalition in a diplomatic bazaar where the most agitated issues are those—like colonialism—that are likely to split the United States away from its N.A.T.O. partners. But there is a fallacy in the assumption sometimes made by Western Europeans that without the United Nations the problem would evaporate. It in turn rests on another common fallacy, which prospers chiefly in high-level French and other continental thinking. This is that the N.A.T.O. nations somehow enjoy common interests not only with respect to Europe, but everywhere. This is unfortunately not the case. The nations of the North Atlantic community have come together in N.A.T.O. around a specific common interest demanding regional protection and defense against the explicit threat of Communist encroachment. But it is a long jump from this to the assumption that there must also exist entirely common interests with respect to all other parts of the world. The cement that binds the nations together in the Atlantic region could, in the face of a real threat to Berlin, for example, probably temporarily override differences in national policy toward other regions. But the differences do exist, and cannot be eradicated simply by invoking the commonality of interests in Europe. The response in the North Atlantic region to a commonly felt interest in that region does not automatically carry with it harmony in other situations.

This truth has been revealed several times by clashes of interest in the Far East, the Middle East, and Africa. American interests with respect to Algeria were never precisely identical with those of France, however much there existed a general interest in stability. At the beginning of the 1960's the United States and France still differ in some profound respects as to the nature, potential, and future of the nationalist movement, and, consequently, as to the broad approach the West should take toward it. British interests in Hong Kong may not in a given crisis correspond with American interests, and certainly Portuguese interest in Indian Goa do not strike any but a hostile chord in the United States. American policy toward Taiwan and the offshore islands has more than once aroused profound European misgivings. The differences are probably narrowing, but they are still profound. Thus the Western nations bring into the United Nations some strains already built into the alliance, many of them stemming from differing attitudes toward the problem of colonialism.

(Another set of strains arises, of course, out of issues indigenous to the United Nations itself. Perhaps the most persistent issue arises out of the conflicting views between the United States and some of its closest associates such as Britain, Belgium, Italy, and the Netherlands regarding the representation of Communist China in the United Nations. Disputes among the N.A.T.O. family on such procedural issues as elections to the Security Council have broken the allied front in the United Nations on more than one occasion. Finally, there are the built-in psychological strains based on the dominant power position of the United States within the alliance.)

In seeking to estimate the net losses and gains to the goal of maintaining allied unity, it must be recognized that the alliance is at a minimum embarrassed and at a maximum genuinely weakened when its soiled laundry is exposed in U.N. debates on these issues. The greatest friends of Atlantic unity thus do not tend to be particularly warm friends of a world organization in which that unity is threatened, tested, strained, and sometimes shattered on issues that perhaps might better have never come up. In a period when Western unity or its absence may be a paramount factor in Soviet estimates about the feasibility of further expansion, it is legitimate to ask whether the existence and operation of the United Nations helps or hinders our larger cause.

Free world unity is, of course, more than a matter of Atlantic solidarity. The choice the United States made in the Suez case was recognition of this fact. If the American stand on colonial issues sometimes frustrates its allies in Western Europe, by the same token it reflects solidarity with a related set of American interests in non-European countries—a fact that our European friends swallow with discomfort. The conflict of interests among Western nations toward non-Atlantic issues is a fact of life we must live with. Without a place to deal with those issues internationally there would be far less opportunity for the United States to influence the nationalist revolution in such a way as to maximize the values of freedom, democracy, and stability. The conflicts would go on but without the corrective influence of even the present level of world order and negotiated diplomacy. The United Nations presents opportunities for us to try to moderate the conflicts and assist the parties to develop new and more enduring relationships.

If the triangular nature of the colonial problem puts the United Nations on the debit side so far as Western unity is concerned, this may be offset by a positive virtue offered by U.N. machinery in supplying important elements of cohesion and strength to the non-Communist states as a whole in the face of recurrent Communist threats and challenges. The United Nations furnishes a means for the free nations to stand together publicly and make unmistakable demonstrations of unity. The United Nations furnishes close contact on matters that might otherwise be handled in isolation and therefore without diplomatic coordination. By the same token its processes of "parliamentary diplomacy" give the lesser members a sense of participation, much as the same process in the North Atlantic Council.

There are some improvements in detail that might help. If we are to live successfully in the kind of United Nations that has developed and retain majority support when it really counts, we must do a number of things. We must be prepared to go a great deal further than we have with our close friends on issues that are of great political importance to them but of only secondary importance to us. These usually represent differences over essentially procedural matters such as elections or budgets or the composition of committees, which have often been the source of more inter-allied friction than any substantive policy issues except Chinese representation or Suez. We might do better not to engage the prestige of the United States on such procedural issues but to save it for the big ones. We might also gracefully accept an occasional minority position on some issues instead of insisting on having our own way, or going over the heads of friendly delegates, or threatening retaliation, however subtly.

The United Nations, then, is both an embarrassment and an asset to the United States in its quest for unity among its principal allies. On balance the United States, under present world conditions, must continue to act not only as a leader of the Western alliance but also, in and out of the United Nations, as a bridge between the defenders and the attackers of residual Western colonialism. Its over-all aim must be to join in harmonious and durable arrangements the developed and the underdeveloped non-Communist states—the industrialized and the nonindustrialized, the former colonial masters and the new nationalist "teen-age" states. The only available roof under which this strategy can be pursued is that of the United Nations.

COLONIALISM AND U.S. POLICY

In the process that has taken place, the United States has been drawn somewhat closer to the anti-colonial states. But the same process has also favored the Soviet Union, which has become a reliable tactical ally of anticolonialism, however hypocritical its pretentions to sympathy and support in the light of actual Soviet practices. The Leninist theories of nationality and imperialism, corrupted by Soviet leadership, have become a temporary link between Asian-African resentments and the interests and ambitions of world communism.

United States policy makers in the postwar years understandably developed American military, political, and economic strategy in terms of the crisis that grew out of Soviet hostility to the West. But this was not the way much of the world insisted on defining the situation. "The crisis of the time in Asia," said Jawaharlal Nehru, "is colonialism versus anti-colonialism."[1] Mr. Nehru's Ambassador in Washington described accurately the use by his compatriots of the colonial issue as the standard for judging all else, in and out of the

[1] Quoted by Norman D. Palmer in "Indian Attitudes toward Colonialism," I *Orbis* (1957), p. 234.

United Nations, when he said in 1956, "The colonial issue in Asia and Africa was an acid test for all those who stood for freedom and democracy."[2]

The United States was very quickly caught between the pretentions of some of its European friends that their beneficent rule was superior to anything indigenous rule could offer and the dogma of Asians and Africans that all of the territories in question, however small, untrained, or impotent, had the capacity to govern themselves and to survive in the world after independence. If the anticolonialists measured American *bona fides* by the extent of its parliamentary support, some of our N.A.T.O. allies made serious tests of friendship of the same votes.

The United States as a consequence of its strategic dilemma tended to find itself in the middle on this issue. It has sought to act responsibly where the Soviet Union could act irresponsibly, and has paid the inevitable price in unpopularity with both sides. The United States could not in good conscience consistently pose as the champion of early freedom from Western rule for every colonial possession demanding it, regardless of its readiness for self-rule or its capacity for economic viability. In some cases the United States, to satisfy its Western partners, tended to equivocate, contenting itself with verbal reminders of its own colonial history. But for good and sound reasons it has often advocated patience, caution, and all the other counsels of moderation which unfortunately rarely do more than irritate forces of nationalism.

As a consequence of all these factors, the United States has generally tended to define its interests in terms of a middle position. It has mediated between the two forces as best it could, and in the process it has received a considerable amount of abuse from both sides. There have always been Americans who complained that their government never seemed capable of adopting a fixed, decisive position against colonialism and in favor of independence for all. Many Americans have felt U.S. policy to be compounded of equivocation and fumbling. Interestingly enough, the State Department itself was never

[2] G. L. Mehta, cited in *Indiagram*, January 10, 1956.

able to arrive at an agreed over-all internal policy toward colonialism throughout the postwar years; one effort after another to formulate a general policy failed even to get to the top levels.

The reason was simple. Within the government two schools of thought existed, each reflecting the argument on one side or the other of the external battle. With equal devotion to the American national interest, each advocate urged on his government a diametrically opposite attitude. The result, as so often happens, was a compromise between verbal high-mindedness and actual expediency. For reasons that are inherent in so complex a problem, there was never any real possibility of a fixed, affirmative stand on colonialism in the abstract, which could be carried out in detail in each instance. In fact such a stand would have jeopardized as many American interests as it served. It is perhaps just as well that we have had vigorous and influential partisans of both positions within our own camp, with the result that each case has been dealt with on the basis of what seemed to be overriding interests at that time and place. Dogmatic and doctrinaire attitudes of pure anti-colonialism—or pure pro-Europeanism—however agreeable to adopt, would not have contributed to acceptable or constructive solutions. The role of middleman, urging greater speed and progress on the European powers and at the same time counseling patience and adequate preparation on the dependencies, was never a happy one. But it was the only role we could honestly play.

No one has pretended that it was either an enjoyable or a thankful role, and President Eisenhower perhaps claimed too much for it when he said:

> America has preserved its position as the friend of all. . . . We have not been drawn into the position of being so completely on one side of a quarrel—any quarrel—due to emotion or sentiment or anything else that we are incapable of carrying out our proper role of mediator, conciliator and friend of both sides when there is any possibility of settling a quarrel.[3]

[3] Informal talk, Washington, D.C., May 31, 1956, *New York Times,* June 1, 1956.

But it was an honest position even when the cost was to irritate our French friends by appearing one day to agree that France should be free "to work out her own solutions" in North Africa, and the next to disassociate ourselves from the taint of French colonialism (and, it should perhaps be said, an earlier French failure to come to terms with reality either wisely or presciently). The United States, unlike the Soviet Union, has a stake in stability and must continue to discriminate between situations where the Soviet Union can seem to pursue an abstract doctrine single-mindedly—and cynically. The United States cannot afford to subscribe to the goal of independence before a territory is ready to administer its own affairs—a point that usually comes earlier than the administering powers acknowledge but later than the independence movement leaders insist upon. American objectives involving greater stabilization in international politics will be served by continuing to assist with the process of liquidation to ensure that it is as orderly as possible, and that the claims of neither side are permitted to rend irreparably the fabric of world peace and order. The Congo experience underlines the point.

THE ROAD AHEAD

In considering how the United Nations can best serve American strategic interests in this stage, we ought to distinguish between the symbolic and the more tangible types of U.N. involvement. The symbolic debates in the United Nations have centered around concepts and images that countries form out of impressions gained as to the attitude of other countries. The racial issue, where little action is foreseen but profound and subtle psychological reactions are nonetheless involved, is perhaps the prime example of U.N. symbolism. In the colonial issue the United Nations' effect has been most concrete with respect to the trust territories, and most symbolic with respect to the rest of the non-self-governing territories over which it has little direct authority. Crucial impressions about foreign policy have been formed and acted upon as a result of purely verbal diplomatic performances by governments such as our own. The debates, however ineffective on the policy of the metropolitan government concerned, evoke the values of highest significance to the anticolonial forces—values of independence, self-respect, self-rule, cultural autonomy, and the whole complex of meanings bound up in the concept of self-determination.

In the light of our experience I conclude that the United States has tended to take too seriously some of the purely symbolic U.N. actions, on the entirely commendable ground that what we agree to we must be prepared to live with. The seriousness of some of these actions is open to question and, consequently, so is the legalism of our approach to them. In November, 1958, the United States suffered one of its comparatively rare defeats on its proposal for an *ad hoc* committee to make a fresh analysis of the problem of self-determination. The United States was able to muster only 16 votes in support, contrasted with 48 against.[4] The symbolism in such a vote is, I believe, of high political importance, not for what any particular state may or may not thenceforth do, but in the impression conveyed of attitudes, concerns, and values. The United States insists on definitions that contain reasonable meaning and are not cluttered with extravagant ideological assertions. The majority, however, tends to view this as nitpicking concealing a lack of enthusiasm for the concept itself. The lawyer's habit of looking for traps in the language and of inserting protective caveats and provisos has not made for good propaganda for this country in a field where favorable propaganda is perhaps the prime payoff for the American national interest. I am not at all certain that such scrupulous legalism is necessary or desirable so long as the debates in the United Nations bear no resemblance to a court of law or even to a treaty-drafting session. The political realities are that the colonial problem is in a historical phase of liquidation, with emotional rather than legal factors the primary criteria for judging relative degrees of sympathy with this process. It is possible that within the realistic limits of policy the United States could improve

---

[4] General Assembly Official Records, Third Committee, 893rd Meeting, November 26, 1958, pp. 290-291.

its general public posture. It can afford to loosen some of its diplomatic and legal stays in order to do better in this particular phase of the battle of ideologies. The United States could feel emboldened to assert its belief in the inevitability of the process that is taking place in the colonial world and subscribe freely to an ultimate right of self-determination—whatever that may mean—for any political community that could reasonably wish it.

In addition to the largely symbolic side of U.N. debates and resolutions, however, there is an area of action which can be geared to our strategy.

In the economic and social fields, the general principle that should govern U.N. programs flows explicitly from our broad objectives. The United Nations is in a unique position to help develop and foster institutions within these countries which in the end will be democratic. Programs designed to train civil servants, create administrative services, and improve the internal foundations for social health and political freedom, all contribute to the objective. The U.N. Economic Commissions for Asia and the Far East, for Africa, and for Latin America, as well as the several technical assistance programs of U.N. agencies, should be regarded as serious means toward the goal, with the special virtue that planning and action are done collaboratively with the potential leaders and with the people of the areas in question. With its multiple avenues of contact with the dependent areas, the United Nations can be reliably counted on to identify and bring to general attention problems in dependent areas that might not otherwise come to the attention of other nations until dangerously late, or that profoundly affect the political possibilities, or that supply significant preconditions for an orderly political transition.

Of course, the effect of U.N. debate has often been indirect and largely a matter of atmospherics. As a recent comprehensive estimate concluded:

> There is no way of assessing with any degree of precision the extent to which the United Nations has helped to bring about the vast political changes that have occurred in non-self-governing territories since the Second World War. . . . The United

Nations helped create the atmosphere that produced these developments, but it participated directly in relatively few of the
constitutional changes that occurred.[5]

Yet the trusteeship system has worked directly on the internal
and external conditions of the trust territories. An incidental
benefit has come from the U.N. visiting missions to these
territories, which have the great virtue of demonstrating to
the wards of the larger community that they command outside interest; an equally great virtue, insufficiently exploited,
is to expose Asian or African members of the mission to some
of the problems that call for responsible judgments rather
than glib slogans. Perhaps the most concrete effect of the
United Nations has been in its capacity to "legitimize" the
status of a territory that has acquired independence, facilitating its ready absorption into the community. In fact, in
special instances such as the Italian colonies, Korea, and Palestine, the United Nations actually "legislated" an explicit territorial change of status.

But this in turn raises the question of the international
status such territories can be expected to have in the period
ahead. As the list of dependent territories, already diminishing
from the 76-odd on which information at one time or another
has been transmitted under Article 73(e) of the Charter,
shrinks still further, so will the relative size of the units involved. This points to a new problem which requires novel
solutions. As the number of micro-states continues to grow and
the possibilities of self-contained existence continue to lessen,
the trend toward integration of smaller into larger communities will rate ever-increasing attention. This process is
actually taking place alongside the process of nationalism,
which otherwise seems to fragment and Balkanize; both trends
are presently discerned in the French Community, for example. The United States should seriously consider whether
advance planning for logical forms of association among these
territories would not be helpful. Here the United Nations
could play a useful role in analyzing possible economic and

[5] Emil J. Sady, *The United Nations and Dependent Peoples,* Brookings
Institution, Washington, D.C., 1956, pp. 44, 64.

political integration arrangements that would increase the political viability and economic health of small-size dependencies that "deserve" self-government but could not and should not be accepted as sovereign states.

One aspect of this planning might be the development of a formula for U.N. status that represents something less than full independence and more than continued dependent status. It is particularly important that this be done before the U.N. majority becomes irreversibly committed to awarding membership to new states regardless of size or ability to make a serious contribution to any international program or effort. It can be conservatively predicted that another 18-20 new states, and possibly as many as 30, will expect to join the United Nations in the next decade, and that all but a few will be African territories of small population and, in some cases, size, with no history or tradition of statehood to fall back on, and in some cases without even the prospect of a qualified governing class for another generation.

There is value in having all people represented at the United Nations, in order to give them a continuing stake in the values we deem paramount. But not all of the dependencies whose status has not yet changed should be permitted to expect automatic election to full membership. The practice of associate membership, which has been used with some success by the U.N. regional economic commissions, should be considered for this purpose. The ultimate purpose would be representation on a limited basis of all groups, wherever located and however small in size.

One use of associate membership would be as a halfway house, as it were, toward independence. Instead of having indigenous representatives attend U.N. meetings as part of the delegations of the metropoles, associate membership could accord the dignity and inherent promise of separate representation to the native population, but without vote or other full privileges of the floor.

The other use would be for the most backward areas such as New Guinea, which might remain associate members even while juridically under the continued rule of their metropoles (or of a U.N.-administered trusteeship, as recommended earlier).

Such a proposal could be misconstrued as an evasion of the question of absolute independence for all dependent territories. But to propose a limited form of U.N. affiliation and identity now, before independence, for all the remaining colonies would go a long way toward neutralizing the effects of the other proposal for permanent associate membership for less than state-size entities.

CHAPTER FOURTEEN

Constructive Alternatives
for the New Nationalism

THE FINAL PLAYING OUT of the drama of Western colonialism
has obscured the more fundamental transformation of which it
is but a part: the convulsive growth of national, racial, and
cultural self-consciousness in the non-Western world. The common cause of anticolonialism has held together and preoc-
cupied much of the Afro-Asian world in a period when individual national identities are being emphasized; but when
the residue of Western colonial rule is finally liquidated, and
the common denominator that now binds the anticolonial
countries dissipated, the interior problems of nationalism itself can be expected to come finally to the fore. Just as the
earlier nationalist movements had to come to such a choice,
the contemporary nationalisms will come to a crossroad where
the choice must be made between further pursuit of foreign
devils and the turning inward to constructive tasks of growth,
modernization, and internal integration.

A major American policy objective which stretches from
the present into the middle-time range of strategy is "to channel contemporary forces of nationalism toward constructive
rather than destructive tasks and purposes," in pursuit of the
broader goals of "developing greater stability and less friction

in international relationships." This being so, what uses can be made of the United Nations to advance us toward these goals?

The first object of strategy here is to make contact with the forces in question. The United States, applying its power with a moderation rare in history, acts with a singular lack of acquisitiveness in wishing self-rule and individual freedom for the people concerned; but because it has not at the same time always made successful contact with their vital social symbols and psychological needs, it has sometimes come out second in winning the confidence of peoples caught up in the surge of new nationalism.

The failure of good intentions to substitute for crucial psychological insights has shown up in several ways. Our notions of what other peoples want and need have too often turned out to be assertions of what they ought to want and ought to need—mirror images of the American interests involved. Only belatedly have we come to realize that genuine neutrality in the cold war, rather than being immoral, is often the best to be hoped for—and therefore striven toward—from countries which in their own way are repeating the American nineteenth-century experience. It has not helped to visualize the contest as between either American or Soviet "leadership" of these countries. Such a concept is unrealistic, and leads to a succession of surprises and disappointments for American policy; international leadership will come from within rather than without the groupings concerned, with successive efforts by a Nehru or a Sukarno, a Nasser or a Castro, a Nkrumah or a Mboya, to be accepted as spokesman for a region or even for the whole.

We have at times seemed unable to comprehend the depth of feeling experienced where whole peoples have been seared by vivid memories of racial "inferiority." The mood of the people we have sought to help is caught in these words of a leading Arab statesman:

> Our young men are inspired above all by an immense need for personal dignity and by an uncoercible spirit of independence.[1]

[1] Habib Bourguiba, "Nationalism: Antidote to Communism," 35 *Foreign Affairs* (1957), p. 648.

But we have sometimes assumed that the paramount concerns of the underdeveloped countries can be met almost entirely by military assistance or economic assistance or a combination of both. President Sukarno of Indonesia touched this chord on a visit to the United States:

> For us, nationalism means the rebuilding of our nations; it means the effort to provide equal esteem for our peoples; it means the determination to take the future into our own hands. . . . Nationalism . . . is the mainspring of our efforts. Understand that, and you have the key to much of post-war history. Fail to understand it, and no amount of thinking, no torrent of words, and no Niagara of dollars will produce anything but bitterness and disillusionment.[2]

The problem of contact—of some ground of common understanding and mutuality of interest on which to meet—is a universal one as we confront the issues of new nationalism. Turning from Asia to the Middle East, here are two comments that spell out the dilemma the United States faces in trying to help non-Western societies to pass successfully through their present period of ferment and settle down to constructive solutions to their problems:

> . . . on the most crucial issues we and the Middle East are essentially talking about different things. Our difficulty is that, while we have a clearly expressed stake in the Middle East, the Middle East has not found an equally clear stake in us. We are for defense against Russia; they are looking for independence and integrity. We are concerned about alignment; they are concerned about national development. Until, in our sympathies and our foreign policy, we find some way to take account of their basic priorities I doubt if the situation can be greatly improved.[3]

> In their competition with communist values in the uncommitted areas . . . Western values labor under a tremendous disadvantage. Western talk about freedom—individual freedom as opposed to group or national independence—is alien, strange, and untrue in the East.

[2] Address to U.S. Congress, May 17, 1956, *New York Times*, May 18, 1956.
[3] John S. Badeau, "The Middle East: Conflict in Priorities," 36 *Foreign Affairs* (1958), p. 240.

It is the same with Western political conceptions. Democracy, representative government, free elections, independent judiciary, constitutions, the evils of autocracy and totalitarianism, the separation of church and state, free institutions such as clubs, unions, societies, newspapers, which are independent of government and even free to criticize it—all these are not generally understood in the uncommitted areas. . . .[4]

What has happened, perhaps inevitably, is that the United States, in its understandable preoccupation with the cold war, has tended to shape policy toward the new nations to meet cold war imperatives, whereas the issues that engage the feelings and convictions of the new countries are not the issues of communism versus capitalism, the "liberation" of Eastern Europe, or the American way of life versus "guided democracy." Recent history tells us that to make a satisfactory impact on the countries concerned and their peoples the United States must give far greater attention to the identification of American interests with real rather than supposed interests of the uncommitted and underdeveloped countries, wherever that is possible. This conviction supplies the clearest insight into the use of the United Nations in the period ahead in dealing with the new nationalism.

The chief values of the United Nations under these conditions are two. First, through the whole complex of developmental activities—the technical assistance programs, the regional economic commissions in Asia, Africa, and Latin America, and the specialized agencies—the organization furnishes an acceptable substitute for the colonial powers in guiding and protecting the new countries. The concerted United Nations program in Guinea could well be a model for other African lands. Emergency administrative assistance to the new Congo Republic in mid-1960 helped to fill a gap as no single nation could.

The second chief value of the United Nations under these conditions arises from the very fact that troubles planners as they count heads in the future United Nations—the position

---

[4] Richard H. Nolte, in *American Universities Field Staff Letter,* from Beirut, dated January 16, 1956.

of political and parliamentary power in the United Nations of the Arab-Asian-African neutralist, anti-colonial, underdeveloped countries. Because the United Nations supplies a forum and quasi-legislature in which their particular concerns must necessarily be heeded, they display a special attachment to the organization and its role in world affairs. In that organization they will increasingly seek to give expression and form to what they—rather than anyone else—conceive to be their urgent interests. Without for a moment suggesting that the United States should forego the pursuit of its truly imperative interests even when they conflict with those of others, I do suggest that in dealing with *these* countries, in a period when *their* problems command their attention, it is in the American national interest to meet them more than halfway and to make every possible use of the United Nations in the process to manifest our genuine and unqualified support for their ambitions and goals.

From the logic of this reasoning, several principles of action regarding the United Nations can be derived:

1. In the area of human rights the United States, with the Bricker type of assault on its foreign policy hopefully in the past, should re-examine its essentially disdainful attitude toward the largely symbolic but nonetheless psychologically crucial multilateral efforts to spell out civil, social, and economic rights. It should be possible by now to evaluate with some precision whether the official policies inspired and symbolized by Mrs. Roosevelt or those influenced by Senator Bricker contributed more to the prosperity of American strategy and the creation of a satisfactory American image in other parts of the world. The whole question of covenant-drafting in the field of human rights should be re-examined from the standpoint, not of whether an isolationist or regional domestic minority will be alienated, but of whether and how the United States, within broad constitutional limits, can recapture the precious international advantage it once held and then squandered. The programs earlier proposed by the United States to identify and acknowledge basic human rights should be redesigned to avoid

compromises that seem to weaken standards achieved in the most advanced Western societies. With ingenuity we ourselves can formulate statements and conceptions of economic and social rights that faithfully reflect the reality of American society.

By evading this task we have left such formulations to the extravagances of irresponsibility and the dogmas of statism. Human rights and human dignity are most important to those who do not believe they possess them; smugness and indifference on the part of those who do yield no less unfavorable results here than in the economic field. Renewed leadership in the area of human rights, while responding both to American beliefs and to the psychological needs of recently suppressed peoples, cuts directly into the greatest vulnerability of communism both in theory and in practice, and the United States betrays both its ideology and its strategy when it forgets this.

2. So long as the United States conducted its day-to-day diplomacy in the United Nations as though the only significant interests to be considered, apart from purely voting tactics, were those of Britain, France, and a handful of other Western European states, the image of genuine American concern for and contact with the other peoples remained highly imperfect, if not downright suspect. The United States has made some headway in the United Nations in altering its traditional diplomatic practice of consulting first and often exclusively with its N.A.T.O. partners, even on issues not necessarily centering around the Atlantic Community. One specific problem has been that often the United States consulted with its European partners and then informed others, as though informing were a form of consultation. True, it is a courtesy to inform in such circumstances, but it is a courtesy that is hollow as compared to serious consultations undertaken in or out of the United Nations on issues of importance before the United States formulates its views. Although many individual exceptions can be cited, the record will bear out the assertion that in the main American policies have been formulated intergovernmentally, and American tactics have developed within

the United Nations, with far less consultation, in the true sense, with *any* government, and certainly less with the non-Western countries, than our best interests dictate.

The United Nations is the natural focus for a policy of intensive consultations with such members as the emergent African grouping, a policy that pays important dividends in conveying to them a suitable sense of importance and consideration on our part. Moreover, it has tactical implications in helping to sort out, for example, genuine African interests from the attempts of the Arab-Asian leadership to gather the entire anticolonial and neutralist world in an undifferentiated policy embrace.

Without going into details, a suggestion made to this writer by a veteran top-level negotiator is to the point. With a hundred delegations to be dealt with soon, it may be desirable to have two or three distinguished citizens in permanent residence at the American U.N. mission whose prestige would make them both welcome and effective in discussions with other delegations in a way that no squadrons of junior liaison officers could. (It goes without saying that adequate entertaining allowances are basic to successful diplomacy here as well as elsewhere.)

3. The longer-term goal of American foreign policy suggested earlier is to "develop greater concepts of responsibility by states, particularly the newer ones, regardless of size or strength."

Perhaps the highest value of the United Nations is as a place for affirming and giving substance to the international responsibilities acquired by a congeries of states which because of past history have not had the experience that customarily underlies such a sense of responsibility. The newer member states are and will be intensely self-centered as a result of their struggles for independence or for a new mode of economic growth or both. The American strategic objective of stability and integration can be significantly advanced by furnishing to these egotistical, youthful states a genuine stake in international order, by making them part owners of the business, so to speak, rather than continuing to regard them as irritating complications to the continuation of great power diplomacy.

True world community can come about, if at all, only by building on common interests and genuine consensus. The chief stumbling block to such community is usually said to be world communism. But a satisfactory consensus even among the non-Communist states and, *pro tanto,* in a world where somehow East and West were to agree on fundamentals cannot come about without the voluntary commitment by the least or the most alienated of its members. General Romulo wrote:

> The Asian peoples will not fight for the vague concept of a free world; they will fight on the side of a free world only if they have a stake in freedom themselves.[5]

This truth was sensed by a group of American delegates to the United Nations in 1955 when they joined in this unanimous statement:

> We can succeed, not by outbidding Communism in sheer amounts of economic aid, but by making newly independent and newly articulate peoples feel that they can best satisfy their wants by becoming and remaining part of the community of free nations.[6]

Such insights have not always been followed by action. The United States has been elaborately cautious in encouraging the participation in international enterprises of the neutralist or underdeveloped countries, except where absolutely necessary, on the sometimes valid view that on East-West matters they might be "neutral" in favor of the Communist position. It was ironic that the small negotiating body on disarmament set up outside the United Nations in the summer of 1959 strained at the gnat of participation by neutral countries and swallowed the camel of parity between the Soviet Union and the entire Western world.

[5] Carlos P. Romulo, "Asia: Ten Basic Facts for Americans," in *The New Leader,* June 21, 1954, p. 6.
[6] Statement of December 9, 1955, quoted in Department of State Press Release No. 14, January 11, 1956.

The educational potential of the United Nations for the anticolonial and neutralist rebels against the West can be realized only by greater collaboration with them in common enterprises which lift their sights above their exclusively nationalistic concerns, and by adopting a policy that encourages them to play a more vital part in international diplomacy and international programs. A British diplomat speaks with some astonishment of the dramatic change in the attitude taken in the U.N. Trusteeship Council by a key neutral country after one of its nationals was given a major role to play in a Trusteeship Council visiting mission. The moral of this lesson is obvious.

4. The behavioral sciences have undergone a revolution in the United States in recent years. The insights of the social scientist have not been well or widely used in policy making partly because of their sometimes forbidding jargon, and perhaps most of all because of the natural suspicions by men of affairs of "theoretical" knowledge. We face a concrete problem, however, in trying to create constructive and trustful contacts with the new countries, and we are obviously hampered by our own cultural affinities and lack of general knowledge of the vital components of such relationships. The most telling evidence of our need is the failure, despite high ideals and financial sacrifice, to establish successful communication with these people. There is a plasticity and a mobility in the societies in question—and in the range of policies we might adopt toward them—that do not necessarily exist in, for example, Soviet-American relations. Our performance in dealing with these countries either individually or collectively in the United Nations has not adequately moved us toward our strategic goals. We need help in formulating a better concept of the problem and its possible avenues of solution, and we need it now. It is here that the systematic knowledge of human and social behavior, of alienation and subsequent integration, and of patterns of rational and irrational conduct, have perhaps their greatest relevance.

I would therefore recommend that a group of authorities in the behavioral fields be officially—or unofficially—invited to recommend an appropriate set of policies and attitudes with respect to the new states, mobilizing in the process the findings and insights gained from studies in the field.

5. One of the probable findings by such specialists can be easily anticipated. The common need for a sense of participation is a need of individuals as well as of the abstraction known as the nation. Two students of the problem recently wrote that

> . . . the central objective of American policy in the transitional areas is to use whatever influences we can bring to bear to focus the local energies, talents and resources on the constructive tasks of modernization.[7]

This is not the place to detail the means, bilateral and multilateral, which, through technical assistance and developmental aid, help the central government to become, in Millikan's and Rostow's phrase, "a major source of energy, initiative and resource of modernizing the economy."[8] But we can recognize that the very heart of the problem, particularly in semiliterate and poverty-stricken countries, is the leadership group, the élite that almost alone shapes the course of events. The supply of educated and trained personnel that new educational programs will produce in increasing numbers will, as at present in India, for example, in some sectors go beyond the capacity of the economy and the national administration to absorb their energies. This phenomenon has already created local instability, and if widely projected can endanger the whole effort.

Underemployed—if not actually unemployed—élites characteristically fall prey to emotions of alienation, discontent, and ultimately hopelessness. A cushion is needed, during this transitional phase, for the excess human energies among this élite. International organizations might be helpful in furnishing such cushions, and I have already suggested that international secretariats be regarded as at least one such cushion. I men-

[7] Max F. Millikan and Walt W. Rostow, "Foreign Aid: The Next Phase," 36 *Foreign Affairs* (1958), p. 422.

[8] *Ibid.*, p. 420.

tioned also the incidental by-product of broadening the relatively narrow and self-centered vision of the intensely nationalist view. Existing international secretariat facilities should be used to the limit with this specific end in view. The multilateral technical assistance programs might utilize more trained personnel from the underdeveloped countries than they now do. The new International Development Authority under the World Bank should adopt a policy of recruiting a maximum number under the direction of those who have the requisite banking and evaluative skills. Any international inspection program or corps created as a result of an agreement, however limited, in the field of disarmament should recruit to the greatest extent possible clerical and inspection personnel from countries where such trained people are in surplus.

6. Our short and middle-range approach to the transitional areas under discussion needs to be geared to the larger political environment which over the longer range we wish to develop. As weak and inadequate new states have emerged from their colonial cocoons into political and juridical independence, we have witnessed numerous instances of the phenomenon of the "morning after." After the first flush of enthusiasm and pride, old problems are often discovered to remain unsolved, and a horde of new problems acquired.

The aim of a more stable world is achievable only as these countries come to settle down as viable members of international society. A great gap is left by the removal of the older administrative fabric, however hated, and the economic ties, however resented. The British Commonwealth, and now the French Community, represent compromises between the ideology of nationalism and the facts of life and economics. Libya and Guinea, to name only two, acquired independence in spite of economic realities, and lack authentic viability to the point where the reality of their independence has been questioned. Something must substitute for the colonial power.

Some of the new countries may come to reconsider the advantages of total independence and total isolation. I have noted the trend toward internationalization and integration that is running parallel with the trend toward nationalistic separatism. The integration trend is still a cloud no bigger than a man's hand compared with the centrifugal force of nationalism. It almost seems as if Asia and Africa must wallow in the most irrational and least promising aspects of nationalism until they ultimately discover that greater vitality, greater prosperity, and greater world influence might be had by joining in one or another kind of wider community with other similar political units, as Western Europe is in the process of discovering. The Governor of Puerto Rico, in explaining his country's answer to the problem, said:

> When the strident chorus of nationalism begins to fade in Europe, Asia, Latin America and Africa, some ingenious formula may permit the rational regrouping of new and old sovereign units on a sounder economic basis, just as the United States and Puerto Rico found a workable formula. The world has become too small, too complex, too interdependent to permit indefinite political fragmentation at the price of widespread poverty. Where blind insistence on rigid, nineteenth-century-style sovereignty exists in defiance of economic logic, new forms of federalism are called for. Puerto Ricans are proud that they are contributing to the American political system a new form of federalism.[9]

In considering the future values of the United Nations the United States should look beyond present appearances and toward the other emergent pattern. The key to the pattern in many cases will be sheer necessity, just as it was in the original motivation for European integration. But other incentives exist. Renan wrote that the sense of nationality is not biological but spiritual: "What constitutes a nation is not speaking the same tongue or belonging to the same ethnic groups, but having accomplished great things in common in the past and the wish to accomplish them in the future."

The purpose of the United States should be to "foster the growth of loyalties to broader communities of common interest, both political and functional, through processes of integration," as part of the larger aim of channeling nationalist forces toward constructive tasks. The principal way in which

[9] Governor Luis Muños-Marin, "Puerto Rico Does Not Want to Be a State," *New York Times Magazine,* August 16, 1959.

the United Nations can aid toward this objective is to identify and crystallize foci of interest relevant to the great concerns of the countries involved. Around these areas of common concern common interests can cluster and action be taken, both national and international, which has as its aim the creation of enduring ties between nations and between peoples.

Part **V**   THE GOAL OF WORLD ORDER

CHAPTER FIFTEEN

The Basis for Planning

WE FINALLY TURN to the third and last category of time in which to explore the possible uses of the United Nations: the long range. We have said that the over-all long-range U.S. objective is:

> To build a more reliable, predictable, and tolerable world order, based on values reflecting freedom and voluntarism rather than totalitarianism and coercion. . . .

We have suggested that this objective calls for strategy designed:

> To substitute processes of cooperation, order, and eventually world law for the anarchy and narrow nationalism that continue to endanger world peace and stability.

The most explicit suggestions for actions toward the realization of this ultimate goal have come from the small minority advocating world government or from those who advocate political union among nations of the Atlantic Community. Such proposals have called for steps going far beyond present levels of constitutionalism and intergovernmental cooperation. As a consequence, although in the abstract they might have appeared logical and entirely rational, they have seemed anything but rational to professionals who were struggling,

217

with only limited success, to bring to life even the multilateral machinery already in existence. Advocates of world federation like to cite the experience of the American colonies as relevant and even analogous, particularly the transition from the Articles of Confederation to the Constitution. But they often miss the point that:

> Those who seek to bring about America's participation in projects for international control and even world government would be well-advised to settle for a vague commitment at the outset and to trust history to define the reality. It seems very unlikely that the American Constitution would have been ratified if it had been clear that the national government enjoyed the powers claimed for it by Marshall in *McCulloch v. Maryland*.[1]

Proposals are occasionally made to "give the United Nations legislative powers," or to "eliminate the veto." Such proposals clearly require acceptance of some basic concepts of sovereignty which have hitherto not been accepted. One of the most encouraging contemporary developments is the evidence of some gradual steps to crystallize a community of interests among certain nations on the basis of a consensus as to specified values or objectives. But it is a far cry from such beginnings to the allocation of genuine legislative power to the General Assembly of the United Nations. That lies on the other side of the Rubicon, and it involves acceptance of a form of international constitutional government which the majority of nations have shown themselves unready to accept.

The argument about world government has all too frequently centered around questions of feasibility rather than questions of values. Much thought has gone into planning governmental arrangements for expressing the technological and administrative interdependence of nations, but little analysis has been made of the values of personal liberty in relation to world government. A world government, while satisfying certain administrative and security needs, conceivably might, by applying a lower common denominator than that which we are used to, jeopardize the high standard of individual lib-

[1] Robert G. McCloskey, "American Political Thought and the Study of Politics," LI *American Political Science Review* (1957), p. 129.

erties painfully acquired by certain Western peoples, as well as reduce the initiative of local governments upon which the bulk of social and economic progress depends.

Another problem, which because of the very nature of the political process must be anticipated, but which is not often cited, is that of providing satisfactorily for the process of change. The nations comprising present world society are characterized by highly unequal stages of economic, political, and cultural development. As it has been in similarly unbalanced civil societies, so under a world government, civil war on a global scale might be the consequence of seeking to deal with the insurrections that would predictably take place against the new established order.

Apart from the theoretical considerations, the chief disability of world government proposals is that they must assume the disappearance, or at least the drastic transformation, of the Soviet Union and Communist China. Both today are revolutionary and imperialistic powers determined to organize the world in their own image; but to validate the proposals for world government they must be postulated into sharers of Western liberal values and advocates of permanent stability.

In short, the debate on strategy to achieve a new world order has almost completely ignored a first truth: that, since the goal of world order depends upon a minimum consensus of political and societal values, unless by world order we mean world tyranny, the focus of logic must be not on the form and structure of a possible world order but on the prior issues; namely, the inescapable prerequisites of consensus and shared values.

American planners have sensed this fundamental fact, but American policy has reflected not so much a conscious consideration of the problems it implies as an acceptance of those problems as an excuse for inaction. American policy, although correct in assuming that a gradual rather than a drastic approach to world order will command the best chance of success, has in using this reasoning given "gradual" the comfortable quality of meaning anytime, or perhaps never. Thus there still remains the operational task of formulating a coherent American strategic doctrine in the political realm that orchestrates the short-range, the middle-range, and the long-range approaches to the kind of world order the United States seeks.

In such planning it is essential to maintain an atmosphere of reality and concreteness when it comes to contemplating the uses and development of international political institutions, and indeed this frame of mind is indispensable if steps are to be taken now to begin to implement our goals. But this is only half of the need. The other half is a fresh willingness to regard our long-term goals as capable of implementation instead of regrettably but safely meaningless. It is not easy to surrender the comfort of dreams in favor of the realities of a program of limited action; but limited action is at least a start toward distant goals, and some such start must be made if any meaning is to be given our concept of world order based on democratic and libertarian principles. Even if the world is not yet ready for a universal version of such a program, we are not entitled to sit still. Burckhardt said it well:

> From time to time a great event, ardently desired, does not take place because some future time will fulfil it in greater perfection.[2]

The starting point must of necessity be a modest one, and progress predictably slow.

But we are powerless to make even limited progress unless we believe that time is on our side in the struggle with communism. If we believe that Western civilization is the Rome of this century, and that it is fated forever to remain on the defensive, the outlook is hopeless. But the truth is that, in the process of defending against assault, the West has begun to create new strengths and to set in motion new energies of its own. Although now it is in a defensive position and cannot act the revolutionary (no matter what verbal gymnastics may be recommended by salesmen for America overseas) the course of revolution invariably produces a new dialectic. The Soviet Union as a new imperial power represents an established order

2 Jacob Burckhardt, *Force and Freedom*, Meridian, New York, 1955, p. 325.

behind whose façade the forces of change are working just as surely as they worked on Rome; and if the West can seek out the dynamic principle of those forces, so to speak, it can consciously accelerate the effect of contradictions within the Soviet empire. Above all, with a positive organizing principle of its own the West can act purposefully to foster its own version of history.

During a period when both sides are generally balanced by a rough equilibrium in technology and, more precisely, in the deliverable megatonnage of nuclear destruction, the primary determinative forces are not military but political and ideological. The kind of political strategy needed by the West is that which can unbalance the nonmilitary equilibrium in our favor, and the present seems a peculiarly auspicious moment to make a start. As anthropologist Clyde Kluckhohn wrote:

> There are moments in the careers of nations, as well as in the careers of individuals, when opposing external forces are about equally balanced, and it is then that intangibles like "will" and "belief" throw the scales.[3]

What follows is not written in a spirit of optimism. Perhaps even the modest steps suggested will require for their implementation a new major crisis, perhaps several trips to the brink of war, or at least a significant further decay in the capacity of Western civilization to fabricate more persuasively the future it offers to mankind. There still remains, however, the chance that the job can be faced up to without the incentive of impending disaster.

[3] Clyde Kluckhohn, *Mirror for Man*, Whittlesey House, New York, 1949, p. 198.

CHAPTER SIXTEEN

The Creation of Community

CONSENSUS AND COMMUNITY

The inexorable rhythms of history, of which our century displays only the most recent examples, offer little prospect for an end to the dynamic interplay between the established order and the invariable rise of forces dissatisfied with the conditions of their membership in it. That dynamic process and its effect on the prospects for world order are the raw materials with which planners must work if they are not to fall into one of the three pits described by Walter Lippmann when he wrote:

> The American refusal to recognize the struggle for existence has in this century crystallized in three recognizable patterns of conduct: in a neutrality which assumes that the struggle can be ignored and avoided; in crusades that assume that by defeating the chief troublemaker the struggle for existence will end; in the sponsorship of a universal society which assumes that the struggle can be abolished.[1]

The basis for true community, political experience tells us, is found in a genuine consensus about the values which the community cherishes. Law, in turn, can become acceptable and effective only if it reflects that consensus. Political community

[1] Walter Lippmann, "The Rivalry of Nations," *Atlantic Monthly*, February 1948, p. 19.

in its ideal form rests on commonly shared values as to the proper role of man in society. Translated in terms of today's world, world government would be a possibility if all the politically determinative sectors of world society shared the same concepts of human rights, political freedom, and economic organization. We know in our very bones that this does not represent a feasible possibility at the present stage of history.

But we also know that, although in terms of world consensus the degree of agreement among nations is still low, there is a highly developed consensus on some limited values—allocation of radio frequencies, epidemic control, weather reporting, mail service, as well as all the importance attached to the process of industrialization and societal modernization; and, we hope, on the mutual interest in minimizing the possibilities of global war. Beyond that, there are some nations that do share primary political and social values, achieving a *de facto* community of interests from which have already come limited experiments in economic integration and in intellectual and cultural harmony.

Finally, we know that among the citizenry of virtually all nations, if not necessarily among the ruling élites, there is a shared longing for conditions of greater international tranquility, material betterment, and individual fulfillment.

There are, then, operational bases for action. They are at present limited, fragmentary, and non-universal; but their very existence argues that the prospects for an improved world order, although they cannot rest on the expectation of an abstract commitment by members of an essentially nonexistent community, may be advanced by degrees by focussing attention on those specific interests, small or large, that are shared by groups of nations, whether they represent the entire world or not. One writer has developed this theme in these words:

> Our actions and attitudes on detailed questions of daily policy, on questions of tariffs and immigration quotas, on technical assistance programs and investment in undeveloped areas will contribute more to the international community, which all far-seeing Americans see in the making, than any abstract commitments to

ideal and impossible world constitutions which some idealistic Americans regard as important. World community must gradually grow through acts of mutual loyalty. Mutual loyalty in situations of great disproportions of power and fortune is difficult but not impossible. . . . Our problem is that technics have established a rudimentary world community but have not integrated it organically, morally, or politically. They have created a community of mutual dependence, but not one of mutual trust and respect.[2]

What, then, is the governing principle around which long-range Western strategy should center? The creation of segments, however imperfect, of true community.

What basic strategy does it call for? To support integration in economic and political fields which minimizes separatist nationalisms and ideologies and maximizes principles of cooperation and common purpose.

What can be done now? The United States can seek out areas of consensus and common interest from those not already formed and creatively support their transition to prototypes of the world order to which we aspire.

THE CREATION OF LIMITED COMMUNITIES

The first category of potential communities that the United States should strive to bring into being embraces the international community of science and technology. We have already commented on the degree to which common interest in science transcends ideological differences, with the caveat that political considerations continue to define the broad limits of intergovernmental collaboration. One prediction that can be confidently made is that further radical and transforming changes are to be anticipated in the realm of science and technology, and that there is no theoretical limit to the need for institutional means to deal with these changes constructively.

We have already noted that the challenge of outer space, beyond its purely military and scientific objectives, offers both need and opportunity for the development of institutional forms of international cooperation on a problem of irrefutably

[2] Reinhold Niebuhr, *The World Crisis and American Responsibility,* Association Press, New York, 1958, pp. 80, 85-86.

common human concern. The recommendation made in the context of internationalizing realms still outside the claim of national sovereignty can be elaborated here in terms of creating segments of community, however imperfect. Soviet abstention presumably motivated American policy makers to support the conclusions of the 1959 U.N. Ad Hoc Committee on the Peaceful Uses of Outer Space that international efforts should be limited to a very modest program of technical cooperation and further study, and that "the world does not yet need an international agency for outer space."[3] But in the words of the House Committee on Science and Astronautics:

> . . . the dangers inherent in acting too soon and with insufficient information [must be balanced] against the dangers of delaying too long and thus permitting the growth, by custom and usage, of vested interests in space—interests which might become impossible to overcome except by force.[4]

The technical and political reasons for a slow start and a cautious approach, that is to say, need to be balanced against the larger requirement that the United States point the way toward a more effective international order. The Soviet Union did rejoin the embryonic U.N. efforts in 1959, and it can be argued that the pace must be governed by the limits of Soviet cooperation. But are American interests best served by this reasoning?

Soviet motives in cooperating in limited ways can be deduced from Soviet doctrine. In general such collaboration as takes place is doubtless believed to advance Soviet ideological aims and Russian national interests. American motives, however, are not so focussed and remain confused, with scientific and military claims alternating on the center of the stage. So long as the United States does not sharply define in concrete organizational and institutional terms the image it wishes to imprint on the space age, the direction which collaboration takes is going to be fixed at every point by Soviet rather than American planners.

[3] U.N. Document A/4141 July 14, 1959, p. 54.

[4] "U.S. Policy on the Control and Use of Outer Space," House Report 353, 86th Congress, 1st Session, May 11, 1959, p. 9.

The United States should mark the desired path by proposing the creation of a U.N. body to ensure the maximum amount of coordination—whether the Soviet Union agrees at this stage or not. The functions of a U.N. agency would be advance registration and reporting of missile firings, international monitoring, and U.N. rather than national sponsorship of probes involving other planets and celestial bodies. These proposals would not tie the hands of the U.S. military strategist any more than our 1953 proposals for an international atoms for peace program, which the Soviet Union ultimately joined after the U.S. initiative won general favor.

If fifty or forty or even thirty nations agreed to harmonize and elevate to a multilateral plane their efforts bearing on the peaceful uses of outer space, a limited but meaningful community on this common interest would come into being. A separate treaty could be signed binding the signatories but reserving their freedom of action with respect to security preparations until *all* countries joined in an appropriately safeguarded program of disarmament comprehending ballistic missiles and space vehicles with a military function. Such an agreement would have the virtue of pooling unclassified research and development. It would also by its nature provide on a world-wide scale for better public information and understanding about the space age, an effort so far generally left to military leaders and technical experts seeking appropriations.

Such a program could bring together into a common enterprise nations other than the United States and the Soviet Union actively engaged in rocketry-missile programs, including Argentina, Great Britain, France, Italy, Japan, the Netherlands, Switzerland, and Sweden;[5] and nations in other continents who now are part of a world-wide network of tracking and monitoring stations, including Australia, Peru, Chile, Ecuador, Iran, and India.[6] It would give a sense of participa-

[5] See Donald Cox and Michael Stoiko, *Spacepower*, Winston, Philadelphia, 1958, p. 33.
[6] Francis O. Wilcox, before House Committee on Science and Astronautics, March 6, 1959, *Department of State Bulletin*, March 23, 1959, p. 403.

tion to other countries whose contribution, although marginal technically, would be significant politically. The parallel with the International Atomic Energy Agency—conceived and prepared for without the presence of the Russians—is obvious, even to the "haves" contributing *ex gratia* out of their stockpiles, so to speak. Perhaps the most effective act of political symbolism well within our power would be to offer our first moon shot to the international community. A "U.N. shot" of this nature could serve as a telling countermove against the spirit of extreme nationalism which frustrates the quest for more genuine international collaboration.

The head of the U.S. Information Agency in reporting on the world-wide reaction to Soviet satellite successes indicated the great symbolic meanings conveyed to peoples:

> Probably the most significant result of the Soviet successes is a change in the over-all impression of the people of the world about the Soviet Union.[7]

The most effective way to convert the image of American weakness to one of superiority would be by transferring the contest to grounds of our own choosing and daring the Soviet Union to compete with the United States in the degree of imaginativeness and creative political statesmanship rather than exclusively in the degree of thrust.

There are other scientific and technological areas in which common interests exist, whether yet identified as such or not, and where the United States can move toward its larger political objective by innovations and experiments in institutionalizing those interests. The International Geophysical Year furnished a world pattern that can and should be exploited. The Soviet representative on the committee that organized the I.G.Y. was reported as urging that it be taken as a model for continuous cooperation in various fields.[8] Scientists have repeatedly argued that the long-range hope for peace lies in the

[7] George V. Allen, before House Committee on Science and Astronautics, January 22, 1960, reported in *New York Times*, January 23, 1960.

[8] Dr. Vladimir V. Beloussov, quoted in *New York Times*, August 8, 1959.

establishment of "trans-national communities" in which scholars, scientists, and others with common interest work together for a new world order.[9] As an official of the National
Academy of Sciences wrote about the International Council
of Scientific Unions (I.C.S.U.):

> I.C.S.U. and its affiliated bodies welcome participation in their
> activities of scientists from any country or territory and . . . such
> participation [does] not carry any implication whatsoever with
> respect to recognition of the government or territory concerned.
> This principle made possible the virtually universal enrollment
> of national scientific communities in the I.G.Y.[10]

Certainly the success of the International Geophysical Year
with its widely publicized emphasis on the international interests of the scientific community was a landmark in international relations. Indeed, some have seen it as progenitor of
completely new patterns of international political relations:

> The I.G.Y. may turn out to be a brilliant new approach toward
> world organization. The geophysicist is inevitably a truly inter-
> national scientist. During current Antarctic operations all con-
> siderations other than scientific have been set aside. Cooperation
> among all participating nations is real.[11]

It may well be that the most fruitful areas of cooperation today
lie in realms that depend sufficiently on the scientists, with
their usually detached political outlook, to minimize political
differences.

But, although scientific contact should be outside the political forum, the importance of the issues of scientific cooperation can be underscored only by giving them the floor, so to
speak, in political forums such as the United Nations. If it
appears that there may be danger that such interconnections
make scientific subjects political, the answer is to concentrate
on nonpolitical bodies, whether private scientific or the U.N.
specialized agencies, for example, for the actual scientific col-

[9] J. Robert Oppenheimer, *New York Times,* April 16, 1958.

[10] Wallace W. Attwood, Jr., "The International Geophysical Year in
Retrospect," *Department of State Bulletin,* May 11, 1959, p. 684.

[11] Laurence M. Gould, "Antarctica in World Affairs," *Headline Series,*
No. 128, Foreign Policy Association, New York, 1958.

laboration and contact, but to use the United Nations for the purpose of institutionalizing such cooperation as a desirable part of the political process for the dissemination of results through the widest media.

The International Health Year for 1961 was proposed by vote of the U.N. General Assembly in 1958, and it can be anticipated that subsequent technical attacks on medical and scientific problems will increasingly be within the political ambit of the United Nations, particularly if the United States makes it its business to see that this happens.

American strategy should program a series of proposals through the United Nations for intensive collaborative investigations and endeavors in various scientific fields that bear on the solution of the common global problems now or eventually affecting every human being. We have noted the problem of overpopulation. Scientists are also in general agreement that solutions must be found for the common human problem of dwindling water supply. One solution is through cheap conversion of sea water, and U.N.E.S.C.O. has made protracted studies of this problem; but it has never been introduced in a larger setting by American leaders in any serious way, or regarded by American strategists as germane to the problems of ends and means they are dealing with. A recent supplement to the earlier U.N. Report on New Sources of Energy and Economic Development, prepared at the request of the Economic and Social Council, revealed exciting progress in the development of practical applications of solar, wind, and geothermic energy capable of promoting higher levels of living and economic development in less developed areas.[12] There are many other comparable problems and comparable promises of large-scale solutions whose social and political impact could be widespread.

One way of moving such vital issues from the technical level to that of maximum public and political impact yet without overburdening the political agenda would be the adoption by the General Assembly of the British Royal Commission method. Blue-ribbon special bodies of both experts and dip-

12 See *United Nations Review,* April 1959, pp. 6, 7.

lomats would be created *ad hoc* by the Assembly to examine the latest developments in a particular field, reporting back with recommendations for action in political, financial, and organizational terms. Such reports could package whole areas which political leadership might otherwise neglect. Clear explanations of the social and economic significance of such issues before an international political body could have a salutary effect, both in focussing international diplomacy on essentially constructive nondivisive issues and in elevating to their proper place some problems that deserve urgent attention and the allocation of significant international resources.

To turn to another base for action, there has been in recent years an accelerating trend, commented on frequently in these pages, toward the integration of the economies and, in some cases, the politics of states in limited association with each other. It has paralleled the sharp upsurge of nationalism during the same time and has been obscured by that more dramatic and vivid development. France, for example, has behaved under General de Gaulle as a state sometimes torn between the pressures of the two opposing trends. The balance has been so fine that limited steps favoring further integration within the Western European community have been accompanied by the withdrawal of some of the established cooperative arrangements under N.A.T.O.; greater collaboration in coalition diplomacy has been offset by nationalistic efforts to establish nuclear and diplomatic parity with France's allies.

Clearly, the quiet trend toward greater integration must contend every step of the way against the forces of nationalism; there is no evidence that purely "functional" interrelationships will lead by any natural or automatic process to political integration, or even that integration as such will eventually be the dominant trend. One recent study basically sympathetic to the integrating trend concluded that:

> Neither the study of our cases, nor a survey of more limited data from a larger number of countries, has yielded any clearcut evidence to support [the] view . . . that modern life, with rapid transportation, mass communications, and literacy, tends to be more international than life in past decades or centuries. Nor

do these results suggest that there has been inherent in modern economic and social development any unequivocal trend toward more internationalism and world community.[13]

The same evidence has been interpreted differently. In a larger historical framework one veteran observer saw the trend as clearly toward confederation and integration:

These processes of coordination and integration have often been interrupted by counter-processes of disintegration, but the trend of history has been toward larger political units.[14]

Whichever view one accepts, we do have contemporary evidence that furnishes a reasonable basis on which to construct a more coherent strategy.

The European community is perhaps the most inspiriting example of the effort to supersede nationalism with community. In N.A.T.O., according to its Secretary General, "little by little, without fanfare or useless publicity, a sort of collective diplomacy is taking the place of individual diplomacy that was for so long traditional."[15] New patterns of trans-Atlantic organization are evident in the new 20-nation successor to the Organization for European Economic Cooperation. In September of 1959 seven Latin American nations—Argentina, Bolivia, Brazil, Chile, Paraguay, Peru, and Uruguay—met in Montevideo to consider moving toward economic integration in a free trade treaty. In 1960 Malaya, Thailand, and the Philippines took steps toward a new Southeast Asian grouping.

Africa will doubtless offer new challenging opportunities for federal and confederal solutions. There are first of all the pan-Africa movements. On a regional level Guinea and Ghana, plus possibly Liberia, seek to form a nucleus of a larger union of independent African states. Competing with this move but at the same time demonstrating the relationship

[13] Deutsch, Burrell, Kann, Lee, Lichterman, Lindgren, Loewenheim, and Van Wagenen, *Political Community and the North Atlantic Area,* Princeton University Press, Princeton, New Jersey, 1957, p. 22.

[14] Quincy Wright, "The Mode of Financing Unions of States as a Measure of Their Degree of Integration," XI *International Organization* (1957), p. 30.

[15] Paul-Henri Spaak, "New Tests for N.A.T.O.," 37 *Foreign Affairs* (1959), p. 358.

between the two trends, other former French possessions in Africa upon being granted independence turned shortly to arrangements that would once again draw together the states of the region. A first step was the customs union involving 20 million people among seven states other than Guinea which formed French West Africa: Senegal, French Sudan, Ivory Coast, Mauritania, Niger, Volta, and Dahomey. This scheme was designed to harmonize financial policies, labor codes, judicial systems, and other common elements. Four of these republics—Ivory Coast, Voltaic Republic, Dahomey, and Niger—formed the Council of the Entente. Union is contemplated by Chad and the Congo and Central African Republics; i.e., former French Equatorial Africa less Gabon. The Mali Federation of Senegal and Sudan was further evidence of the confederation trend in the area, although it is also part of the parallel separatist trend toward complete independence.

Other areas which earlier separatist forces broke up are once again moving toward coalescence: the British and former Italian Somalilands are united in the new Somalia, which in turn will put pressures on French Somaliland. Tanganyika and Nyasaland may one day come together, if plans for the Rhodesia Federation have to be changed. Even the old German Cameroons could be a model for its successor territories to emulate, and conceivably the whole former East African pattern could be recaptured. Other indices of the pattern are obvious: the Council of Europe, the Scandinavian Union, the Federation of the West Indies, the United Arab Republic, the new federal union of Malaya; other regional associations such as the Organization of American States, S.E.A.T.O., and the Arab league have at least the potential for more substantial economic and political functions of a federalizing nature.

The United Nations has only a limited role to play in facilitating or even affecting this trend. But it has already taken some constructive steps which should be encouraged and built upon. Perhaps the earliest was the decision of the General Assembly in 1949 to incorporate Cyrenaica, the Fezzan, and Tripolitania into the new state of Libya, and the related decision in 1950 to federate Eritrea with Ethiopia. It is not generally realized that the common market for Central America, which technically went into effect in June 1959 with the ratification of Guatemala, was sponsored by an organ of the United Nations—the U.N. Economic Commission for Latin America—which as early as 1952 set up a Committee for Economic Cooperation of the Central American Isthmus to encourage re-establishment in some form of the abortive Federal Republic of Central America. On another continent, the U.N. Economic Commission for Europe implied new interorganizational relationships when, over Soviet opposition, it resolved to take account of the existence of new "subregional groupings" such as the European Common Market.[16]

I suggested in Chapter Twelve that the United Nations be encouraged to look beyond the stage of technical independence or self-government for independent territories, recognizing that the moment of independence represents merely one critical watershed in the political and economic life of the territory, after which new arrangements may be required to sustain its viability and effective international existence. It should also look beyond the problem of postindependence status. To stimulate such a new approach the United States should propose that a new study be undertaken under the auspices of the General Assembly or Trusteeship Council (which will have little to do by 1961) with a view to recommending appropriate arrangements on a regional or other federal or confederative basis for territories slated for eventual independence. Few issues are more sensitive, but few require study and rational planning more acutely. Regional and functional integration will of course normally take place without reference to the United Nations itself. But it should not be regarded as competitive to the principle of universality. Confederations of the sort described above, far from being rivals or threats to the United Nations, are building blocks of consensus and community and political stepping stones toward the universal society of which the United Nations is the forerunner.

[16] *New York Times,* May 5, 1959.

The United States, as the largest contributor to the United Nations and the leader of the non-Communist forces within it, and with a clear interest in promoting and encouraging the expansion of loyalties on a widening geographic basis, should be in the forefront in a new approach to the problem of independence, an approach that accepts neither colonial status nor isolated independence as definitive, but rather introduces as its own principle of action the growth of larger-than-national communities of common interest and peaceful purpose. The ultimate issue cannot be stated better than it was by Salvador de Madariaga:

> The trouble today is that the Communist world understands unity but not liberty, while the free world understands liberty but not unity. Eventual victory may be won by the first of the two sides to achieve the synthesis of both liberty and unity.[17]

[17] *New York Times Magazine,* October 11, 1959.

CHAPTER SEVENTEEN

Toward a Rule of Law

IF WE SEEK to make progress toward a world community now, we must be looking at areas that reflect common interests not only in regions but also across the board, so to speak. For there are interests among nations in all continents and all regions that are not being reflected adequately in the world's institutions. Beyond the areas of common interest already considered, is there possible any more fundamental approach to world order? Specifically, can anything be done to foster the rule of law in the world without waiting for the formation of a universal political consensus on which to base it?

Since law and order can flow only from communities of common interest characterized by a consensus on certain fundamental political values, the communities of interest must themselves be created before the law can be superimposed.[1] Even in the realm of international law, however, it is believed that the United States could sponsor limited action now which would be realistic, positive, and constructive in advancing our grand strategy.

The road toward the sort of world order we aspire to is treacherously blocked. Among the many issues which lie athwart it, two are of unusual moment: the problem of mak-

[1] For a more thorough exposition of this point of view, see the author's *Law, Politics, and International Disputes*, in *International Conciliation*, No. 516, January 1958.

ing greater use of legal methods in the settlement of international disputes; and the problem of building a legal order
in the absence of a true universal community, or of the shared
political and social values upon which genuine community
must rest.

LEGAL AND POLITICAL DISPUTES

The first problem—legal solutions for international disputes—
raises once again some long-debated issues about the role of
the law in fostering or inhibiting the processes of political and
social change. This relationship has some fixed qualities which
cannot be disregarded, however powerful our impulses toward
reform.

There has long been agreement that in its essence the law
represents stability, in distinction to the political process, which
is dynamic in nature. The law, in this oversimplified but nonetheless historically striking equation, reflects the *status quo*.
Significant and needful changes in the established political,
economic, and social order cannot be brought about by appealing to the courts, since it is the function of the courts to
uphold that existing order. Adjustments between those sharing the same ground rules can be accommodated by the law.
But changes in the ground rules themselves—in the basic distribution of power or status—can, so the argument runs, be
brought about only by altering the law.

Even in the most harmonious domestic setting, parliaments,
rather than courts, generally alter the law in the sense of resolving the great conflicts of interest between component parts
of society as to the allocation of political power and social
strength. These conflicts and their accommodation are the very
stuff and substance of the political process. Of course, the law
has a role even here, in ensuring that the process stops short
of violence, in guarding the larger public interest against the
contenders, or, in a different sense, in rendering decisions
which show that it too understands the dynamics of the society
it serves. But when all is said and done, in a well-integrated
society the means by which the basic constellation of internal
forces is rearranged without violence are legislative and not

judicial. In an unintegrated society, revolution, or—on an international scale—war, is the traditional vehicle for such changes. It is quite evident that we have some distance to go before we can achieve the preconditions for genuine international legislation, with all that it implies. And such a task is Herculean in an age in which the engines of history are political forces with warring ideas about how to organize society.

The international dispute-solving process thus functions under extraordinary handicaps, and still encourages a sterile black and white dialogue between those who insist that if only men would be rational all disputes could be adjudicated and those who dismiss legal methods as permanently irrelevant to world politics.

The matter is of course anything but black and white. Even when political disputes were most intractable, it was true that courts did sometimes change the law, often after, as it were, reading the election returns. The doctrine of *rebus sic stantibus* at least theoretically permits obsolete treaties to be legally invalidated. The United Nations, like the League of Nations before it, has machinery available for peaceful change. In the case of the United Nations a genuinely new bias exists toward change and away from the status quo—for example, in the realm of colonialism.

But perhaps the greatest challenge to traditional thinking about law and politics is that the legal order is no longer always synonymous with the political *status quo*. The international *status quo* today is a multiple array of established orders against each of which large-scale forces are in revolt. It bears little resemblance to the two-dimensional confrontation of the 1820's which still colors much of our political imagery.

The shifts in the political equations are in turn reflected in the mirror that law holds up to society. The principle of domestic jurisdiction—the very keystone of modern international constitutional order—yielded with high drama in March of 1960 to the conviction of a growing number of states that South Africa's internal racial policies were not only reprehensible but constituted a potential threat to international peace and security. The latter concept too had changed when such a threat could engage the Security Council even though no armies were mobilized, no borders violated, no ultimatum issued. Cuba's invocation of the Security Council in her dispute with the United States in the summer of 1960 further illustrated the trend to broaden the meaning of "international."

The new plasticity in legal concepts is not limited to the colonial area. The very notion of territorial inviolability and privacy has already been shattered by orbiting satellites, and more sophisticated successors can be counted on to appear. Only when such intrusion becomes institutionalized by the organs of international society will the law ever again catch up with the reality.

These are all among the reasons why the present, although a time of change, could also be a time of opportunity. A serious *détente* between East and West, if it ever comes about, could permit the processes of evolution to erect new conceptual bridges between the Communist states and the West, draining some presently intractable disputes of their revolutionary quality, and turning the mutual focus away from issues involving the legitimacy of the present distribution of power and wealth. Such an evolution in the East-West contest may be in the far distance, particularly considering the international dynamics of Chinese communism. But as newly independent countries come to reaffirm what President Lleras of Colombia called their decisive stake in Western civilization, as they come to regard the legal order—such as it is—as the guardian rather than the thief of their patrimony, the international consensus can grow and with it the possibilities for law and, by the most natural process of all, government.

Thus issues which may not be justiciable at one time could well be at another time because their adjudication would not be seen as placing in jeopardy the existence or relative power of a nation. And surely there are many matters which are non-justiciable now only because there exists no custom or habit or expectation or pressure for adjudication.

A discriminating brand of statesmanship can isolate legal aspects of political cases and, with strong leadership and proper timing, make better use of the potential of the law. The Suez crisis of 1956, for example, may well have offered opportunities at one stage to seek a World Court ruling, by mutual agreement, as to the obligations Egypt bore regarding free passage under the Constantinople Treaty of 1888. But at no time after July 26, 1956, was it realistic to expect Egypt to consult the Court as to the proper ownership of the Canal itself. The question of sovereignty had become a closed question, but the more procedural issues might not have been. If we achieve a better international environment for the settlement of differences there may be factors, some of which are now lacking, that will favor their submission to the World Court or to impartial arbitration.

But there are two basic preconditions for improved use of the law in the settlement of international disputes. Both reflect hazards to which Americans are peculiarly prone.

One hazard already touched upon is the persistent delusion, popular among a few professionals and many laymen, that one of the things man strives for is to substitute law for politics. At its most extravagant, this fantasy sees the objective of foreign policy as being the creation of a world in which there is no conflict or tension, and an end to the dynamic processes by which history spins itself out of the thrusts and responses of man and nature.

I have tried to show that under the most favorable conditions the legal and political realms have their natural and legitimate roles to play in ordering social life. In taking a forward step toward greater use of international arbitral and judicial machinery, nothing could be more damaging than to underrate the distinction between the legal and political realms into which constitutional society, if it is to survive and flourish, characteristically and naturally divides itself.

The other hazard is the tendency to take temporary easements in world conditions as a signal to slacken off drastically on major international tasks considered imperative when under pressure. A rather new order of maturity will be required of us if the incentives to community building do not recurrently atrophy if pressures are lifted in a more relaxed environment. By the same token, continued tensions will also supply a permanent excuse for inaction unless there is the same degree of purposeful action and example by leading countries such as the United States.

A MORE LAWFUL WORLD ORDER

It is with respect to the distant vision of a more lawful world that frequently enunciated long-term goals seem most abstract and unreal. So long as those goals depend on a universal consensus, the prospects for advancing toward a more satisfactory international society are dim indeed. But are there no steps we could take before this distant millennium, given the promising raw materials out of which to construct meaningful segments of community?

I believe there are, but they require us to modify some assumptions about the nature of a world legal regime. One assumption is that a community upon which to base such a regime already exists—which is patently untrue. Another is that, to subject nations to a compulsory rule of law, such a total community would first have to come into being—which relegates the possibilities to an indefinite future. To make any progress at all toward the larger goal, for the foreseeable future we must, in the words of Andrew Jackson, "elevate them guns a little lower." We must revise the all-or-nothing premise that underlies much contemporary thinking about the rule of law in the world. For if progress toward a rule of law depends upon a genuine sharing of fundamental political values between the West and the Communist states, we are lost before we begin.

High American officials offered the disturbing suggestion in 1959 that the place to make a start was in relations between the United States and the Soviet Union, by requiring that disputes about the terms of agreements reached between the two be adjudicated. This was disturbing not because it is undesirable but because it was the only concrete suggestion made by American political leadership to implement what seemed a promising initiative.

Such a proposal implies that the only alternatives are either no effective international law at all or law that would span the world's two most incompatible societies. By this reasoning, we would rest our hope for greater use of the legal method in resolving international disputes on the least attainable form of agreement.

Certainly the dominant attitudes in the Communist outlook may change, and we should encourage this change in every way possible. But on the evidence so far, Communist leaders reject the notion of impartial judges as between systems; according to their doctrine one is either for them or against them. We seem to envisage so-called peaceful competition as a way in which we can "win" in accordance with civilized ground rules; it is not at all clear that the Communists can contemplate losing gracefully or in any other way. I can only conclude that the most promising prospect for enlarging the rule of law today takes the form of agreements between the *most* like-minded rather than the least like-minded states.

A considerable number of nations share certain values in common that would be relevant to the formation of a legal community. One shared value is their relative satisfaction with the established order in broad terms, implying their general willingness to live within it. This in turn suggests that a willingness probably exists to let their legal disputes be arbitrated or adjudicated by an impartial body if they are guaranteed mutual reciprocity from other nations similarly bound, and if they feel they can count on recognizable justice from the mediating third party.

There is a deep tradition of jurisprudence in North America, Western Europe, and Australasia which can be built upon; the legal habits developed by Latin American states on international questions are already strongly embedded. In other areas, as one after another newly independent state comes to reconstruct satisfactory and trustful relationships with the older parts of international society, a similar tradition could develop.

The nature of a potential legal community is to some extent identified by the character of the 39 states whose declarations regarding compulsory jurisdiction of the International Court of Justice are still on the books—13 are European, 10 Latin American, and 10 Afro-Asian, in addition to the United States, Israel, and the four older British dominions. It will be noted at once that such a community would not be limited to any one region or continent, nor would it make a politically myopic distinction between "have" and "have not" nations.

Actually, the nations outside traditional Western systems have had little or no opportunity to demonstrate their willingness to submit even their legal disputes to the legal process. Moreover, they have not been influenced to do so. The United Arab Republic was never seriously challenged by the principal powers to submit the legal aspects of the Suez Canal dispute to adjudication; India and Pakistan have never been pushed to arbitrate their differences over Kashmir, or the Netherlands and Indonesia to adjudicate the West New Guinea dispute. In some cases, of course, one or the other party knows only too well what the law's reply will be, and does not wish to hear it. But in an improved environment, with great powers such as the United States setting the example, the pressures to make such modest progress would doubtless intensify, always, however, with the clear understanding that the legal process can be expected to encompass only the legal questions that arise between nations, not those that are basically political.

The Latin American states seemed prepared, in the Bogotá Conference on Pacific Settlement of Disputes in 1948, to agree that *all* disputes, whether justiciable or not, be submitted to a process of adjudication. This goes too far, and feeds the fear that any step at all would involve an unacceptable cost. But political disputes frequently have aspects that can be formulated in legal terms and upon which a legally based judgment would be acceptable. This leaves a not inconsiderable body of issues that can be so handled, and it is a counsel of despair to hold that even the most advanced nations would consider *any* serious dispute political and would refuse to be bound by a third-party legal judgment.

I do not believe the germ of truth this assertion contains is sufficient to deter the United States from making a fresh start, on the assumption that greater willingness to use legal processes for legal questions would be forthcoming under appropriate political and constitutional conditions. The place to make a fresh start is among those nations throughout the world presently sharing a minimum consensus of values and political beliefs, constituting them a core legal community open to all who will join it, but without awaiting the reconversion of the Communist nations to the Western versions of jurisprudence and political philosophy.

The first step of course is repeal by the United States Senate of its damaging reservation to the American adherence to the Statute of the International Court of Justice, specifically the article reserving to the United States the determination of whether a dispute is within its domestic jurisdiction or not, a decision that the Court would otherwise make. As a consequence of the American example eight countries—Mexico, France, Liberia, South Africa, India, Pakistan, Britain, and the Sudan—followed suit. The number of acceptances of the Court's compulsory jurisdiction declined to 39 out of 84 nominal parties to its statute, and the result has been that the present Court enjoys less stature in the world than even its predecessor before the war.

But India, Britain, and France have reconsidered and dropped their self-judging reservations. The abrogation by the United States of its reservation is an indispensable step toward pointing the way to more orderly methods of settling international differences. Once done, it furnishes a new basis for action that should be followed without losing the momentum of the act itself.

The United States should undertake the formation, now, of a legal community consisting of those nations willing to live under its rules. Such a community would not be limited to any one region or continent, and would be open to all nations willing to accede. Within this legal community all legal disputes of the nature contemplated by Article 36 of the Statute of the International Court of Justice would be recognized, without reservations, as coming within the jurisdiction of international jurisprudence. This is of course the obligation nations assume when they accede to the optional clause of the Statute of the Court, but in the light of the progressive deterioration of this obligation in the recent past, a fresh beginning is needed.

How can the United Nations assist in this endeavor?

Other organizations than the United Nations have taken promising steps toward a more lawful world order. The Council of Europe established, in January 1959, the Court of Human Rights to which individuals can bring grievances against a state—a step that goes beyond anything embraced by present international law. By late 1959 the leading members of the Council of Europe had not yet agreed to recognize decisions of this court, but it may well create a new precedent, and should be encouraged. Beyond this, proposals have been made for a Court of Justice for N.A.T.O., for example, based on the same kind of reasoning applied here but limited to the members of N.A.T.O.[2]

It would seem far more appropriate to extend such a proposal on the broadest basis and to the widest variety of cultures consistent with the willingness of states to submit themselves to the regime of law. The United Nations would seem to be the most obvious place to act, since we would wish to attract to our policy the maximum number of nations from all walks of political life; these can best be reached collectively through the United Nations.

The U.N. Legal Commission, on call of the General Assembly, should be asked to prepare a new protocol that would make the Court's jurisdiction mutually binding on the signatories thereto. The protocol would address itself both to primary legal disputes and to those aspects of political disputes that are realistically justiciable. In addition, the protocol would bind states to establish bilateral or other arbitration tribunals and to arbitrate claims and disputes that might arise out of treaties drafted in the future. It would also include a fresh appraisal of the need for regional or other subbodies of the International Court, which were not needed up to now because of the paucity of Court business but conceivably

[2] Proposal by Charles S. Rhyne at Atlantic Congress, June 6, 1959, *New York Times,* June 7, 1959.

might be needed in the future if enough nations followed this new lead. The United States would indicate its willingness to be the first signatory of the protocol.

If other nations initially were cautious about a new commitment of this sort, it would not be a reason for abandoning the effort. The 39 nations whose declarations regarding compulsory jurisdiction are operative—with or without reservations—constitute the basic membership of a legal community. A limited legal order encompassing those countries can be established now. Other nations ready for more enlightened patterns of relationships—and there are obviously some—will be offered a concrete means of taking action instead of continuing to be dragged down to the level of the most narrowly nationalistic or isolationist.

In order that countries not members of the United Nations —Switzerland and the small principalities of Europe, as well as semiautonomous territories—might also accede anew, the protocol would be negotiated and drafted at a plenipotentiary conference called by the United Nations but of an *ad hoc* nature. The protocol would come into force with respect to any pair of states as soon as those states had ratified the protocol by their own constitutional means.

If the Russians did not come into such a limited community for another fifty years, we would still have provided a new beginning for a more lawful world with respect to legal disputes, the adjudication of which would be in no way dependent on agreement with the Soviet Union. Under this proposal the continued antisocial international behavior of the Communist nations would no longer serve as an excuse for the almost automatic rejection of legal methods among non-Communist nations. Indeed, the position of the Soviet Union would be quite irrelevant. In no way threatened by our proposal, it would be hard put to attack it on plausible grounds (although once aware that the United States was actually taking a concrete step toward its own variety of world order, the Soviet Union would doubtless appreciate the scope of our challenge).

Such a proposal should commend itself to the American

public and to the Senate, which, apart from abrogating the American reservation, must ratify the proposed commitment. The crucial point is that such a step binds the United States only with respect to states that equally bind themselves. So long as the rule of law is limited to those states that agree in advance to live within it, and actually only affects a limited sector of their international relationships, the safety and security of the United States remain free of any jeopardy.

The positive argument is even more compelling. Nothing will take the place of example and leadership in designing new patterns of international behavior which nations will be prepared not just to applaud but to act upon. The Western-oriented nations, by acting decisively and courageously, can give content and reality, however modestly, to their version of the proper course of history and the shape of the political future. The United States, once freed of the self-imposed incubus of the Senate reservation, can apply its influence to encouraging other nations to follow suit, not least of all the Communist nations at such time as they cease to repudiate the existing rules of the game and finally decide that they can live and prosper within the kind of mutually tolerant legal and political framework toward which we should now be bending our efforts.

A Perspective

PROBABLY NOTHING is more important in determining the role of the United Nations on the world political stage than the picture of it that leading statesmen hold in their minds. Whether or not those images are accurate or even rational, they define in broad terms national attitudes toward the United Nations. Moreover, the process is a reciprocal one, with national attitudes in their turn affecting the prospects of the world organization. Of all its members, the United States has for obvious reasons had the greatest influence in shaping the organization as it is today; for less obvious reasons the United States has had perhaps the greatest difficulty among the principal members in defining its national attitude toward the United Nations in terms of a coherent and integrated strategy.

For many Americans the story of the first fifteen years of the United Nations had three parts: early hopes and dreams, rapid disillusionment, and eventual relegation to that cherished but quiescent role assigned to unattainable moral purposes. With the special poignancy with which men react to illusions that never quite materialize, the hopes nurtured in 1945 for One World and for wholehearted international cooperation have been repudiated by those who woke from the dream, and clung to by those who believed that the reality rather than the dream was at fault. The issue between the two has continued to be success or failure measured in terms of the original vision; meanwhile, fifteen years of experience have accumulated, and during that time a number of important things have happened to change the very nature of the problem.

The meaning of the strategic issues confronting the United States and the West have become far more explicit than they were in 1945. The alternatives realistically available to deal with those issues have in turn become increasingly well defined. Simultaneously, the United Nations, although profoundly influenced by external forces, has itself undergone organic growth, acquiring qualities of uniqueness and individuality according to its own laws of internal development.

It now becomes not only possible but essential to redefine the touchstone in terms of which an American strategic doctrine for the role of the United Nations is formulated. The vision with which, perhaps asking too much both of men and of their institutions, we created the United Nations requires to be brought into new focus and related to what we are, what we have, and what we must do from here on.

Thus any estimate of the potential role of the United Nations in the years ahead necessarily takes its cue not from the original premises of the institution itself but from a realistic concept of the United Nations as it is today. It is this concept that must be related to the dictates of the national strategic problem.

The great tasks of national strategy—deterrence of general war, a modus vivendi with the Soviet Union, and safeguarded disarmament agreements—represent a proper first claim upon national resources. To succeed in them, the United States is utilizing the entire range of instrumentalities—diplomatic, military, economic, and psychological—that are available to it. These tasks, seen in the large, have been essentially beyond the reach of the United Nations except in marginal terms.

But in reality, as our breakdown of national goals indicates, these massive problem areas are not the vast and undifferentiated wholes that rhetoric makes them seem. Each is composed of many smaller parts, some of which are entirely national or bilateral in significance, but others of which reveal important opportunities for international institutions such as the United Nations to contribute to their solution.

The possibilities of action through the United Nations to attack significant segments of the short-term problems emerge from our analysis with perhaps the greatest clarity. It is not difficult to demonstrate that U.N. neutral forces and third-party presences fill a serious gap in purely American or Western capabilities, minimizing the dangers in the use of force while discouraging take-overs and preventing the deterrent situation from being undercut by irresponsible national leaders. With a more consistent role, the United Nations can take purposeful preventive actions, help to damp down local conflicts, and dispense a form of international justice so that peaceful change can take place.

Of course, in the light of the over-all strategic problem the United Nations is secondary to other instrumentalities—national and collective—in meeting the basic short-run issues of survival and security. But even here, when measured against the specific goals of American foreign policy, it reveals possibilities for maximizing the qualities about it that are unique —its inclusion of neutral nations, its capacity to act as the indispensable third party, and the larger symbolism communicated by the presence of its physical agencies.

When we lift our eyes from the short term, the most striking fact about contemporary history is the acceleration of the processes of change. Once the scope and drama of those processes are grasped, a different perspective begins to emerge regarding the connection between the short run and the middle and more distant future—and, by the same token, regarding the potential uses of the United Nations. Because the process is dynamic and not static, we may accept the limiting realities of the present regarding the role of the United Nations, but without letting these continue to determine the limits of policy actions open to the United States.

The processes of change with the greatest capacity to affect the contours of world politics are those taking place in the underdeveloped countries and in Soviet society. These have important implications for the United Nations as an institution linking East with West, and North, so to speak, with South. In Western-Soviet relations, assuming as we must that the process of deterrence is successful, there will open up possibilities of limiting and regulating armaments as both sides come to perceive common interests that are still not mutually explicit; from this tangible expression of common interest, as well as from the common interests arising out of scientific and technological transformations, can flow unforeseeable tasks for the United Nations. In the area of revolutionary nationalism, the processes of modernization and development in the underdeveloped countries is by definition a process of nation building and institution building in which the United Nations can play a crucial role.

The dynamics of change thus govern strategy itself, and a strategic doctrine for the United Nations, if it is to serve us adequately, must be dynamic and not static. Forces of change are at work that organically connect the short range with the long range, and national strategy that persists in keeping them in separate compartments, the one representing today's ineluctable reality, the other merely tomorrow's idle dream, has an unpromising future.

What happens during these historical transformations can profoundly reshape history. A false step in the process of seeking Soviet-American rapprochement might jeopardize the chances for peace; the way in which the modernization process is or is not steered into wholesome and constructive channels can reorder the strategic map; and what happens now to enhance the power and clarity of the ideological forces at issue in the world can give a decisive advantage to the value system preferred and propagated by one or the other of them.

If the political configurations that emerge from the present conflict are to reflect the value system preferred and practiced by the ideological force representing freedom rather than tyranny, national strategy must encompass a far larger enterprise than the tactics of maneuvering safely through short-term crises.

Conceived in this broader perspective, the United Nations opens opportunities to the United States and the West to stamp with the desired mold a larger segment of international affairs, and to help accelerate the growth of a broader consensus and consequently a broader world community.

But for every opportunity there is a danger. A valid net judgment comes only out of weighing in the scales of national interest the aggregate of assets and liabilities, and separating the possible from the impossible.

Today it is not possible to assume a situation of harmonious and trustful collaboration between the Soviet Union and the United States. But it is possible to focus intensely on the common interests that do exist between the two or might be brought into being, and to study attentively the possibilities offered by the only political institution joining the two for making those interests concrete and giving them form and operative meaning.

It is not possible to rely on the automatic or inevitable dedication of the underdeveloped countries to the values of political democracy and economic liberalism, or to be certain that the United States will not wind up outnumbered in the United Nations by a solid and growing bloc of newly independent states. But it is possible to utilize the opportunities offered by their presence in the United Nations, and by their political attachment to it, as a means of identifying our interests with theirs. It is possible to apply the institutional resources of the United Nations for constructively influencing their internal development and international maturity, without too much concern about who wins the popularity contests at any given moment.

It is not possible today to execute a policy that recognizes that in reality the United Nations is not at all the privileged club of like-minded states we have insisted it to be, but a world forum in which virtually all the nations are represented or soon will be, and in which on any rational grounds we ought to insist that membership should be regarded as a mandatory obligation of all states, with no one permitted to remain unaccountable and free of the obligations other governments have assumed. It is not possible to adopt such a view of the United Nations, however sensible and consistent with our broader strategy, until the problem of Communist Chinese representation is settled, an event that will probably take place not by the resolution of any abstract or legal issue but because at some future moment progress in the field of disarmament or related areas of scientific or technological action as a practical matter cannot be institutionalized without the participation of a country covering a significant portion of the earth's physical surface and containing a quarter of its inhabitants.

What is possible now is for American policy making to reconsider the implications of universality in the light of a concept of international responsibility and accountability, and to begin to enable the serious values embedded in that concept to be discussed rationally. What is not only possible but essential, if we are to keep faith with both the Chinese Nationalists and the people of Taiwan, is to plan for suitable institutional devices which, even after the present leadership no longer rules, will keep that island within the perimeter of the free world, its people suitably represented in the United Nations and afforded the same ultimate right of self-determination that is extended to other peoples.

Finally, it is not possible to wish into existence a world in which the forces of extreme nationalism yield consistently to the larger interests of mankind. But it is possible to view extreme nationalism as a malignant disorder of an historical epoch, and nationalism in its benign form as the zealous guardian of individual liberties and the uniqueness of diverse cultures. National sentiment may be the undoing of the Communist empire before it runs its course, and the United States must perceive the value of continued separate membership in international organizations and other means of sustaining the identity of states held in thrall.

It is possible to sharpen the utility of the United Nations as an agency for lessening—and in this sense civilizing—the virulence of self-centered nationalism, by using it to give greater encouragement to the parallel trend toward consolidation and integration, and by international activities, programs, and institutions that transcend the concerns of individual nations and reflect a common interest, however limited to start with. We risk perpetual failure and disillusionment when we falsely postulate a true consensus where none exists. But where there does exist a legitimate prospect of a genuine community of interests around a specific—rather than an abstract—need, we have every cause to move and move vigorously. If the communities of interest are less than universal in scope and size, they need not fragment the larger edifice so long as they are fostered within the framework of the United Nations.

In sum, even measured against the realistic limits, the United Nations represents an opportunity for the United States and the West. Of course it could become a potential danger to American interests if national strategy is passive in the face of the strong incoming tides of political movement and change. It could become a danger if the Western powers misinterpret their larger destiny and shrink to the stature of a bitterly embattled minority, hopelessly out of tune with history. It could become a danger if communism and state socialism appear to offer the only available organizing principle for new societies, with the West smugly insisting on conformity with its standards and piously reiterating slogans that often seem empty of meaning.

But the United Nations furnishes an equivalent opportunity for supporting and reinforcing a dynamic Western view of the future trends of political life. For all that it is a noisy and often ineffective bazaar for everyday international relationships, the United Nations is a symbol of the kind of world society in which American values and concepts of political relations would best flourish—including the values of pluralism, of individuality, and of home rule.

With all its imperfections, the United Nations typifies in embryo that which we want to see emerge beyond the cold war between East and West and the civil wars between North and South. It symbolizes the sweep of our own vision of a more perfect union, and it challenges anew our capacity to make plans befitting that vision and our will to transform those plans into reality.

The Mechanics of U.S. Participation
in the United Nations

AMERICAN SPONSORSHIP of and active participation in the United Nations during and after World War II represented a radical departure from the past. Isolationism, if not dead, was dying fast. The United States had to create a revised set of attitudes toward the rest of the world; and it had to improvise an understanding of its dominant role in the new organization. This book has attempted to suggest ways of refreshing and renewing that understanding in the light of 15 years experience and of rapidly changing conditions and needs.

The historic break with the American past symbolized by membership in the United Nations was inevitably reflected in the machinery employed to conduct the nation's foreign relations. Here, too, some radical departures from the past were needed if the United Nations was to play its new role effectively. What follows is a thumbnail sketch of how the machinery for this unprecedented American diplomatic responsi-

This appendix is based largely on two articles by the author, published elsewhere as noted: "How the U.S. Government Is Organized to Participate in the U.N. System," *Department of State Bulletin,* September 17, 1956, pp. 435-444; and "American Policy toward the U.N.—Some Bureaucratic Reflections," *International Organization,* Winter 1958, pp. 1-16.

bility was created, used, sometimes abused, and ultimately assimilated into the larger bureaucratic structure of American government.

The first postwar unit of the State Department devoted to the preparation and execution of U.S. policy in the United Nations was the Office of Special Political Affairs (S.P.A.), established January 15, 1944. Parallel to, and technically equal with, the geographic offices, it continued for a time to report to a Special Assistant to the Secretary of State, Leo Pasvolsky. With Mr. Pasvolsky's departure in March 1946, the Office of Special Political Affairs remained, still technically speaking, on a par with the four geographic offices but without representation at the assistant secretary level.

When the geographic offices became "bureaus" on October 3, 1949, so did the former S.P.A. (which on January 21, 1948, had been rechristened the Office of United Nations Affairs). The Hoover Commission report of February 1949 recommended endowing all *five*[1] bureaus with assistant secretaries—the five assistant secretaries "at the action level." References at that time were to "five operating vice-presidents." The only distinction was reflected in the injunction that the Bureau of U.N. Affairs should normally secure substantive area policy guidance from the appropriate regional bureau—which it does.

Functions were added to the Bureau from elsewhere in the Department; for example, the narcotics control, international health, and social welfare interests from the now disbanded Division of International Labor, Health, and Social Affairs in 1948 and 1949. The Division of International Conferences was acquired on April 1, 1949 from the administrative area of the Department.

On August 25, 1954 the name of the Bureau was changed from U.N. Affairs to International Organization Affairs. There were sound reasons for the change, including the Bureau's responsibility for many aspects of U.S. participation in the specialized agencies as well as in the Caribbean and South

---

[1] Now seven: the five regional bureaus, the Bureau of International Organization Affairs (formerly U.N. Affairs), and the Bureau of Economic Affairs.

Pacific Commissions. But the change was also made with the tacit acknowledgment that the new label would not inflame quite so many members of Congress who had become disenchanted with the United Nations.

Many of the Bureau's officers were recruited during the war to assist in the preparations for postwar organization, preparations that were largely of a research nature. The roster of officers on this staff prior to 1946 reveals some names now familiar outside the Department as professors, college presidents, and research directors. Others stayed on after coming in from the academic world, or at any rate from other than the regular service, and for some years were keenly aware that as a group they were often regarded, particularly by the more traditionally minded in the geographic bureaus, as "dilettantes" of diplomacy, "intellectuals," even "visionaries"—at any rate, not quite members of the "in-group."

Such distinctions as were drawn were magnified because the vast majority of officers in U.N. Affairs were members of the Department's civil service, while at the same time most of the *key* officers of the geographic bureaus were Foreign Service officers. New integration legislation, signed by the President in August 1954, changed all this. A steady flow of replacements began to stream into the Bureau from field duty. The long-term effect of this change can be salutary both in terms of the diversity of experience it offers former civil service personnel and career Foreign Service officers and in terms of the needful institutional amalgamation and acceptance of the U.N. segment of our foreign affairs machinery and policies.

In the years since 1944 the United States has built up what is unquestionably the most elaborate policy-making and policy-executing structure of any of the members of the United Nations. At the top of the chain of command of that structure is, of course, the President. The President is responsible for the formulation, execution, and coordination of foreign policies. As chief executive, as commander in chief, and as chairman of the National Security Council, he presides over the process of defining U.S. objectives in the world and coordinating activities to achieve those objects.

In directing U.S. participation in international organizations the President under his constitutional authority determines policy and designates representatives and agencies for its execution.

The National Security Council advises the President as prescribed by statute and acts on major policy problems arising in the United Nations in the same way as on other foreign policy issues.

The Secretary of State is principal adviser to the President in the determination and execution of U.S. foreign policy and is charged with the responsibility for all the activities of the State Department. In directing U.S. relations with international organizations, he performs his functions in the same fashion as he does in all fields of international relations.

The Assistant Secretary of State for International Organization Affairs is one of the seven assistant secretaries with action responsibilities who, in the words of the Hoover Commission, have "responsibility for decisions within clearly defined limits" and "serve as focal points of contact between the Department and the overseas and international organization missions in both substantive and administrative matters." The Hoover Commission described the Assistant Secretary for International Organization Affairs as "in charge of relationships with international organizations, including the United Nations and its affiliated organizations" and as "the channel for instructions to and from United States representatives and delegations at the United Nations" as well as to certain other international organizations and conferences.

The Assistant Secretary for International Organization Affairs acts as the headquarters office, so to speak, for the U.S. Representative to the United Nations and U.S. delegates to other U.N. agencies (and some non-U.N. bodies). He ensures that these representatives of the United States follow national policy.

The U.S. Representative to the United Nations is, as prescribed by Executive Order 10108,[2] the chief of the United States mission to the United Nations (U.S.U.N.). The mission

2 15 *Fed. Reg.* 757.

includes other U.S. representatives and deputy representatives (i.e., those serving in the U.N. Economic and Social Council and its commissions, the Trusteeship Council, Disarmament Commission, Military Staff Committee, etc.) and the deputy representative on the Security Council. There is also a second deputy for the Security Council.

The U.S. Representative coordinates "the activities of the Mission in carrying out the instructions of the President transmitted either by the Secretary of State or by other means of transmission as directed by the President." Thus he is responsible for directing U.S. activities at U.N. headquarters, administers the U.S. mission, is the chief U.S. representative in the U.N. Security Council, chairman of the U.S. delegation to the General Assembly, representative ex officio and principal U.S. spokesman in any U.S. body at the U.N. headquarters, and principal U.S. negotiator with the U.N. Secretariat and representatives in New York of other member governments.

The U.S. mission to the United Nations, although unique in many ways, is comparable to a major U.S. embassy abroad in terms of its normal working relation with the State Department. Just as the Bureau of European Affairs is the home desk for our London Embassy, so the Bureau of International Organization Affairs is the home desk for the U.S. mission to the United Nations. U.S. ambassadors in both cases are appointed by and responsible to the President. The appropriate assistant secretary of state, acting for the Secretary, is in both cases responsible for ensuring that they are instructed and advised, that such instructions and advice represent the coordinated views of the government (including where necessary the decisions of the Secretary, the N.S.C., and the President), and for receiving the information they report and seeing that it is used in Washington. Under special circumstances, the head of the U.S. mission, like other ambassadors, occasionally receives his instructions directly from the Secretary of State or the President. The head of the U.S. mission takes an active part in the formulation of U.S. policy and tactics both prior to and during U.N. meetings and recommends changes in policies if, in his opinion, conditions require them.

The basic functions of the U.S. representative to the United Nations were stated by the so-called U.N. Participation Act of 1945, as amended in 1949,[3] and by President Truman's Executive Orders of 1947 and 1950.[4] Warren R. Austin was the U.S. Representative at the time. Henry Cabot Lodge succeeded him in 1953. Both men had been influential Republican senators. But there was one important difference: Lodge was also made a member of the President's Cabinet.

The formal responsibilities of the representative did not change, but his domestic political stature was sharply upgraded, particularly by contrast with his nominal "home desk" in the person of the Assistant Secretary for International Organization Affairs.

There was one immediate effect in the General Assembly delegation. The Department's practice during the years 1946-1953 had been to furnish the U.S. Representative with what was in effect a ready-made Assembly delegation each fall, cooperatively planned, to be sure, but characteristically "chief-of-staffed" by senior officers of the Bureau. All this changed in 1953, and the directing staff positions in the Assembly delegation became fixed to the permanent mission. This practice remains, but with passage of time and the renewed realization of the benefits from harmonious relations between the field and Washington, the procedure of selecting and briefing delegations was once again cooperative.

Undoubtedly many policy initiatives have been pressed on Washington by the U.S. mission in recent years, although it is not generally appreciated how often these are, for public relations reasons, inspired by Washington. An instance was the unanimous declaration of the U.S. delegates to the Tenth Assembly on foreign economic aid,[5] which could only mean support for a more positive U.S. attitude toward economic development programs through the United Nations. Dramatic as

[3] Respectively, Public Laws 264, 79th Congress, and 341, 81st Congress.
[4] Executive Order 9844 of April 28, 1947, amended by Executive Order 10108 of February 19, 1950.
[5] Announced by Secretary Dulles in *Department of State Press Release* No. 14, January 11, 1956.

this declaration was, it has had little perceptible effect on U.S. policy. Despite all that happened, the shifts of prestige to New York have not much affected national policy. The U.S. delegation to the United Nations is, as always, an instructed delegation in the technical sense and, more often than not, in the real sense. Perhaps the sharpest reminder of where the levers of power are in the U.S. government was furnished during the succession of postwar crises such as Korea and Suez, during which the permanent staff of the U.S. mission in New York functioned tirelessly and skillfully as servants and executors of policy made by the hour, as it were, in Washington. It could not be any other way, nor is it any other way in U.S. missions elsewhere in the world, where the lines of authority and responsibility are perhaps in better equilibrium than in New York.

In the policy-making echelons of the U.S. government, the key figure regarding U.N. participation is the Assistant Secretary of State for International Organization Affairs. This presidential appointee must be able to maintain a relation of mutual confidence and respect with two personages central in our government who both outrank him: the Secretary of State and the U.S. Representative to the United Nations. If these relations break down, the Assistant Secretary's usefulness is, of course, critically impaired.

Protocol places a handicap on the Assistant Secretary of State in carrying out his duties. The U.S. Representative, particularly when he sits as a member of the President's Cabinet, outranks the Assistant Secretary through whom he normally receives his instructions. (A problem which some anticipated but that does not seem to have arisen concerns the ambiguity of the U.S. Representative's role vis-à-vis his superior, the Secretary of State—both Cabinet-level officials.) All U.S. ambassadors, of course, enjoy nominal relations with the President that transcend, again nominally, their obligation to the Secretary of State's deputies. These deputies, however, are clearly in a command position, both over the cables and in their functions as regional chiefs of mission meetings, over which a regional assistant secretary generally presides.

In the New York setting, where protocol governs to a heavy degree if only because of the sheer number of functionaries and dignitaries present, the Assistant Secretary tends to remain far more of a background figure vis-à-vis the mission chief. The primary responsibility of the Department U.N. Affairs chief is, of course, to advise the Secretary of State in Washington. Nonetheless, unlike some of their counterparts in foreign governments, the U.S. Assistant Secretary or deputy has not often been designated even an alternate representative on a U.S. General Assembly delegation, and up to 1960, when Francis O. Wilcox was named a representative on the U.S. General Assembly delegation, he had never been a full representative. In the first six years or so, with only a few exceptions, the "home-desk chief" or his deputy usually sat at the right hand of the delegation chairman at Assembly sessions and functioned as *éminence grise* as well as source of government policy. There was a shift in this relation in 1953, as indicated.

One consequence of the Secretary of State's confidence in the assistant secretary charged with U.N. affairs has been the preoccupation of the latter with political, as opposed to economic, social, trusteeship, technical, and other facets of his responsibilities.

The reasons for this preoccupation are several. The most obvious one is that great political crises have dominated the foreign policy scene over the last decade. Another basic institutional factor resided in the dominantly political interests and proclivities of Secretaries Byrnes, Marshall, Acheson, and Dulles, whose attention to U.N. affairs was characteristically limited to the more acute political aspects. (With Secretary Herter the emphasis was not quite so pointed, perhaps because of Undersecretary Dillon.)

Nonetheless, the other problems claimed the assistant secretaries' attention and had somehow to be dealt with. The utilization of two deputy assistant secretaries has from time to time resulted in a fairly sharp division of responsibility. At one time one of them followed the economic and social work of the Bureau, and the other oversaw the administrative decisions and often certain specialized interests, such as inter-American organization matters and, at times, refugee problems. Later the division was between economic, social, budgetary, refugee, and other international administrative matters on the one hand, and assistance on political, atomic energy, disarmament, and related problems on the other.

Since the objective of U.S. participation in the United Nations is to realize this nation's role and forward its interests in multilateral diplomatic bodies, there are two objects in organizing and disciplining the government machinery for participating in this process: (1) to ensure that the United States speaks with one voice on issues arising in the international forums, and (2) to ensure that this voice represents the best judgment and skill that can be brought to bear on problems of foreign policy.

U.S. participation in international organizations works like a funnel. At one end, experts in government agencies recommend policies for the United States to adopt in the United Nations on a wide variety of topics. At the other end, U.S. spokesmen in international forums are expected to state these policies with clarity and authority. This presents the government with a formidable task of coordination.

The stages at which the coordination process comes to light are the instruction of U.S. delegates and representatives and the expression by them of the official policies and views of the United States at meetings of international organizations. In addition to the permanent mission in New York, the United States has permanent missions at the International Civil Aviation Organization in Montreal, at the International Atomic Energy Agency in Vienna, and in Geneva for liaison with the U.N. European Office and the several specialized agencies located there. (In Geneva this function is handled within the framework of the American consulate general by an augmented staff.) There are also U.S. liaison officers for F.A.O. at Rome, for U.N.E.S.C.O. at Paris, for the Economic Commission for Latin America (E.C.L.A.) at Santiago, and for the Economic Commission for Asia and the Far East (E.C.A.-F.E.) at Bangkok.

The central point for the coordination necessary in this funneling process is the Bureau of International Organization Affairs, which through its five offices—U.N. Political and Security Affairs, International Economic and Social Affairs, Dependent Area Affairs, International Administration, and International Conferences—furnishes staff support to the U.S. Representative to the United Nations and to U.S. delegates to other U.N. agencies and some non-U.N. bodies.

(1) It coordinates the policy views and technical requirements originating in other parts of the Department and other agencies, so that the U. S. representatives in international organizations can be sure they are always stating consistent and unified U.S. positions.

(2) It develops U.S. policy on questions that are peculiarly multilateral in nature, that cut across the bilateral functions of the geographic units and the specialized subject units in other agencies, and that no other office is staffed to handle. Examples of these questions are collective security preparations, parliamentary tactics that have been proved best by experience in specific U.N. agencies, international secretariat problems, operations of the U.N. trusteeship system, and problems of non-self-governing territories, world health, social welfare, narcotics, human rights, interpretation of the articles of the U.N. Charter, international budgets, and the U.N. aspects of arms regulation and control.

(3) It assembles in one unit the knowledge and experience the United States has built up in the field of multilateral diplomacy so that the government can most efficiently prepare itself to uphold its interests in international organizations. This means chiefly the political and organizational work of the U.N. bodies—questions of credentials, elections, budgets, secretariat organization and practices, agenda and procedural problems, and the relation of other multilateral bodies to the United Nations.

A considerable part of the coordinating is done through informal day-to-day contacts between the Bureau's desk officers and "subject specialists" elsewhere in the Department or other government agencies. Often this is the only way in which deadlines can be met at U.N. meetings or prompt action taken to deal with imminent votes or sudden shifts in position by other countries. In this way also the countless routine matters that arise in international organization operations can be resolved with a minimum of formal clearance.

In the political field, when there are indications that a political problem will come before the United Nations, a team is formed. The representative of the Office of U.N. Political and Security Affairs usually chairs the group, prepares papers for its consideration, and drafts instructions for the U.S. Representative. His responsibility is to ensure that the views of all interested offices are secured and that any information required is obtained from Department and overseas files. He furnishes the knowledge of the U.N. Charter considerations, precedents in U.N. bodies, past performances of delegations and delegates, voting probabilities, and the operation of regional and special-interest blocs in the United Nations. He frequently acts as principal adviser to the U.S. Representative during U.N. meetings when the political problem is considered.

Also on the team are U.S. representatives from the affected geographic areas, who furnish information as to the general U.S. policies toward the countries in question. These policies, however, must be reconciled where, for example, one desk officer is speaking of U.S. interests with respect to France and another regarding our interests in North Africa, as in the Algerian case in the General Assembly. In addition, they furnish knowledge of geographic factors, national idiosyncrasies, and official personalities; and often they participate in General Assembly or Security Council sessions as political liaison officers with delegates from countries in their areas. To harmonize the work of the geographic and economic bureaus with that of the Bureau of International Organization Affairs, each normally has a full-time adviser on U.N. affairs, who collaborates with officers of the Bureau on relevant problems affecting the region.

These teams frequently include representatives of the legal adviser's office and, when necessary, of the public affairs, economic, and research officers. The member from the Office of U.N. Political and Security Affairs often consults informally on military aspects of the cases with officers in the Defense Department. The team members turn to their respective assistant secretaries, and these in turn consult higher echelons, as required, before approving U.S. positions. Many political issues in the United Nations require decisions by the Secretary of State, and in some cases the President. Either the Bureau of International Organization Affairs or the geographic offices undertake consultation with appropriate U.S. missions abroad and foreign envoys in Washington.

A similar process takes place within the Department on economic and social questions before the United Nations and specialized agencies. Since the clearance process here involves not only many different units within the State Department but also other government agencies, a group of interdepartmental committees furnishes the chief means of coordination. Unless another agency clearly has a predominant interest (for example, the Department of Agriculture, for F.A.O.), the State Department furnishes the chairman or secretary of the committees. Within the State Department, the Bureau usually provides either or both.

The same process also operates when dealing with problems of dependent and colonial areas. Here the Office of Dependent Area Affairs teams up with the geographic desk officers for the task of harmonizing both within the U.S. government and in the United Nations the traditional U.S. attitudes toward colonial peoples, on the one hand, and the special problems of the administering authorities, which include close allies of this country, on the other.

In the process of developing U.S. policies, the Department of State, through the Bureau of International Organization Affairs, consults the U.S. Representative to the United Nations, who in turn consults his diplomatic colleagues in New York and has the benefit of constant contact with high officials from close to 90 other countries.

The Office of International Conferences screens invitations to international conferences, recommends as to U.S. participation, negotiates throughout the government the makeup of the U.S. delegations, assists, when appropriate, with preparations of U.S. positions, allocates funds, makes travel and housing arrangements, and, in meetings away from the U.N. headquarters, furnishes the service staff of the delegation, and, after the meeting, makes sure that responsibilities for official reports, documents, and other items are properly discharged.

Still another function of the Bureau of International Organization Affairs is, like other areas of the Department, to provide the U.S. Information Agency with policy information on important aspects of U.S. participation in the United Nations.

Index

Acheson, Dean, 262
Afghanistan, 68
Africa, 10, 12, 21, 26, 33, 67, 81, 100, 107, 113, 120, 129, 131, 138, 156, 173, 177, 187, 189, 193, 197-199, 207, 212, 231, 232
Afro-Asian grouping, 1, 10, 11, 14, 54, 192, 201, 205, 207, 242
Agricultural surpluses, 181, 185
Agriculture, U.S. Dept. of, 266
Albania, 122, 131
Algeria, 14, 15, 120, 139, 141, 143, 158, 163, 189, 265
Allen, George V., 227n
Amman (see also Jordan), 88, 148
Antarctica, 36, 166ff, 228
Apartheid (see Union of South Africa)
Aqaba, Gulf of, 166
Arab League, 232
Argentina, 166, 226, 231
Armenians, 131
Articles of Confederation, 218
Asia (see also Afro-Asian grouping), 6, 10, 21, 26, 69, 73, 113, 129-131, 138, 156, 173, 187, 189, 192, 193, 197, 198, 203, 212
Atlantic Congress (see also North Atlantic Treaty Organization), 177

Atoms for Peace program, 79, 125, 226
Attwood, Wallace W., Jr., 228n
Austin, Warren R., 260
Australasia, 21, 241
Australia, 166, 226
Badeau, John S., 203n
Baghdad Pact (see Central Treaty Organization)
Balkans, U.N. Special Committee on (U.N.S.C.O.B.), 148n
Baltic states, 130
Bangkok (see also Thailand), 263
Barrau Pelaez, Manuel, 176n
Bases, 61
Batista, F., 85
Beck-Friis Mission, 152, 153
Behavioral sciences, 209-210
Belgium, 25, 68, 190
Beloussov, Vladimir V., 227n
Berkner, Lloyd V., 127
Berlin, 57, 113, 139, 147, 153, 158-160, 162-164, 189
Berlin blockade (1948), 46, 52, 56, 120
Bogotá Conference, 242
Bolivia, 176n, 231
Bourguiba, Habib, 202n
Brazil, 68, 181, 231
Bricker, John W., 205
British Commonwealth (see also Great Britain), 10, 122, 211, 242

269

Date Due

J